NEVER TO
RETURN

NEVER TO RETURN

A MODERN QUEST FOR ETERNAL TRUTH

SHARON JANIS

BLUE DOVE PRESS
SAN DIEGO • CALIFORNIA • 1998

Blue Dove Press publishes books by and about sages and saints of all religions as well as other inspiring works. Catalog sent free upon request.

BLUE DOVE PRESS
P. O. Box 261611
San Diego, CA 92196
Phone: (619) 271-0490, FAX:(619) 271-5695
E-mail: bdp@bluedove.com, http://www.bluedove.com

FIRST EDITION

Rumi poem, p. 277 © Coleman Barks, by Rumi, translated by into English by John Moyne and Coleman Barks and contained in Say I Am You, *Mapop, 1994*

Cover and text design:
 Brian Moucka
 Poppy Graphics, Santa Barbara, California

The names of certain people appearing in this book
have been changed where deemed appropriate

Special thanks to Mary Kowit for help
in the preparation of this edition

ISBN: 1-884997-29-5

Library of Congress Cataloging-in-Publication Data:
Janis, Sharon, 1959-
    Never to Return :-a modern quest for eternal truth /
    Sharon Janis.
    p. cm.
    ISBN: 1-884997-29-5
    1. Janis, Sharon, 1959-   . 2. Spiritual biography-
United States. I. Title
BL73.J37A3 1998.
291.4'092--dc21
[B]   97-44497
                                                  CIP

*"Never to Return" is a cry of the soul
that longs to break free from the illusory world
of limitation and confusion
and rediscover its own true nature*

For You

TABLE OF CONTENTS

PROLOGUE

IT STARTED AS A LOW RUMBLING. I had barely sunk into the arms of exhaustion after a hundred-hour work week when the world went mad. The earth itself, metaphor for all that is stable and dependable, was dancing. But this was not a gentle dance; it was the dance of destruction. This was a display of force unlike any I had witnessed.

Instinctively, I jumped up and ran to the alcove I had designated as the "earthquake spot" just days earlier, when two small shocks rumbled through town. During my five years in L.A., we'd had a few temblors. I'd always enjoyed and joked about them, impressing co-workers and friends with my bravado. Those small tremors were nothing like this.

I had just spent a year editing the "Mighty Morphin' Power Rangers" television show. With my apartment shaking violently from side to side, I visualized one of the big monsters from the program picking up our building and shaking it, as all the contents spilled out. Holding tightly to the door frame to keep from being tossed around, I wondered for a moment if I was dreaming.

A glass shower door upstairs shattered, and my neighbor's

35" TV smashed against the wall. What devastation must be occurring all around me? In my mind's eye, I envisioned a jagged line running up the coast. This might only be the edge of something huge. I imagined the entire west coast crumbling at its seams, perhaps swallowing thousands of lives with each quaking gulp.

I truly believed this was the *big one*. I was about to die. The ceiling could crash down any moment, squashing my body like a bug. These were my final moments as me. From within an expanded sense of time, the twenty- to forty-second earthquake seemed to take hours.

"Now what am I supposed to do? I should know this!"

I thought I had made peace with the idea of death many years earlier. Yet now, as the walls closed in on my life, my pounding heart cried out with anguish at the large gap between *me* and where I'd hoped to be during my last moments of life. Once upon a time, I had anticipated that my death would come as a great merging into the Grand Source of all, as promised in one of my favorite Indian texts:

> *Whatever state of being a soul remembers*
> *at the moment of death,*
> *he goes to that very state of being.*
> *Therefore, at all times meditate on Me*
> *(the Supreme Soul),*
> *keep your mind and intelligence fixed on Me.*
> *In this way, thou shalt surely come to Me.*
>
> —*THE BHAGAVAD GITA*

Now it was too late. I had fallen off the path of spiritual evolution and wasted my precious time. I had been meditating on TV shows and worldly success. Why couldn't my death have come when I was beyond personal identification, living a life completely devoted to God? Why did it have to come when I was just like everyone else, afraid of losing things that never truly existed?

Even greater than the fear of death was my embarrassment at having discarded the precious gifts given to me through the years. I cowered before my God and couldn't recognize Him. First I tried to paste a face on him, invoking the images of my spiritual masters. Then I repeated my mantra, in hopes that it could magically lift me up. I wanted to leave this world from a mountaintop of elevated awareness, instead of from the valley in which I had been dwelling. How could I make the leap? Was it even possible to break through untold layers of illusion in these last few moments of personal existence? Could I become immortal at the threshold of death itself?

The rumbling stopped.

The cacophony of smashing, crashing and creaking also stopped. There was dead silence and blacker-than-black darkness.

A voice pierced the stillness. "Holy shit!"

I had to chuckle. It was one of the guys who lived on the second floor.

I was in my body, on the floor, still on earth — and in shock. I had been given another chance. Next time, I had to be ready.

Having pursued several avenues for growth in the past, it was clear I now had to find a more personal way to relate to this unnamable, perhaps unknowable, Truth. But first, I had to remember what had already been learned and forgotten.

There is only the fight to recover what has been lost
And found and lost again and again;
and now, under conditions
That seem unpropitious.
But perhaps neither gain nor loss.
For us, there is only the trying.
The rest is not our business.

—T. S. ELIOT

NEVER TO RETURN

Life is a series of awakenings.

—SIVANANDA

1.

AWAKENING

AT TWO AND A HALF YEARS OF AGE, I discovered the
existence of grace. Life was comfortable at the time.
My family lived in a small house in a reasonably safe
area of Detroit. My sister spoiled me as though I were her personal doll, and our grandmother lived just down the block.

Our folks were not exemplary parent material. One
benefit of this unfortunate circumstance was that it supported
my development as a freer spirit. I had a great deal of
independence to wander about.

One Sunday, I jumped out of bed early. Everyone else was
sleeping, so I unlatched the back door and went to play
outside. Our yard was surrounded by a medium-sized fence,
which I had recently been eyeing as a possible challenge to

overcome. Several times I had even tested the fence out, putting my feet in the holes and pulling myself up off the ground. This time I decided to climb to the top. Carefully, I inched my way hand by hand, foot by foot, up the fence. Suddenly I was falling, and then landed with a bump on the other side.

Everything shifted. I had never been in this big field before. There was my house, but it was behind the fence. I was not quite ready to repeat the whole process again to get back home. What to do?

To my left I saw a familiar spot, though from a new angle. It was the church, two doors down. I didn't know that it was a church or even what a church was, having been brought up without any religious exposure at all.

My sister and I used to play with stones in the church parking lot. That seemed like a comforting diversion at a confusing time like this, so I walked toward the lot. I heard music coming from the building, and looked up. The windows were glowing with bright colors! I walked over to get a closer view.

As I got to the door, it opened like magic. The entrance to this colored light palace opened right up for me. I wasn't afraid at all. It was kind of like being back in the dream world again. At age two, the two worlds are not as easily distinguished. Whatever is happening is what is happening.

As the door opened, I saw a woman's legs and knees, just above my eye-level. With a big smile, she lifted me up and carried me into the room. What a party! The room was filled with pictures, candles, and smiling people dressed in bright colors. It was even better than the birthday parties I'd often attended for the neighborhood kids.

I had been in our backyard, then over the fence, then in the parking lot, and now in this magical place. In my own nonreligious way, it felt as though the "gods" were smiling upon me.

After the party ended, several women gave me a cup of juice and asked what my name was. To their surprise, I gave my full name and address, as well as my parents' names. I told them my family lived two houses away and that they were still asleep. I knew how to get back home by myself, but they kept an eye on me as I walked down the front sidewalk to my house.

From then on, I went to this Episcopalian church every Sunday. I never told my parents about it. Maybe I was afraid that if I talked about it, the fun might end. I became a regular there. Surprisingly, nobody ever asked to speak to my parents. The church did put our family on their mailing list, but the flyers went unnoticed.

One day, I came home from church wearing a lapel pin with a cross and the words "Jesus Loves Me." That afternoon, my mother saw the pin and asked where it came from. I told her it was from church. She called my father and they took the pin away. They told me I could never go back to that place again, because I was *Jewish*, whatever that meant!

This was a devastating blow to my young psyche. Although I had been upset about not getting my way many times before, this was a more painful frustration. The energy in this church had lifted me to a magical, colorful, and love-filled place, more wonderful than anything else I knew. Now I was not allowed to go there anymore. This was as upsetting as anything else I had encountered during my two-and-a-half years of life.

Nonetheless, I am grateful to have had a chance to enter a place filled with spiritual power at such a young age, especially while growing up in an atheist (though officially Jewish) household. After this glimpse of heaven amidst my daily experience, I always believed in magic. I knew things could change unfathomably for the better, in the blink of an eye.

However, the disappointing side of this early experience rippled through my subsequent personality development as well. Whenever I'd discover something really beautiful, precious, and magical, I would often clench my muscles in fear that it would be snatched from me. Or I'd move into a space of aloofness to distance myself in hopes of numbing the pain of separation that seemed to be inevitable with any personal attachment.

A few months later, I turned three, with another surprise on the horizon. All my friends came to our house for the big party, laden with gifts for me. I was the *birthday girl*. This was the first time my mental structures had really assimilated the concept of *I'm special*. Until this age, *I* couldn't be special, because *I* was all there was. Everything else existed only in relation to me.

But today *I* felt special. I was queen for the day. I was different and unique, an individual worthy of being celebrated. I was separate, and it felt pretty damn good. The seeds of egocentricity were planted.

While unwrapping my presents, I held up a mirrored toy and saw my own reflection. That was me. *Me*. I had only recently realized that the face I saw in mirrors was not an imaginary friend. I had sometimes wondered who that little girl was, walking with a lady who looked an awful lot like my mother. Not so very long ago, I had figured out that it was me. *Me*. I stared into the mirror, entranced by my happy face. As the world and party faded away, I began to think, "I'm three, I'm three, I'm three." Just the other day, my mother had explained to me what *three* was. I had been *one*, then *two*, and now I was *three*. I looked at my face in the mirror, and had one of the most startling realizations of my life.

One day... I would be five!

What a shock! I would not always be exactly the way I was in that moment. Time slipped its noose around my neck. I realized I was a separate being, locked in a linear world. I was going to keep getting older and older. Change was inevitable. Life would never again be so simple.

Illusions command themselves to us
because they save us pain
and allow us to enjoy pleasure instead.
We must therefore accept it without complaint
when they sometimes collide with a bit of reality
against which they are dashed to pieces.

—SIGMUND FREUD

2.

NEVER TO RETURN

AT AGE SEVEN, I OPENED my mother's psychology course notebook to the first page and read: "The average person likes to believe he knows most of the time why he thinks, feels and acts as he does. Psychoanalysis holds this is not true. All the things we think, feel and do are largely dictated by the unconscious over which we have little control."

My parents had just begun teaching psychology classes in their respective high schools. The bookshelves in our house quickly filled up with the hottest new psychology discoveries: books on gestalt, transactional analysis, multiple personality, autism, dream symbolism, and more. For years, there would be a steady stream of new psychology books flowing through the shelves in our den. Even at age seven, I enjoyed reading the interesting ideas in these books.

And so, when my parents signed up to take a three-month course in hypnosis, I decided to take the class as well. I thought hypnosis would be a fun skill to learn. Even though the class was intended for adults, our instructor allowed me to register. This course radically expanded my understanding of the mind, in terms of both its power and its vulnerability.

On the first day of class, our instructor, Paul, hypnotized a woman. He told her that his finger was a lit cigarette, and touched the tip of his finger to her arm. The woman winced with what was clearly a real sense of pain. It was disconcerting to see someone so uncomfortable for no reason at all. I didn't know whether to feel sorry for her or not.

The following week, the woman returned to class with a very normal-looking blister where the "lit cigarette" had touched her arm. I was amazed.

I realized in that moment that our experience of what is true or false, painful or pleasurable, may have absolutely nothing to do with what is really going on. How could I ever again be certain that *any* pain, even with physical evidence, is real? During the first few weeks of this course, I discovered the sobering fact that there was no way to really know anything.

A few weeks later, Paul hypnotized another woman and gave her a posthypnotic suggestion. He instructed her to jump up and down and act like a gorilla every time he said the word "Yes." He also told her that she would not remember being given the suggestion.

The woman came out of trance and walked back to her seat. One of the adults prompted Paul with a seemingly innocent question, while we all watched with smirks of anticipation. As soon as Paul responded with the magic word, there she was, jumping up and down, doing a gorilla dance, complete with sound effects. The woman looked perfectly normal and well-dressed, but she was acting absolutely nuts.

This demonstration of blind obedience had profound implications, and was entertaining to watch as well. But what shocked me most was the woman's response to seeing this ridiculous behavior coming out of herself. Here she was, in front of all these people, acting very strange without any conscious explanation for her own bizarre behavior. She was, after all, acting like a gorilla.

I would have expected her response to be one of shock or confusion. "Why am I jumping up and down acting like a gorilla?" Maybe she'd figure out there had been a hypnotic suggestion. But no. The woman smiled nervously, and made up a completely lame excuse for her behavior. "I've always liked gorillas and when I get silly I like to act like them." Her mind filled in this blank space of irrationality just as proficiently as it fills in the blind spots of our visual fields, with false, manufactured, memory-based misinformation.

Without reading the latest neurophysiology research or the ancient texts of yoga, I learned at age seven that *the world as we know it is a mirage*. This nebulous process of life-experience is created and projected by our sensory receptors and mental creativity. It is the fairy-dust of illusion that makes us feel that what we experience is independently real, honest, and authentic.

The idea that I was in control of a stable world shattered, as I realized that *whatever I think I know may have nothing to do with the way things really are*. This intelligent woman actually believed that she had always acted like a gorilla when she felt silly. The other woman's skin had been burned by a cigarette that didn't even exist.

Because of my youth, this discovery may have impacted me more than my older classmates. At age seven I hadn't yet learned to ignore the implications of what I saw. I had not yet developed all the defense mechanisms we use to keep our world-views consistent, filters that make incongruous experiences palatable to our accepted belief systems. After all, at age seven our impressions of the world are constantly being usurped and updated by new information, new responsibilities, and new experiences. I was still in the foundation-laying stage of personality development. It wasn't so strange for me to see shocking new evidence that forced me to rethink my belief system. It happened all the time.

After witnessing these hypnosis demonstrations, I understood that even experiences which seem to be coming from the external world might be created solely by my mind. Many years later, I would rediscover this idea in the scriptures of Indian philosophy. *"Ya drishti, sa srishti: the world is as you see it."*

According to this principle, all of creation as we know it manifests according to our vision. *"The world is as you see it"* goes beyond the notion that if we are pessimistic or in a bad mood, we will see things as being worse than they are. *"Ya drishti, sa srishti"* means, "As your vision is, so this creation is." It takes the *"are"* out of "seeing things as they *are*." There is only the process of *seeing*. This is a difficult concept to grasp. Physicists who study quantum mechanics have been trying to do so for decades, having discovered that the very act of viewing affects and changes what is being observed.

I now understood that this world was created by my mind, literally. I knew things were not the way people pretended they were. I could see that people were getting totally wrapped up in nonsense, trying to put out painful, burning cigarettes that were, in reality, nothing but benign fingers. I had peeked through the veil of illusion, at least a bit.

At one point during the three-month course, we split off into pairs to practice hypnotizing one another. My subject was an older man (although at age seven, anything over twenty was considered "old"!). We went into a separate room so I could put him into a trance.

I used all the techniques we had been studying, and to my excitement, the man started showing signs of going under. His facial muscles relaxed and his eyelids closed without fluttering at all. His breathing became deep and even. I walked him down the imaginary staircase into his unconscious mind. "You're going deeper and deeper...."

He replied, "Deeper and deeper...."

The man started to repeat everything I would say, in a very monotone voice. It was like a good cartoon. He was under *my* power!

I was amazed and proud of myself. I had actually hypnotized somebody. But then, the man began to improvise. "Going deeper and deeper, beyond the world...."

Well, this was strange. Our teacher hadn't prepared us for a runaway subject. It turned out the man had been practicing self-hypnosis for some time. Once I brought him to the threshold of his subconscious mind, his familiar methods had kicked in. But at the time, I had no idea what was happening. He continued to drone, "Deeper and deeper...beyond the earth; beyond the galaxies; past the universe...never to return."

O my!

I frantically tried to bring him back with my squeaky 7-year-old voice. "Back to the universe, back to the galaxies, coming back to earth!" I didn't want the rest of the class to think I was too young to do it right. My hope was to bring him out of trance quickly, so nobody would know what had happened.

But he continued, "Far beyond the galaxy. Beyond the universe. Never to return."

I ran to get the instructor!

It took Paul more than ten minutes to bring the man back to his normal consciousness.

That night I lay in bed, thinking. I contemplated my fear that this man would get lost somewhere out in the universe, and a question boomed through my awareness: "Where did he go?" It appeared that this man's mind was not in his body, yet he was *somewhere*. According to the evidence before me, he had apparently traveled out into the universe.

While lying there contemplating all this, I felt myself rise up out of myself. Just by imagining this man's journey out into the universe, I was able to see stars as well. The vision was similar to science films which pull back from a spot on earth, expanding by powers of ten through the solar system, galaxy and universe. But I had never seen any such films at the time, and had no real context through which to understand the experience.

Nevertheless, this was another momentous day for me. A new possibility entered into my world view: that our minds have the ability to expand far beyond the body, in a way that feels experientially real.

I thank God for my handicaps, for through them,
I have found myself, my work and my God.

—HELEN KELLER

3.

I CHOSE THIS?

IN MODERN NEW-AGE CIRCLES, there is a belief that the soul who reincarnates into our many lifetimes has chosen the specific circumstances of each life, theoretically to learn certain lessons. If this is so, then why did I choose my parents?

Neither my mother nor my father had any siblings and both were somewhat narcissistic, with little interest in taking care of anyone else. They had been forced into these parental roles by a society that dictated, at the time, that it was required of them. If the cultural tides had not shifted during my generation, perhaps I too would be in the same boat right now, forced to take care of children I may not really want, instead of having an opportunity to live life more according to my more independent nature.

I suspect the maternal instinct was bred out of our family's genetic pool a few generations back. When I was a child, my mother told me, "If you want to be happy, don't ever have kids." This was during one of the rare moments when she actually spoke to me. At the time, I took her words somewhat personally. Still, this statement ultimately gave me the parental permission I needed to break free of the templates of cultural expectation. I didn't have to follow the same path.

My parents were not prepared to have children. Emotionally, they were children themselves. They were barely twenty when they got married. At age twenty, I could hardly keep my plants alive!

Both of them came from controlling families, and had married one another mainly to get away from home. What they really wanted was to be free, but first they had to satisfy all the expectations of their friends and relatives. Even before the wedding cake crumbs were cleared away the inevitable next question came: "When are you going to have children?"

So there we were, my sister and I, more products of society's expectations than of love. Within a few years, my parents realized that they had nothing in common. Over the years, they grew to despise one another. Our house was filled with a constant backdrop of yelling and screaming, insults and accusations. If this had happened today, they would have simply recognized their mistake and gotten a divorce. However, this was the early 1960s, and society frowned upon divorce. My parents certainly did not want to be ostracized by their families and peers! No, they were stuck with one another, and with us. Their marriage lasted for nearly twenty years, with each going through a series of affairs and relationships in an effort to achieve at least a taste of freedom and affection.

Not that they were very affectionate people. I cannot remember a single time throughout my childhood that either parent touched me in anything but punishment. There was never a hug, a kiss, a whispered "I love you." This entire arena of parental care was completely unknown to my sister and me, though we did receive some affection from our grandparents. If I was looking for the golden sky peeking through this particularly stormy aspect of my childhood, it might be that the lack of physical affection gave me a certain self-reliance. I learned to find comfort inside myself, and did not spend the rest of my life seeking external relationships that might recapture some sweet, comforting affection of childhood.

From an early age, my sister and I were more or less on our own. Our parents started to hang out with a partying crowd, and we never really knew when they would be coming home. But we liked it that way. We had the whole house to ourselves. Only upon hearing the sound of the garage door opening would we run up into our respective rooms and close the doors. Most of the time, we just wanted to be left alone. We were both independent, and did not like being told what to do, ever.

Not surprisingly, my sister and I lacked certain social skills. Because of this, we were teased mercilessly throughout elementary school. For the most part, our childhood life was not fun.

Sometimes I lie awake at night and ask, "Why me?"
Then a voice answers, "Nothing personal,
your name just happened to come up."

—CHARLIE BROWN

Yet all this turmoil brought with it some unique opportunities. Even the disdain of my classmates served a wonderful purpose when viewed with optimistic objectivity. I learned to depend on myself. I spent massive amounts of time alone. During recess, instead of hanging out with the other kids, I would sit off to the side, observing them. Or I would spend the time watching a squirrel gathering food.

In the fertile ground of inner silence, I would think about life. I didn't become quite as indoctrinated into the limiting ideas of the society around me. I evolved my own morals, my own desires and goals, at least to some degree.

Along with this, I managed to avoid a common habit many people seem to have developed, of putting themselves down. Maybe because so many others were available to do this for me, I learned to support and stand by myself no matter what. If I made a mistake, it was simply a mistake. I've always been shocked to hear acquaintances say things like "I hate myself." Such thoughts would never enter my mind or heart.

I can imagine myself in that space before this life-breath, choosing these parents who would give me the independence required for the lessons before me. Although our family situation may seem undesirable from society's viewpoints, the lack of parental support and expectations did have its appropriate place in my soul's journey through this life.

4.

THROUGH THE YEARS

Snapshots from an album
of personally significant childhood memories

AGE 1 At age one, I learned to speak. While most infants were grunting out *"Ma-ma"* or *"Wa-wa,"* I was using complex sentences such as, "Mommy, would you please change my diaper?" It is likely these early language skills had some beneficial impact on my ability to store bits and pieces of memory information, even at this early age. Some of these earliest memories are composites of the stories told to me years later and actual memory-based images.

I also loved to sing and learn songs. At one-and-a-half, I was able to sing the song, "O where have you been, Billy Boy," including all the verses. My mother was a show-off, and had me sing for people all the time, basically turning *me* into a show-off. My audiences would be amazed and shocked to hear such songs coming from an infant. I was a little performer, always ready to please mommy by showcasing my abilities.

This was the beginning of a pattern between my mother and me. On a personal level, there would be little affection or interaction of any kind. But when friends and family were around, we would act as the ideal mother and daughter. She would suddenly become Mrs. Cleaver and talk to me the way other mothers talked with their children. And I would jump right into my "good daughter" role and act as though her motherly behavior was typical.

Nevertheless, as soon as the guests left, our conversation would be reduced once again to sentence fragments: "Go to your room." "Stop that." "Good." "Go away."

Both of my parents were high-school teachers. They needed to find someone to take care of my sister and me during the day. My sister was three, old enough to begin nursery school. When we signed her up, my parents asked if I could also attend. The administrator said that wasn't possible, because they would only accept children over three years of age. I was not even two. But then my mother had me sing "Billy Boy" and talk to the woman. She was impressed. "Your daughter speaks better than the three-year-olds!" So I got to go to nursery school after all. This made me happy because the school had a very enticing, big yellow giraffe to climb on.

At one and a half, I encountered my first major obstacle. Since I was mature enough to ask, "Mommy, would you please change my diaper?" my parents decided that I should also be capable of using the potty. Why should *they* have to do this nasty task, when clearly I was intelligent enough to take care of it myself? Thus began the great potty battle of 1961.

I was not used to having to know ahead of time when digested foods and liquids were ready to leave my body. It had never been an issue before. The process and sensations were definitely intriguing to me, but I certainly did not want to have to be in charge of it all. Suddenly, I was expected to catch the foreshadowing moment, put down my toys, walk all the way to the bathroom, and get properly adjusted on the seat, all before anything was released. I thought the whole thing was ridiculous. Why go through all that trouble when you can just wear a diaper?

AGE 2 Age two was a time of increasing independence for me. At stores, I would often separate from my mother. I loved to wander about. Many times I'd hear my name over the loudspeaker, "Calling for lost child, Sharon Janis." I liked hearing my name being announced like that, and made sure to disappear as often as possible.

Most of the time I was left with babysitters, relatives, or family friends. Between nursery school and all these different caretakers, I learned to be fairly social. I trusted nearly everyone, and was at ease even with strangers. In those days, it wasn't quite as essential for parents to warn their children about "bad people."

❧

My grandmother was worried about my habit of wandering outside. To discourage me from going out at night, she made up a little story. She told me there were monsters that roamed the street after dark.

Monsters, in our neighborhood!

While lying in bed one night, I looked at our window and saw the shadow of one of these huge monsters, moving right outside our house! I couldn't tell anyone about it for a long time. Every night I would lie in fear, watching the monster outside the window. My sister and I shared a room, but I was too frightened to move or make a sound to wake her up. What if the monster saw or heard me?

Then the next day would come with all of its activities and challenges. In the brightness of daytime, I would forget the previous night's terror. The experience would dissolve like a forgotten dream. But as darkness descended, once again I'd enter my own personal battle with evil.

The monster turned out to be the large pine tree in our front yard, waving with the wind.

AGE 3 I used to wander around our block, but now I became bolder, and started to cross streets. Every few days, my parents would have to search the neighborhood to find me. Once, they spent hours driving around, getting more upset and worried as time passed. Finally, they found me napping on the bedroom floor between our two beds.

We lived in Detroit, with a house full of toys and a swing-set in the backyard. I had good friends to play with, and life was pleasant enough. My mother saw potential in me, and began to teach me how to read. This was one of the few activities we ever did together. She liked to see how quickly I could catch on.

This Christmas, I had a chance to meet Santa Claus. This was a very exciting event for me. Even though we were Jewish atheists, my parents still allowed me to believe in Santa Claus. He was the closest thing I had to the idea of God. He knew if you were bad or good and brought wonderful new toys to play with.

I went up to meet Santa with great excitement and awe. He gave me a big smile and lifted me up to his lap with a "Ho, ho, ho." He asked me some questions, and seemed delighted at my answers. I really liked Santa.

As we talked, I saw that he had a piece of tape stuck on his beard. He probably didn't know it was there. I reached up to remove it, and his whole beard came off! I was dejected to learn that Santa was a fake.

AGE 4 At age four, I proclaimed to all my family and friends that I was going to die in a car accident when I was nineteen. Okay, so I wasn't psychic.

I think this may have been my way to encourage people to talk about death. Even my richest sources of information were reluctant to discuss the topic. However, I was intrigued by the idea that people could just completely disappear. On my third birthday, I had realized I was a being in time, and now came the knowledge that I wasn't even going to be here one day. Every single person was going to die. What an intriguing concept.

Our grandmother lived just down the street. Every morning, my sister and I would walk to her house and stand at the back door shouting, "We want breakfast! We want breakfast!" She would welcome us with a loving smile, and serve us scrambled eggs, toast, and a few drops of coffee in a cup of warm, sugary milk.

My grandmother loved to feed the birds and squirrels. I also learned to relate to these little creatures. I had a favorite squirrel, Timmy, who would follow me around the yard gently taking peanuts from my hand. Once I even let him into my grandmother's house. She was not too thrilled about this. He was, after all, a wild squirrel. Fortunately, he behaved himself and left quietly.

It was time for my sister and I to get our measles vaccinations. We were going to a clinic where the shots were being given to a large group of kids all at once. During the drive, my 6-year-old sister was getting more and more scared about the impending injection.

I, on the other hand, was feeling quite brave about it all. I took over the role of big sister, and proceeded to give her some wise advice about getting shots.

"It will happen so fast, you won't even feel it. There's no reason to be scared about a little shot." I was enjoying this new position of authority, and used it to preach a wonderful sermon about the importance of giving up fear. My parents in the front seat were clearly impressed with my maturity, as was I. This may have been my first tangible experience of pride.

When we arrived at the clinic, I don't know what happened to my little wise soul. All my bravado fell away, and I was overcome with terror. "Oh no! A shot!!!"

Screaming at the top of my lungs, I ran to hide in a corner. On this day, I learned that it is much easier to give advice than to follow it.

AGE 5 Kindergarten had been easy and fun, consisting mainly of games, naps and cookies. But now I was in first grade. This was where my rebellious nature first expressed itself into the world. I refused to do homework. I didn't want to do it, and I wouldn't do it.

Part of the problem was that I already knew most of what was being taught. I was reading on a fourth grade level. In fact, the teacher often asked me to help the other students with their reading. You might think that would have made it easier for me to zip through the assignments, but it didn't work that way. I was bored by it all.

During this time, the word *lazy* was introduced to my world. My teacher told me I was lazy, and my parents told me I was lazy. Looking back, it is remarkable how much of my adult life was spent trying to convince the world and myself that I'm not!

❧

Concerned about my scholastic incompetence, my parents took me to have my IQ professionally tested. My mother had been tested with a 160 IQ, and was a member of Mensa. She was much relieved when I surpassed the test boundary of 160.

This meant there was no excuse for my laziness and refusal to do schoolwork. A new battle ensued. At one point, my parents told me if I brought home one more note from school, I would be severely punished. So when my teacher handed me the next note, I didn't bring it home. Instead, I put the envelope in my coat pocket and conveniently forgot all about it. The next day, I told my first outright lie.

As I was leaving the classroom that afternoon, my first-grade teacher asked if I had given her note to my parents. I said "Yes." Then she asked if they had sent back any response, and I said, "No."

Before this I had never really considered lying as a viable alternative to getting in trouble. I was surprised by how easy it was to lie, although there was an uncomfortable knot in my stomach at the same time. What if she had asked a specific question in the letter and was expecting an answer? Unfortunately, I had forgotten to read the note myself.

She didn't say anything more, and it looked as though I had gotten away with the deception, until one of my classmates came running into the room with my still unopened envelope. It had fallen onto the hallway floor through a hole in my coat pocket. The teacher took the envelope and looked at it. She rose up and pointed her finger at me. "Now you're really going to get it."

As she walked out the door, I followed, begging her not to get me in trouble. But she wanted to teach me a lesson. She *wanted* me to be scared. After all, at age five I had just lied to her face. While walking up the school stairway, she continued to describe all the trouble I was going to be in. I stayed at the bottom of the stairs, crying and pleading for mercy, hoping to avoid the inevitable spanking. It didn't work.

I think this early lesson may have been the one that taught me not to lie. If so, I will always be grateful to my first-grade teacher.

AGE 6 One of my first memories of jealousy happened when I was 6 years old. We weren't quite ready to move into our new, improved neighborhood yet, but the school semester was beginning. It didn't make sense to spend one month in one school and then change, and so Frona Foner came into the picture. Frona was a teacher at the elementary school we were going to attend. My parents knew her through some mutual friends, and asked if she would be willing to drive my sister and me to the new school for the next month. She agreed, and early every morning, my mother would drop us off at her house. There, we would wait in the front room until it was time to go to school.

Frona had, if I remember correctly, three children. We hardly ever saw them, since they only had to come through the front room to leave the house. There was a doorway between where we sat and where the kids were getting ready for school. And what we heard and smelled through that doorway shocked and enticed us. What kind of family was this?

The kids would be watching cartoons while their mom made breakfast. We could hear the shows but not see them.

Then we would smell all kinds of wonderful breakfast aromas. We had usually not eaten anything before leaving our house, especially since it was so early in the morning. My mother never cooked breakfast for us. That had been our grandmother's territory. Now we were leaving the house much too early to go to her house, and so we didn't eat breakfast at all.

Through the sliver of open door, we would hear all these *family sounds* of kids getting dressed. "Where is your blue shirt?" "Come here, honey, let me zip that up for you."

My sister and I were shocked. We had never even imagined a family scene like this. There was warmth, caring and laughter. These people actually seemed to like each other! I think we were more surprised and intrigued than outright jealous.

Sitting there for so long every morning, my sister and I did manage to entertain ourselves. We'd pretend we were begging for pieces of toast, and end up cracking up so hard that we'd have to stifle our laughter.

AGE 7 At age seven, my favorite toy was a massive chemistry set. Since both of my parents were high school teachers, they were able to bring home chemicals and instruments from the chemistry departments in their schools. I had a Bunsen burner, two high-powered microscopes, and shelf after shelf of chemicals.

Sometimes I would follow experiments described in the high-school books, but most often I would just heat stuff up and mix it all together to see what happened. Some of my creations smelled really bad, others fizzed over on to the table.

Most just changed color or did nothing. Fortunately none of them blew up the basement!

My sister and I became instant outcasts at our new school. I think the main reason for this was that we were quite unkempt. Nobody helped us to get dressed in the morning. Not surprisingly, we put together some strange color and texture combinations. This did *not* build a positive image for us in our affluent new school.

There were, for example, the orange tennis shoes. They had been on sale for five dollars each, and my thrifty mother snatched up ten pairs: five for my sister and five for me. Pointy-toed, bright orange tennis shoes, with our pink dresses, green skirts, and purple blouses. My sister and I walked into our new school looking very strange indeed.

Suddenly, after six years of pleasant relationships with my peer group, I was an *outcast.* At first, I didn't know how to respond to this new experience of being teased. I would answer back with some clever or sarcastic answer, but that didn't seem to work at all. The other kids wouldn't appreciate my humor. Clearly, there were no extra points given for cleverness in this new game of teasing the outcast. Anything I said made things worse, so I learned to stay silent.

Upon reflection, I can see some important lessons that came from this tumultuous time. First, I had to learn to control my anger. I learned to remain peaceful, even in the face of injustice.

Also, I learned to feel content while just being alone with myself. Although I would form some valuable relationships and friendships later in life, they were not based on neediness.

If destiny brought a relationship to me, I would experience it in the moment. But I didn't seek out relationships to fill a gap in my life. And when my karmic connection with someone began to wane, I would usually be able to move forward with little disruption.

So, as with all life circumstances, whether outwardly favorable or unfavorable, this situation brought valuable benefits along with the adversity.

Another problem arose for me during this time. In my old school we had been learning to print. I'd learned to read and print before even starting school, and had been far ahead of my classmates. Now I was going to a much better school, and these kids already knew how to write! I hadn't even started to learn handwriting. Suddenly, I went from being the class genius to the class dunce, and an outcast to boot. Life really began to crumble at age seven.

AGE 8 By this time my parents actively hated each other. And my sister and I, or "the bastards," as we were often called (as in "Get the bastards in the car,") were the reason they had to stay together and suffer. Their resentment was tangible.

One day I got into a bit of trouble at school for swearing. While standing in the lunch line, a particularly hyperactive kid jumped in front of me, pushing me back. Being the outcast often meant being at the end of the line for things. I was upset at being pushed back, and called him a "bitch." Who knew it was a bad word? It was a an often used thread in the argument tapestry at our house.

Our family no longer ate meals together. My mother had finally become tired of slaving over a hot stove cooking "Hamburger Helper" every night. She and my father discovered that they could afford to eat every meal in restaurants. From then on, my meals consisted of TV dinners, canned soups, toast, and/or ice cream. The closest thing I got to wholesome meals were the none-too savory school cafeteria lunches.

Around this time, my sister and I discovered the occult. Our mother was a violin player for the local philharmonic orchestra, and every other Friday we'd have to sit through a two-hour concert. If we moved around or talked, we'd get in trouble for disturbing the audience. So we came up with a little game. We would choose a nearby, unsuspecting candidate. My sister would try to use her will power to make the person scratch their ear, and I would direct mine to making their nose itch. Whichever area was scratched first decided the winner of the game.

We also began to use an ouija board to answer questions, and held seances, trying to evoke disembodied spirits. We read spooky books, and religiously watched our favorite shows, "The Twilight Zone" and "One Step Beyond." We played constant ESP games, and were absolutely convinced that we were able to access paranormal powers.

Our parents did not discourage these interests. In fact, they were teaching about the various categories of paranormal phenomena in their ever popular high-school psychology classes. Our mother even seemed to think she had some special psychic abilities, or at least wanted others to think she did. Around this time, she started hanging out with "a group of witches." I never knew much about them, except that she liked to impress them with her friend, the Wizard.

First, my mother would have one of her witch friends pull a card from a deck at random, let's say the six of diamonds. Then she would phone our house. I'd answer the phone, and she would ask "May I speak to the Wizard?"

This was my cue to play the game. I would begin to recite the four card suits, "Spades, clubs, diamonds. . ."

As soon as I said "diamonds," my mother would say, "Yes, I'll hold," and I would begin to recite the card numbers.

When I reached "six," she would say, "Hello Mr. Wizard."

Then my mother would hand the phone to her friends, and I would speak in my deepest, most wizard-like voice, "Your card is the six of diamonds."

Her witch friends were amazed. All they heard was, "May I speak to the Wizard? Yes, I'll hold. Hello, Mr. Wizard." And there would be the Wizard with their randomly chosen card.

From this game, I learned that apparently paranormal events may ultimately have an everyday explanation.

AGE 9 At nine, I began to babysit. Despite my young age, I looked like a teenager and was often trusted with more responsibility than other kids. I started by babysitting for the twin babies of my parents' friends.

The adults would usually stay out past midnight. There I would wait, bobbing in and out of consciousness for hours. I'd keep the television set on most of the time, trying to stay awake. Even though I was *allowed* to fall asleep, still I felt guilty when I did. After all, I was being paid by the hour to babysit.

Little did I know these efforts were stretching my consciousness. The practice of trying to stay awake while sleep descends takes a lot of mental self-control. I would stay right on the edge between wakefulness and sleep for hours on end. It was uncomfortable, yet there was also a blissful transcendence in moving through various degrees of unconsciousness with just a sliver of awareness.

This was the year we took our first family vacation overseas. My sister and I were excited about the trip, but knew that being with our parents full-time was not going to be a barrel of fun. We were right!

Right after landing in France, I started feeling stomach flu symptoms. While walking through the Louvre, I was getting increasingly nauseous. At first, I didn't say anything, hoping the queasiness would go away. However, as we stood examining the Mona Lisa for what felt like way too long, I realized I was going to throw up. I told my father, and he helped me find a "water closet."

This French bathroom was unlike any I had ever seen before. Two very large, metal footprints stuck out from the floor, with a large drain-hole between them. I stood on one of the footprints and puked my guts out. When I returned to the gallery, my parents were arguing about what to do with me. They were upset that I was sick. How dare I try to ruin their vacation like this?

My parents believed that all illness is *psychosomatic*, created by the mind. This was a theory they had picked up while doing research for their psychology classes. My mother's class notes explain, "We sometimes condition behavior that is not wanted inadvertently. For example, a child is ill and the parents make a big fuss over him with positive reinforcements of gifts and attention. Illness should be checked and basically ignored. It seems cruel, but doesn't reinforce the illness."

Although this philosophy may have value on a theoretical level, it created a rather distorted response to disease in our family. If I got sick or even injured, it was thought to be intentional. When ill, I would be ignored, sometimes for days on end. I remember my mother once saying, "If she gets hungry enough, she'll decide to get better." I don't think they responded this way with the specific intention of inflicting cruelty on us. Nevertheless, it served as a convenient excuse for them to avoid acting as caring parents, even during our most needy times.

Here we were in beautiful Paris, and I was sick to my stomach. There was some discussion of whether I could be dropped off at the hotel, but that didn't seem acceptable. So we continued on to the Eiffel Tower.

In order to see the view from the top, it was necessary to walk up many flights of stairs. We began the trek, but soon I was lagging behind. I felt so sick that I had to use my hands to help pull me up each step. At first, my parents accused me of being overly dramatic, then they just walked on. My sister stayed behind to help me.

Eventually, we arrived on a level with an elevator. My parents were waiting there, still irritated with me. "Because of you, we have to take the elevator!" I felt bad, but was relieved not to have to crawl up any more steps. Fortunately, it ended up being only a 24-hour flu.

The trip continued through Austria, Germany, and Hungary. We were making the trip with a book my father had found: *Europe on $5 a Day*. There were few things my father loved more than saving money. His father had lost all his money in the Depression, and never recovered from the loss. My father was left with serious money issues because of his father's trauma. So here we were two generations later, staying in the crummiest places so we could experience Europe on $5 a day.

In Vienna, we spent more than two hours trying to find the cheapest place. We found it. The room was filled with flies. We had to keep calling the front desk to come up and kill them. The beds also had bugs, and we had to have all the linens changed. But there was my father, happily keeping track of how little we had spent, so he could go back home and impress all his friends. This was our "luxurious" trip to Europe!

Germany presented another problem for me. Most of the food in Germany looked like sausages, all wrapped up in intestines. I had recently watched a cooking show and discovered what that chewy wrapping on my hot dogs was really made of. From that day, I never touched one again.

So in Germany, I lived for several days on nothing but bread and beer.

My parents weren't upset to see me drinking beer. They thought it was cute that I liked alcohol. Truthfully, I wasn't really as crazy about the flavor as I tried to appear. It was just a way to get positive attention. It had started when I was five. We visited my great-aunt for Passover dinner almost every year. It was the only slightly religious thing our family ever did. I would get smashed on Manischevitz while all the adults laughed. "Look how cute, she likes the wine!" At the time I relished whatever positive attention I could get.

Germany was also significant for another reason. My father was absolutely obsessed with Hitler. He was teaching several history classes at the time, and included a very detailed study of Nazism. Our four days in Germany were spent mostly at Holocaust museums and sites. We went to the Dachau concentration camp and saw the barracks, gas chamber, ovens, and shocking photos of the victims. It was all very sobering. Seeing this level of pain and suffering made me grateful to have the life I had, even with its difficult times.

After Germany and Austria, we went to Hungary where we took a trip with some distant relatives who lived there. At one point, the adults wanted to go off on their own, so they left my sister and me with our two Hungarian cousins at a youth communist camp for several days. We had to wear the official khaki shirts with red scarves. Every morning we would stand for a half-hour while all the kids chanted communist slogans. My sister and I spoke almost no Hungarian, and nobody there spoke any English at all. But there was a swimming pool and campfire dances at night, and we had a reasonably good time nonetheless.

AGE 10 School was getting worse. As my peers grew older, they became more obnoxious in tormenting us few unlucky souls, the school outcasts. In a way, it was like being famous, except the attention was negative. We had songs composed about us and our families. Sometimes we were tripped or pushed around physically. Our every move was scrutinized.

Now that the initial stress of being an outcast had worn off to some degree, I was starting to settle in to my new role. Even though it looked bad from the outside, really, it wasn't so bad. This situation brought me a sense of freedom. I came to realize that it wasn't necessary for me to be like everyone else. I didn't have to try to make the other kids like me, because they wouldn't anyway. I could be eccentric; I could be aloof. I could be myself without putting on masks to please others. I could be alone with my thoughts. I didn't even want the other kids to like me at this point. Most of them were so obnoxious and immature that I had no desire to be friends with them. Inside, I would often laugh at their nonsense. One girl who wore big glasses even started to call me "four-eyes." I guess she didn't quite understand the term.

By this time, my parents had all but disappeared. It was 1970, and they had entered the hippie world of free-love and pot parties. We never knew when they would be coming home. My sister and I received generous allowances of $20 per week, allowing us to eat regularly at fast-food restaurants. Far from lacking material possessions, I had my own room, a private phone line, and an excellent quadraphonic audio system.

One fateful day, our mother decided to try to cook a meal. It had been years since she had done such a thing. I don't know what got into her. She bought a fish and put it in the oven. My sister and I took one look at this fish with its head still on and started laughing, making fun of it. "We're definitely not going to eat that!"

Our mother became very upset. Here she was trying to act normal and motherly, and we didn't even appreciate her efforts. She yelled, "You are going to eat it, or you can go to hell!"

My sister and I went upstairs for a meeting. We decided to run away from home, rather than eat that nasty-looking fish. We gathered our savings, and left a note: "WE WENT TO HELL."

Proud of our boldness, we slithered down the roof to our bikes, and took off. We had a lovely dinner at Burger King, and visited a couple of the neighborhood stores. Then it got dark. We hadn't really thought about what we were going to do at night. Where would we sleep? We tried to come up with an alternative, but finally had to surrender and return home, knowing we would be punished. The end result wasn't too bad. Our bike privileges were revoked for a month, but at least we didn't have to eat that awful fish!

AGE 11 At this point, my sister and I became film makers. We'd use a little super-8 camera to create all kinds of "masterpieces." The first was, "The Adventures of Super Squirrel," featuring all of our stuffed animals moving across the screen frame-by-frame, saving one another from peril.

By this time, I had become the quintessential bratty sister, but my sister was physically stronger than I. She won every fight, though I never seemed to give up. We both had a substantial amount of sublimated frustrations, and were often aggressive with one another. Since our parents were hardly ever home, we'd have the whole house available as our fighting space. We would stand on opposite ends of the living room, with piles of boots and shoes. Then we'd throw them at one another as hard as we could, one by one. Whoever was the least injured by the end was the winner. Or we'd run around the house with glasses of water, splashing them over each other's head.

One day, I stood behind the door frame, poised with a big pillow. I was waiting for my sister to walk through so I could slam the pillow down on her head. I stood there patiently for a long time. Finally she came through, and I smashed the pillow down with all my might. Oops! It was my mother. She was too shocked to even get mad.

Although she wasn't a model parent, my mother was quite an interesting character. The high-school kids lined up to take her fascinating psychology class. She once hired an artist to create a huge scenic painting of a deer walking through the woods on our garage door — to make it easier for friends to find our house. "We're the house with the deer on the garage."

Unfortunately, it also made our house easy to find for her inevitable few disgruntled students. We spent many hours cleaning eggs and tomatoes that had been thrown against our windows, and the beautiful deer painting was eventually sprayed over with graffiti.

Our mother was clever and punny. Actually, her puns often got on our nerves. Once I fell off my bike and broke my big toe. It quickly became swollen, painful, and dark purple. I was barely able to make it home, hobbling with my bike. When I showed my mother what had happened, she quipped, "Well, I guess we'll have to call a tow (toe) truck!"

AGE 12 At the age of twelve, I entered junior high school, where things improved considerably. Blue-jeans were now standard wear. It's hard to mismatch anything with jeans. There was a whole new group of kids at this school, and I found new friends and a niche for myself. School became a fun place, and I met my best friend, Larry.

Larry was special to me. He was an adorable boy who looked as though he could be a rock star. We hit it off right away. He used to laugh for hours as I told him all the horror stories of my home life. It was so healing to be able to laugh at these things with my new best friend.

From this point on, my reaction to difficult family circumstances was transformed from distress to glee. Whenever my parents were acting particularly insane, I would be chuckling to myself at how much Larry was going to laugh when I told him about *this* one. Without changing the external circumstances at all, my experience of family life was transformed. With just a shift of perspective, the pain became pleasure. The idea that my family's craziness was good fodder for conversation elevated my whole perception of it. I almost looked forward to the next shocking event, knowing how much Larry would be entertained. And I didn't usually have to wait very long!

Around this time, I started to take amphetamines. I took them for nearly two years. My mother had befriended a "diet doctor," who had access to pure speed, and I decided to join her in this new adventure. Though neither of us were more than a few pounds overweight, we would go every Tuesday afternoon for a shot of pure speed and pills for the week. Every week there would be different tablets and capsules in the packet. We were studying drugs in school at the time, and I learned some of their street names, such as "Christmas trees" and "pink ladies."

As a child speed-freak, I found myself needing much less sleep. Some nights, I would sleep for a single hour before going to school. My brain was buzzing all the time. One positive side-effect of the speed was that it made me really, really smart. All of a sudden, I loved math. I loved algebra. I loved geometry. I loved crossword puzzles and logic problems. I'd stay up all night reading, thinking and going through, at times, two full crossword puzzle books in one night.

After years of receiving C's and D's throughout elementary school, I was now placed in the most advanced math class. I wrote an essay for my seventh-grade English class, contrasting Freud's topological and structural theories. I was still interested in psychology, and continued to read all the latest books being used in my parents' classes. I liked the idea of tracing behaviors back to different theories. It seemed to be as important as anything else I was learning at school.

AGE 13 At thirteen, I got my first real job as a waitress in a nearby restaurant, "The Purple Pickle." According to law I had to be over eighteen to work there; however, I had a fake I.D., and looked old enough to pass.

Still on speed, I'd leave school at 3:30 p.m. and walk to the restaurant. I'd work from 4:00 p.m. until midnight, when one of my co-workers would drive me home. Then I would spend the rest of the night doing homework, reading, and solving logic problems or crossword puzzles. My speeding mother was always up all night as well, so we did manage to spend some time together during this phase. Occasionally, we even managed a little conversation.

I'd work at the restaurant Monday through Friday, and on weekends I would babysit. Most Saturdays, I would take care of three kids whose mother was away in a mental institution. The funny part of the situation was that the oldest girl I was babysitting for was half a year older than I. But the family didn't know that; they thought I was eighteen.

This was a fairly happy time. I was busy and making a lot of money. Plus I was hardly ever home. And when I was home, I was usually stoned. After my encounter with speed, I had discovered other drugs. First, I took THC and mescaline, and then marijuana.

I believe that addiction tendencies are genetic, because that is my only explanation for why I did not become addicted to drugs. I was able to self-monitor when I was becoming dependent on them, and pull back.

This year, our family went overseas again, this time taking a trip to Spain. While there, we took a "nice family drive" through the mountains. As usual, my parents were arguing. My father was dishing out one of his favorite retorts to my mother, "Be nice! If you can't be nice, be normal!"

As we drove higher and higher, my mother began to insult my father more and more vigorously. He was a nervous, insecure man who hated being insulted by her. Finally, he snapped, and started to scream, "This is it! I've had it! We should all die rather than be subject to your constant bitching! If you say another word, I'm going off the cliff!!!"

We were driving on a road barely big enough for two cars to squeak past each other slowly, and there was no guardrail. Our father sped up until we were careening around the curves, more than once touching the edge of the cliffs. My sister and I sat in the back seat, clinging to one another. We were crying and begging my mother to stop nagging him. Instead, she told him he was a "stupid ass."

He began to yell louder and louder. "This is it! We're all going to die! Anything to get away from you!!!"

My sister and I held each other, and prepared to die.

Somehow, we did survive and managed to make it back to the hotel. My sister and I had a room adjoining our parents'.

We slipped into our usual technique for diffusing anxiety, and started to make fun of their ridiculous behavior. We took turns being my father and mother in the scenario, as we nagged and yelled at each other. We tried to do it quietly, but they ended up hearing us. We actually got in trouble for imitating their craziness!

My mother was once written up in the local newspaper in an article called, "The Coupon Queen." She had boxes upon boxes of coupons, organized by type of item and expiration date. She knew when each store had their double- or triple-coupon days, and would often manage to get bags of groceries, practically for free. For example, if an item costs $1.00 and you have a coupon worth 35¢, then a triple-coupon store would have to give you the product for free. One particularly generous checkstand clerk even gave my mother some change along with her free bag of groceries.

If you opened a closet door in our house, you would not see a box of Kleenex. No, you would find two hundred boxes of Kleenex. Need a new tube of toothpaste? Help yourself from one of the toothpaste shelves. When saccharin was outlawed as an additive to soft drinks, my mother purchased more than 10,000 bottles (yes, 10,000), because she liked soda pop. When there was an occasion for me to receive a gift, I would just head down to the toy shelf in the basement and choose one. It was like living in a store.

AGE 14 At age fourteen, I experienced my first opening to the remote possibility of the existence of God. The memory of my initial church extravaganza at age two-and-a-half had been long buried beneath a mountain of subsequent experiences. I'd avoided learning anything about religion. I was a total atheist, as was the rest of my family. It's not even that I denied or disliked God; I simply never considered such a thing as a possibility. It was a non-issue. The only time I can remember the word "God" being spoken in our house was during a party when my father got drunk and ran around the house yelling, "I am God!" And even that carried a bitter memory, because I mumbled, "Yeah, spelled backwards" and was sent to my room.

Somewhere along the line I had heard the word "Jesus." I knew he had something to do with religion, but had made it to age fourteen without knowing the story of Jesus at all. I wasn't even sure what the Bible was, though I knew it was some kind of religious book.

The movie theater near our house had matinees for one dollar on Wednesday evenings. One week, I went to see "Jesus Christ Superstar: A Rock Opera." I almost didn't go because of the title. Obviously, a movie about Jesus was bound to have something to do with religion. But it was the only movie playing that I hadn't seen, so I decided to go.

This musical dramatization may not have been authentic in details; however, for someone who had never heard about what supposedly happened a couple thousand years ago, it communicated the archetype of this event. The story touched me in a way that nothing ever had, and brought forth feelings I had never known. I walked into the theater in one world, and left in quite another.

The actors seemed to have really tapped into the essence of the historical figures they portrayed. Their passion was potent, and sparked a new shift inside me. I was inspired by Jesus' intimate relationship and personal dialogue with God. He even yelled at him during one song. Many times, I would have liked to have had a God to yell at!

One of the most touching moments for me came during Jesus' second meeting with Pilate. He had been beaten and led all over the place by Roman soldiers, then dragged into the arena. There, Jesus stood before Pilate, a man with the political clout to kill him. All around were the very people who had worshipped Jesus fervently, now turned against him.

To powerful strains of rock music, Pilate had Jesus whipped fiercely, until he fell helplessly to the ground. Then, with the tenderness of a mother, Pilate lifted Jesus' head. He did not want to kill this man.

Pilate began to sing, "Where are you from, Jesus? What do you want, Jesus? Tell me. You've got to be careful, you could be dead soon, could well be. Why do you not speak when I hold your life in my hands? How can you stay quiet, I don't believe you understand!"

With eyes that seemed to look beyond his own pain into another world, Jesus sang with sweet defiance, "You have nothing in your hands. Any power you have comes to you from far beyond. Everything is fixed and you can't change it!"

This was an extraordinary lesson for me. Jesus didn't buy into the illusion. He didn't apologize or change his belief system to fit in with the ignorance before him. Rather, he took refuge in this *God* who was so tangible to him.

During difficult phases of my childhood, there had been no sense of any higher being to pray to, ask for blessings, or watch over me. It's not that this movie immediately transformed me into a believer, but it did open up a previously untapped spiritual passion deep inside my soul.

AGE 15 In high school now, I was part of a clique (a nonviolent version of a gang), hanging out in a neighborhood several miles away from mine, with a group of kids who had less money but were friendlier and less pretentious than those in my neighborhood. Most of my new friends were barely making it through school, but at least they were fun. Many had a certain street-smart intelligence that wouldn't necessarily be evident to those who might judge them from their external looks and behavior. We drank and took drugs regularly. We also became troublemakers, and would sometimes go into construction sites and wreak havoc. It's a good thing we were never caught, or I might be writing this from a jail cell instead of a cottage by the ocean!

In my school, there were two groups of kids, the *freaks* and the *straights*. The freaks were the wilder kids, while the straights were generally more intellectual and focused on school. I straddled the two worlds. I was definitely one of the freaks, and spent most of my time with them. On the other hand, even with my wild nature I was able to get good grades and chat intelligently with the straights. I think it was during this time that I realized it was not necessary for me to fit neatly into any mold. I learned to meet each person on their own level. I didn't have to be stuck in any one persona. I could kick back with the freaks one minute, and discuss philosophy with the intellectuals the next.

By this time I was spending less and less time at home. My family never ate meals together, and I had subsisted on junk food for many years. My friends' parents seemed to feel bad about my home situation and often invited me to join them for meals. Nearly every evening this year I ate dinner at one of my friend's houses.

Larry's very loving and devoted mother was so upset by his stories about my family that she offered to adopt me. I wanted to take her up on her proposition more than she knew. But it seemed as though the attempt would just make things worse. My parents would never go for it. I had to wait it out.

During this year, I learned how to be a winner. One day, I was listening to the radio. Every now and then there would be phone-in contests for various prizes. I never really paid much attention to them, until one day when I heard they were about to give away some record albums I'd been wanting. I dialed the number and won. Free albums! I developed a new interest in this phone-contest game and decided to learn the ropes.

Most of the stations scheduled their contests at the same time every hour. Some had so many phone lines that you would have to call *before* the contest was even announced to have a chance of winning. I spent hours practicing dialing each number really fast. It was like going to work, only better. I was winning free things nearly every day. Sometimes, I'd win two or three contests in a row.

From this venture I also learned about the tides of destiny. Some days I could feel that the energy around me was low. I knew I wouldn't win, though I'd still try. Other times, I knew even while the phone was ringing that I would be the correct caller.

Within two weeks, each of the stations told me I could no longer win their contests, since I had already won so many times. I put together a list of all my friends' and my parents' friends' names, keeping track of which prizes needed to be picked up from where and in whose name. I was a phone-contest entrepreneur. Within a few months, I had won tickets and transportation to a Kiss concert in Chicago, many T-shirts, $150 cash, a one-year supply of spaghetti, and hundreds of record albums. I had so many albums that my parents went out and bought me a full-sized record display case from a local store that was going out of business.

Once, I won 25 albums with one call. First, you had to be the right caller. Then, you would have ten seconds to say as many albums as you could, title and artist. You would win whatever albums you could name in the ten seconds. I really practiced for this. First, I made a list of the shortest album titles that also contained the artist's name. That was easy because there were many live albums out at the time: *Bowie Live*, *Kiss Live*, *Frampton Live*, etc. Then I would call the number for "time." A woman's voice would continually say, "At the tone, the time will be X hour, X minutes and X seconds. Conveniently, her declarations were exactly ten seconds apart. I practiced my list for hours, and then managed to make it through as the right caller. The seconds ticked away as I executed my well-rehearsed stack of words. The buzzer went off, and the radio DJ said, "Wow, that was great! You must have gotten at least eight to ten in there."

Most people could only say four or five titles and artists in the ten seconds.

Still on the air, I said, "No, that was twenty-five titles and artists."

He said, "I'm sorry. There's no way that was twenty-five."

I suggested that he play the tape back at slow speed. He agreed, and came back on after the next song to announce that I really had won all twenty-five albums.

It was around this time that I started to play pinball. We had full-sized pinball and ski-ball machines right in our basement. Through this game, I once again learned to sense and ride the tides of fate. There were times when I knew every ball would shoot down the middle, clearly predestined for extinction. Then there were other times when I would slip into an extremely confident space. With deep mental focus, I had a sense of stepping back out of myself. I was there, but more as an onlooker, allowing my subconscious abilities to come through without mental judgment or interference. I would orchestrate the game strategy, while my hands served as proficient soldiers.

Around this time, my parents finally split up. My mother had been seeing my father's best friend for eight years. We all knew about the affair, and now that my sister and I were older, they wanted to get married. Thus began the divorce fiasco.

If life wasn't stressful enough before this, now my sister and

I were used as pawns so my parents could hurt one another. Each parent trashed the other, and sent mean-spirited messages back and forth through us. Our mother called our father "that bastard," and he called our mother and her fiancé "the infant and the child." It was all very complicated and messy. I couldn't wait to get away from these people.

AGE 16 Within six months, my mother and her fiancé had married, and my father found a new girlfriend who soon became wife number two. Jean had been one of my father's students years earlier. After my sister and I visited their apartment for the first and only time, she told my father that she didn't want us coming over anymore, because "they messed up the magazines on my table." By this time, not much could faze us. We just took it in stride when our father stopped calling.

To jump ahead in my narrative, it was more than a decade before I saw my father again. While visiting Los Angeles during the winter of 1987, I unexpectedly found myself staying just two blocks away from where he was living, now with wife number three. I decided to pay a surprise visit to dear old dad.

Through the screen door, I saw him sitting at the dining room table. I called out, "Hello! I'm home!"

He came to the door and asked, "Can I help you?"

I snickered and replied, "Yes, I'm here!" I opened the door, walked into his house, and put my hand on his shoulder, looking him right in the eye. He was probably worried that I might be one of the many women he'd had affairs with during his wilder years.

He looked closely into my face and asked, "Don't I know you from somewhere?"

Eventually, he figured out that I was one of the two people he had brought into the world. We kept in touch for a while, then he disappeared from my life again with wife number four. Neither of us seemed interested enough to maintain long-term contact.

Coming back to age sixteen, I had been developing as a visual artist for several years. By this time, I'd even sold some of my paintings. One of my art teachers began to take a special interest in me.

Ms. Mack was an artist and filmmaker. She invited my friend and I to a screening of some of her work, and sponsored us to join the local film group. Ms. Mack had made films to two contemporary songs, and I was moved and impressed by her work. I decided to make a film too, and my friend, Debbie, agreed to help.

We made a short movie to David Bowie's song, "Rock and Roll Suicide." I was the director and camerawoman, and Debbie was the actress. Debbie was quite the little alcoholic at age sixteen, and enjoyed having a chance to act out her not-so-secret desire to commit suicide.

As part of Ms. Mack's class, we also learned about an artist who made movies by hand-drawing directly on each of 24 tiny film frames per second. I enjoyed focusing my mind on painstaking, creative work, and decided to make one of these as well.

I had already been accepted by the University of Michigan, and no longer cared about my high-school grades.

Indulging my rebellious nature, I went from class to class with a big box containing film, ink pens, and two roller mechanisms. While each teacher gave their lecture, I would be sitting in the middle of class, working away on my own little project. One of my teachers forbade me to work on it during her class, while another thought it was a bold and humorous thing for me to do. Yet another expressed personal interest in the artistic merits of the project. The rest just ignored my unconventional behavior.

By this time I had quit taking any hard drugs. Some THC pills laced with strychnine had been sold around school, and I'd taken one. Although the effect wasn't too traumatic for me, it was uncomfortable enough to inspire me to stop taking more than the occasional smoke of a joint.

> *Men do not know themselves,*
> *and therefore they do not understand*
> *the things of their inner world.*
> *Each man has the essence of God*
> *and all the wisdom and power*
> *of the world in himself.*
>
> —*Paracelsus*

5.

Exploring
the Unconscious

AT AGE SEVENTEEN, my time for freedom arrived. My mother and stepfather drove me to the University of Michigan in Ann Arbor. I would be living in a dorm room on the north campus with a very sweet, conventional girl from Massachusetts. Though we got along well, I'm sure Mary Jo often wondered about her unusual roommate. While she was out enjoying the college life, I would sit in our room for hours at a time, with my eyes closed.

Freed of the family constraints and stresses that had kept me in a state of perpetual anxiety for so long, I now had the space to decide who and what I would be. My first interest was to learn more about my mind and the reality it presented to me. I began to use the self-hypnosis techniques learned at age seven to explore my inner consciousness.

Every day, I would sit in the dorm room, and turn my mental focus inward for hours at a time. I'd begin by using the standard techniques for putting myself into a hypnotic trance state, but then something strange would happen. I would enter into a state of mind completely different from any other I had known. I could often feel the physical energy patterns of my brain shift as this opening took place. There I would sit, watching as new understandings began to move through my awareness like a flowing river of insights.

These exploration sessions became more important than anything else in my life. From the space of higher perspective, it felt as though what I had been calling and thinking of as "the world" was just the *baby fingertip* of the real, whole, universal world. It was all so big, so full, so rich and symphonic. Delving deeper into the uncharted waters of consciousness, I withdrew my attention more and more from the "outer" world, becoming more reclusive. Though I was still able to maintain a facade of chit-chat with my schoolmates, I didn't even *try* to discuss the grand spaces I was accessing inside myself during these journeys. They seemed to have no place in the external world, especially in those "pre-New Age" days.

With these sessions, my notion of *self* also began to shift. Through introspection, I began to see my personality, not so much as a solid entity, but more as a biological system made up of tissues and cells of personalities. At times, I'd see tendencies of my family members expressing through me, or reflections of old friends laced through what I had previously considered to be *my* behavior. It was as though human personality was a series of mirrors, receiving and reflecting back patterns of thought and character features of everything and everyone before us.

I watched as my personality spontaneously adjusted itself to whomever I was with. Their nature would resonate with my mass of personality potential, evoking from it aspects that resonated with their own. While chatting with scholars, I would find myself speaking with a more intellectual flair. While hanging out with art students, my eccentricity would be more noticeable. I was sometimes able to learn about a person just by the tendencies, thoughts and speech patterns their presence would elicit inside myself. I was discovering what some ancient texts call "the power of company."

From age seven, I had studied my parents' psychology books religiously. Many of them dealt with multiple personality syndrome. I had found this area to be the most fascinating of all. Several personalities could live inside one body. They would have different voice patterns, different allergies, different talents and abilities. Some would need glasses, while others didn't. One woman even had three menstrual cycles every month, one for each personality. Now there's a good incentive to get healed!

I began to see a less dramatic version of this fragmentation in myself and other people. My friends and parents were not just individual, solid objects. They were each a symphony of personality potentials, with various tendencies becoming predominant at different times. I liked some *parts* of them, and disliked others. I also liked some parts of myself better than others.

Delving into the previously subconscious layers of my psyche, it became clear to me that personality is inherently multiple. For example, I was no longer the same personality I had been as a child, though there seemed to be an essential palette of colors from which all my various character tendencies had been drawn. I watched as my fellow students would get drunk during our dorm parties, acting completely different than they did in class. If I was feeling confident and supported in a group, my personality might expand into being the life of the party; whereas other times I might appear to be very serious and indrawn. My internal and external responses to any particular event could shift drastically depending on my "mood."

Through this contemplation, I came up with a new view of personality. It wasn't that those who suffered from multiple personality disorder had grown an entire biological structure that had nothing to do with that of a so-called normal person. The thread that created and maintained personality consistency appeared to be dependent on memory storage and retrieval. In the case of someone with multiple personality disorder, the various aspects of themselves were no longer communicating with one another. They were hoarding memories.

I began to observe my thought processes with a more objective eye, breaking down what I had thought of as *me* into more organized components. No longer was "I happy" or "I sad" or "I sleepy" or "I enthusiastic." The mirage of *I* opened up, revealing countless levels of physical, electrical, chemical, and ethereal processes that projected all these experiences into the stillness of nonidentification.

A few warning bells did go off as I began to peel back the layers of personality skin to investigate the inner workings of consciousness. Did I really want to do this? I was tampering with some delicate frameworks, the foundations of reality. I was sneaking into "programmers-only" territory. What if I ended up institutionalized, babbling some abstract phrase for the rest of my life? Did I really want to know more than the people around me?

These concerns only arose when I thought about the situation with my rational mind. From the *other side*, I knew that these inner explorations were more important than anything else in my life.

I stopped smoking cigarettes, which had been a habit since age twelve. Suddenly, previously bland vegetables began to taste delicious. My tastebuds were no longer numbed by nicotine. I had been paying for the habit not just financially or with my smoker's cough, but even with the enjoyment of flavor. This newfound appreciation for vegetables, coupled with the fact that the meat dishes in our dorm cafeteria looked quite unappetizing, inspired me to become a vegetarian.

I wish the word "vegetarian" had been around during my childhood, when I resisted eating animal meat and was often punished for my refusal. The idea of gnawing flesh and veins off the ribs and breasts of animals was unappealing to me. As a child, I hadn't come up with a list of reasons why eating animals was wrong. The idea didn't seem to require any justification. It was as obvious to me as if someone from our country landed on an island where natives regularly sliced and gobbled up roasted human flesh.

Nonetheless, during my childhood it was unacceptable for someone to be a vegetarian. There were no such things as veggie-burgers or tofu-dogs. Everyone ate meat. You had to eat meat; it was not a choice. So I came up with a rule. I would only eat meat that was well disguised, such as hamburgers or sandwiches, and I refused to eat animal flesh off of bones.

Now I was in college and could make my own decisions. I swiftly became a vegetarian. Years later I would discover that many people in India are vegetarian, based on the idea that a nonmeat diet is not only compassionate, but beneficial for meditation and yoga as well. Maybe the intuition made available by my inward focus led me to make this spontaneous dietary change that would allow me access to even more subtle recesses of my mind.

Sitting quietly in my dorm room, I continued to move more deeply into my inner thought-structures, world-views, and physical sensations. I could experience the functions within my body, my heart beating and my stomach working to digest food. I could feel the peristalsis in my intestines, the blood pumping through my body, and into different areas of my brain. Once I visualized my stomach churning like a factory to digest and process all the food I had just eaten. This image gave me chills whenever I'd eat for some time afterwards. I had always thought I was throwing food down some nondescript hatch.

During this time, I became intrigued by the physiological aspects of psychology, and started reading about the electrochemical interactions that create personal experience. This field of science brought reality down to shockingly basic terms. Vision was simply a serious of receptors and translators of information, combining with stored memory information to create the internal experience of external images. This new way of looking at the world was fascinating to me. I enjoyed the idea that the whole universe could be boiled down to the cellular level of my own brain functions.

I wanted to unravel the mystery of personal experience. Armed with a bit of knowledge about the mechanisms behind sense experience and mental structure, I began to pinpoint various processes as they occurred in my brain. Once I ate an apple in a state of heightened awareness, and was able to separate the individual textures, flavors and smells from the mirage we commonly refer to as the apple's *flavor*. I could taste the starchiness of the apple and feel its potato-like texture on my tongue. I could discern and separate the fructose sugars woven through it; I could detect the importance of smell in creating this experience of "eating an apple." Through experiments such as this, I began to separate sensation into its more basic components.

I was also able to *manufacture* the semblance of experience internally. Once, I decided to fast for three days on water mixed with lemon and honey. During the fast, I continued my daily practice of going into trance. I decided to try an experiment, and created a huge, delicious meal in my mind.

Through conscious imagination, I was able to orchestrate the various aspects of my brain to create a very realistic experience of eating. I sat there during all three days of the fast, savoring the most wonderful foods. I was surprised to find myself eating even more delicious meals in my mind than I had ever eaten in real life. Everything tasted exactly the way I liked it. Each spice was in balance, and every crust was perfectly crispy. Each dish was a combination of all the specific elements I most liked about that food, and on top of all that, the experience felt real! This was what it might be like to eat a favorite meal in heaven. With the physical element removed, there was just the internal image-maker, who fools and entertains us every night with the convincing images of our dreams.

The same creative mechanism that makes our dreams feel sometimes more real than the waking state is what I tapped into while eating these "astral" meals. It was the essence of the best experiences I remembered from previous meals. That's what I was eating really, the essence of my own memories. It was a quick hop from here to the topic of pleasure.

A psychology article I had read told of experiments where mice would be left in a cage with two levers. One lever would directly stimulate the pleasure centers in the mouse's brain, while the other would bring food into the cage. The mice invariably starved to death. They chose pleasure over food, even though they could have had both.

As I gained more awareness and control over my brain, I wondered how I could make this exploration more fun. Well, I could explore the nature of pleasure. I could learn to stimulate my own pleasure centers without using any wires or levers. Surely, based on everything I knew about the brain, it was possible to use one's will to create experience at its root level…pleasure without an external cause.

If the energy of electrodes could elicit pleasure from a mouse's brain, why not the energy that comes with attention and willpower? I knew from personal experience that eliciting a memory that had originally been perceived in a pleasurable light would bring back many of the chemical, hormonal and brain patterns associated with the experience of pleasure. Surely mental intention could also stimulate the pleasure centers of the brain, through increased blood circulation and oxygen, or another, unknown process. If that woman in my hypnosis class could form a big blister on her arm because she *thought* the teacher's finger was a lit cigarette, then what should be so difficult about eliciting a little bit of pleasure?

I practiced stimulating my pleasure centers at will. It worked surprisingly well. While sitting completely still, I would start to feel a blissful throbbing in my body. It was the sensation of pleasure itself, unqualified, without an object. Everything felt good. The air meeting the surface of the skin on my arms felt like a lover's touch. The sensation of air moving in and out with my breath brought waves of ecstasy.

I began to enjoy this game more and more. In fact, pleasure took over as my main motivation for *turning within*. Alas, human nature can be fickle. We may start doing something for a noble reason, such as the desire to explore the unconscious, but then we get sidetracked by a little bit of pleasure. This is probably why the yoga scriptures warn seekers not to be distracted on their journey toward self-realization by all the amazing inner experiences and supernatural powers that may pop up along the way. These are considered potential traps for one who aspires to higher states of awareness.

Once we open up to the flow of energy within our body,
we also open up to the flow of the energy in the universe.

—*WILHELM REICH*

6.

FAITH-HEALER

WHILE EXPLORING MY UNCONSCIOUS, I became
more sensitive to energies in general. I could feel
the energy that pulsed through my body with
every breath, and eventually, I could even direct it to some
extent. I believe this to be a skill anyone can acquire. It was a
matter of intention and practice, no different from learning
anything else.

Through these inner explorations, I unexpectedly
developed certain paranormal abilities. Without having ever
considered the idea of *faith-healing*, I now understood that
it was possible to move my energy into other people. I was
also able to move a person's own energy within their body
using only my mental intention and willpower. Right there,

on the University of Michigan's north campus, I became a faith-healer.

Once I was called to a room down the hall to heal a girl who had caught a terrible cold. She was sneezing and coughing and could hardly breathe. With important exams coming up in her classes, she was too ill to study. Having heard that I was experimenting with healing people, she asked for my help. I held my hands a few inches above her head, and began to circulate my energy into her body with my mind. I moved my awareness into her sinus system and cleaned out the disease, almost as if I were sweeping debris from a hallway. I simply understood at a deep level how to do this. And just as a good gambler knows when they are right in the flow, I could tell that my efforts were paying off. There was a subtle knowing, a certain tangible sense that my intentions were creating a healing effect in her body.

While I swept away the gunk in this girl's throat, she started to make small coughing noises that got clearer and clearer as I went on. Then I remembered that she also had some kind of recurring knee injury, and so I thought while I was in there, I could work on that as well. I moved my awareness down into her knee and began scraping away at the illness. It was almost as though I were using a tool to do all this, except that it was a subtle, nonphysical tool. Since I was already in her leg, I thought it would be a good idea to move all the way down and clear the whole leg, into her toes. I was standing silently behind her with my hands just above the girl's head, doing all this with my mind. All of a sudden she asked, "Hey! What are you doing in my toes?"

This was my first outward confirmation that my ability to move healing energy was more than just imagination or the power of suggestion. This girl had no reason to think I would be doing anything in her toes. I raised my hands away from her head and she opened her eyes. The cold was completely gone. No stuffed-up nose, no scratchy throat.

I didn't really feel too terribly egotistical about the sudden appearance of these abilities. My focus was not so much on impressing people as on the search for what existed beneath surface appearances. Still, it was fun to play the role of eccentric dorm psychic.

Another time, one of the girls in the room next to mine was really upset. She had a term paper due the next day, which she had put off until the last minute. Now she couldn't find the notecards for this paper anywhere! She was in tears, having torn apart everything in the room. I offered to help. I could feel, once again, that I was in the flow.

I sat on her bed and put myself into a trance state. Within moments, I could see an image of the index cards, sitting on the bottom of the wire basket that was molded into her desk. I walked over and began to take things out of the basket, and immediately found her notecards, hidden amidst some other papers.

The practice of inner exploration seemed to have opened up latent abilities that had not been previously accessible to me. When I would dive beneath the surface waves of this external world, I'd enter a stream of knowledge, a flow of profound insights about deeper patterns of the universe.

Every now and then, I would try to bring an especially delightful understanding with me into my normal consciousness. If I could bring back even one morsel of this treasure, I thought, it could transform the entire world. But by the time an insight came through the porthole of consciousness and was wrapped in the clothing of language, I would be left holding a frustratingly inadequate form of what had been so clear just moments earlier. It was as though I was allowed into this room every day, where delicious secrets of the universe were completely accessible. But when I left the room, only the smallest crumbs would fit through the door. These psychic and healing abilities were a few of those crumbs.

My newfound intuitive connection also had benefits in terms of schoolwork. After all, I was attending classes all day long, and was spending hours each evening exploring my unconscious mind. Who had time to study? I began to write my term papers in this state. Most were written in one sitting. My papers didn't necessarily show the standard depth of research required or expected for the assignments, since the investigation was done inside my mind. I would go into trance with the intention of receiving a personal vision regarding the topic of the paper. After entering into a more expanded, more objective perception, I would cast my thoughts upon the topic. This would often enable me to see patterns or aspects of the subject matter that may not even be available through library research.

During my sophomore year, for example, I took a medical school class on the "Psychobiology of Epilepsy" with one of the world's foremost neurobiologists. Technically, I wasn't even supposed to be in this class because everyone else there was enrolled in the university medical school. But someone had neglected to put the proper prerequisites into the computer, and I discovered the discrepancy and took this opportunity to see what the big kids were learning.

The entire grade for the course was based on one paper we were supposed to write throughout the semester. Just two days before the due date, I sat before my typewriter with a slight sense of desperation and moved into trance. I completed fifteen pages in several hours, and spent the next two days polishing and retyping the paper. The professor gave me a B+ for the project and for the course. He later called me into his office to say, "I can't say that I agree with all your hypotheses, but it was the most entertaining paper I've ever received."

Around this time, I took a workshop based on the teachings of Milton Erickson, who is considered by many to have been the most skilled hypnotist of all time. Erickson was afflicted with polio as a child and had been confined to a wheelchair during his youth. From this vantage point, he observed the body language and subliminal speech patterns of people around him. He learned how to manipulate normally subconscious processes with conscious intention. Fortunately, he was a good guy who used these skills to help his patients, and not to convince shoppers to buy a fluffier, whiter-than-white laundry detergent.

Milton Erickson could put someone into a hypnotic trance just by reaching to shake their hand, using what he called the *confusion technique*. He would move to shake the person's hand, then pull back a bit and hesitate, and then move forward again. At the exact point when the person's mind had stopped in confusion, he would simply command "*Sleep*," and the person would instantly enter a hypnotic trance.

He would also tell stories with specific lessons, voice inflections, precisely orchestrated pauses, and word choices, to heal a particular psychological difficulty the patient might be having. Often, these were simple stories from his own life. Many patients were healed of long-term psychological problems after hearing just one of his tailor-made stories. The implication I learned from this was that even the simple stories of life can be used as a kind of medicine to heal.

After this workshop, I appreciated more than ever the power of my subconscious mind. A particular attitude would not only change my subconscious expectations and outward demeanor in the world, but it seemed to somehow get underneath the very fabric of life, creating undeniable modifications in the world around me. Even without a specific context through which to understand and integrate this new sense of personal potency, I began to appreciate my own channel of input into the heretofore random waves of life.

This was the time to decide what I really wanted. The doors of possibility opened wide. Should I become beautiful? Famous? Wealthy? Brilliant? Respected? Loved? I sorted through all the desires that came up and one by one tossed them to the side. In an objective light, each of these potential desires crumbled into insignificance. They were based on goals that had been injected into me by contemporary society; they were not my own.

What did I really want from life?

I wanted to do whatever was right, based on a big picture I could never see. I wanted to be whatever I was meant to be, and to be happy with whatever my destiny brought. How could I ask for specifics when I was embroiled in cultural illusions? How could I ever know what was really important in life?

After casting aside a long list of potential goals, I realized that all I really wanted was to be content. No matter what porridge of experience was placed before me, I wanted it to taste good. I wanted sweet times to taste good, and I wanted sour times to taste good as well. I wanted to move with the natural flow of life, instead of asking that my short-sighted whims be fulfilled. I wanted my desires and actions to align with whatever was meant to be. I wanted to be in tune with the universe. Clearly, the all-pervasive intelligence that guides the atoms and galaxies to move with such perfection could choose the best path for my life. My best course of action was to get out of the way of its flow, and to be happy with whatever unfolded. Why not break experience down as I had the flavors and textures of the apple? Why not *choose* to be happy? Unknowingly, I had tapped into the secret of *surrender* as a path to happiness.

It often takes time for the seeds of our prayers and affirmations to germinate and bear fruit. First, I had some disturbing lessons to learn.

7.

HIDDEN PERSUADERS

A SOBERING DISCOVERY AWAITED ME near the end of my first semester of college. I read a book called *The Hidden Persuaders*, which documented the use of subconscious, subliminal manipulation by the advertising industry.

Anyone who watched television, read magazines, or listened to the radio at the time was bound to notice certain obvious manipulations. Not all were subliminal or well-disguised. Sexy women were often posed next to cars, implying that this was one of the extras one might expect with the purchase. Cigarette commercials told us, "It's not how long you make it, it's how you make it long," or "It's round and firm and fully packed," or "Taste me, taste me, taste me!"

But *The Hidden Persuaders* revealed an entirely different layer of deception, the realm of subliminal influence. The book showed images of skulls that had been airbrushed into ice cubes in whiskey ads, based on studies showing that alcoholics had a subconscious attraction to death. According to this author, the word *sex* was embedded in everything from magazine photographs to the surface of Ritz crackers — and he had the photos to prove it. Many readers probably found these bizarre claims fascinating but unbelievable. However, because I was exploring my unconscious for hours every day, the subliminal realm had become more available to my conscious mind. I found myself suddenly able to detect subliminal advertising.

One advertisement showed a fun-loving couple, river-rafting down the rapids. But if you looked closely, it was obvious that one of the woman's arms could not possibly have been coming from where her body was. This subliminally suggested a third person joining in the fun. Other couples would be laughing with large, orgasmic smiles, holding all kinds of poles and rod-shaped objects. Subtle drawings were etched in background trees, hidden messages woven through page after page of advertisements. None of these images was meant to be seen by the conscious mind. They were intended to trigger our subconscious minds into taking notice of the wonderful brand of cigarettes the orphan hand was holding, or to associate a particular brand of mascara with the word *sex* subliminally drawn into in the woman's hair. I could even hear commands embedded in the background audio tracks of particularly intrusive television commercials. The potential of these efforts made sense to me based on my understanding and experience of the subconscious mind. It was a form of mass hypnosis.

At first, I was entertained by this new project, looking for subliminal manipulation in the advertising world around me. I had always enjoyed the feeling of discovering secret layers of reality, and this one was available everywhere. Just walking into a store or flipping through a magazine became an adventure. But then my concern for humanity took over, and the excitement turned sour. The structures of our society were being manipulated subliminally by forces of greed. I saw a bleak future ahead of us. The keys to the control panels of our desires and behavior were being used for the purpose of getting us to buy more stuff! The burden of the world fell heavily on my teenage shoulders.

I began to feel sad, exhausted, and at the mercy of decision-makers I could not trust to do the right thing. At every turn was another marketing strategy, looking to screw around with my precious subconscious mind. And none of my friends seemed to really care, even when they believed it was happening. But I couldn't sink into apathy about this. For me, the implications were appalling. We were being told exactly what to think, using techniques that bypassed our conscious minds. With all the political activism taking place at the time, why wasn't anybody protesting this intolerable psychological pollution?

My closest friend became concerned about my well-being. It wasn't so much that she questioned whether my ideas were accurate, as that she felt I was entering dangerous territory. She thought I had stumbled into matters we were not supposed to know about. I began to have my own concerns about where my explorations were leading me. This was a frightening and confusing time for me, as I realized that I had no control over information that was being constantly injected into the receptive tissues of my subconscious mind.

It concerned me deeply to see intelligent people buying things they didn't really need, feeling things they didn't really feel, and thinking things they didn't really think. The ever-evolving belief systems of humanity were being engineered by the limited vision of a few greedy companies. And ultimately, even the CEO's of those companies were nothing but puppets of ... of what? What controlled it all? Who held the puppet strings?

It was all much bigger than I could handle. I was growing increasingly isolated and frustrated. Nobody seemed willing to join my agonizing exploration. Who would want to see through my glasses and enter this madness, *especially* if it were true?

At this time, I experienced another shift. I began to see worlds of subliminal communication and symbolism in nature. It was not only the advertising industry that was manipulating us through subliminal control. It seemed as though these subtle communications were woven throughout the texture of life itself.

I had discovered the symbolic quality of the universe. I noticed that certain events would be foreshadowed symbolically before they took place. Objects with particular significance to me seemed to appear in correspondence with my mood or the situations at hand. It was like stepping into a dream and being able to interpret symbolic elements while they were occurring.

Not only did I perceive symbolic expressions in the world around me, but I was surprised to find myself using subliminal tactics on others, without my conscious intention! Who was speaking through me? Who orchestrated the sexual innuendoes behind my word choices when I spoke with someone I was physically attracted to? Who moved my body in ways that would announce my innermost thoughts? And who was receiving the information?

> *I understood that there is something in me*
> *which can say things that I do not know*
> *and do not intend, things which*
> *may even be directed against me.*
>
> —CARL JUNG

Messages were being sent through me, without my conscious participation! This went way beyond noticing an occasional Freudian slip. I began to see subliminal communication as a constant and all-pervasive thread of reality. I watched as brilliant subliminal expressions moved through people who were not even aware of their own brilliance. They thought they were saying one thing, while woven through their apparent conversations were prophecies, synchronicities, commands, insults, flirting, and so much more.

It was becoming clear to me that we were not just simple objects called "people." Everything about us and everything coming out from us was intricately designed. It was impossible to hide anything about ourselves. Even sitting completely still, our posture would nonetheless reveal our character. Maybe somebody's surface consciousness wouldn't know if I slipped a mistruth past them, but their subconscious mind would know that and much more. Here I had thought I was in charge of this body and its actions, and now it was becoming clear that my ownership had been a fairy-tale. I was just a process, as was everyone and everything else.

The spacing of my written words would tell the universe

if I was feeling miserly or generous; the way I wrote the letter "I" would reveal intimate details about my self-image. Even the lines on my palm and the time of my birth seemed to carry information about me. Symbolic shapes were often subconsciously incorporated into my and other people's signatures. One book I read during this time showed a woman's signature with an unusual loop she'd always add to the top. When a Gestalt psychologist guided her to identify with being her signature and describe herself, the woman replied, "Well, there's... a hump.... " She then realized that this loop represented a hump she'd had on her back as a teen. It was during those years, in fact, that she had added the representational hump to her signature.

I could have pretended to be a psychic, based on my ability to perceive and translate subliminal expressions of people around me. But this was no time for games. Everything was so much bigger and more complicated than I had ever imagined. My isolation became inescapable. It was becoming more and more difficult for me to deal with the surface level of the world, dealing with classes, studies, and social interactions when so much was going on beneath the illusion of simplicity. While my classmates worried about what girl or boy liked them in which class, I was unraveling the guts of reality.

8.

THE
THRESHOLD
OF LIFE

I was far from my goal of constant happiness. Instead, I
had a recurring feeling that I just didn't belong in this
world. I knew too much. I wasn't meant to be living in
this dimension, while being able to see past it just enough to
feel panicked and out of control. It wasn't fair, and it certainly
wasn't comfortable. I did not want to play this game anymore, and decided it would be preferable to *not exist* than to
live with this deep distress. Perhaps death would hold the key
to my freedom.

The decision to take your own life overrides the most
basic human instinct of self-preservation. You don't even have
the luxury of dying for your country or for God. You simply

choose to leave, on the chance that whatever comes next might be less painful than whatever is tormenting you. At the time, even the possibility of dissolution into eternal nothingness seemed preferable to the loneliness and confusion I was suffering.

Many people who contemplate suicide must feel some guilt regarding the family and friends they'll be leaving behind. But I couldn't think of anyone who would even cry for me, except perhaps my grandmother. Maybe my sister would be sad as well. The blunt truth was that nobody in this world was really going to miss me. This thought was sobering as well as liberating.

❧ *Journal notes:*

**My farewell poem, written one week
before the scheduled "journey," at age 18**

*will someone tell me why I look in
as an outsider when I am forced to be a part
that I cannot be for I am apart*

*and given the choice
wouldn't I choose to see reality
unfogged by experience*

*and shouldn't I use this gift for betterment
for personal gain that I cannot appreciate
for external gains hang meaningless
set by someone else's standards
one who won't who doesn't want to see to understand*

and have I the right to feel anger
when they have their ignorant satisfactions
and all I have is painful understanding
that brings only frustration

yet when I realize that if I really try
to block out truth to conform
I know I can't pretend
when deep down I'll always realize
there's more than is being admitted

and how could I accept that fate
how can I put myself under control that I can see
the hidden strings of the puppeteers that block my way

should I connect myself to these strings
and I know I cannot for they would break
and how could I commit such an injustice
against myself
when I can retain my dignity

for I cannot help cannot stop fate I tried
but no one cares they just move with each twitch
and they laugh and pretend and refuse to see past the fog
and I cannot blame them for I am wrong

I have no right to change this fate even if I could
it's too late no turning back now
I must withdraw cannot interfere
can only understand

I decided to commit suicide. I would do it during Easter vacation, while visiting my parents' house. This decision had a drastic effect on my state of mind. I was able to relax in a deep new way. I no longer had to worry about my future, or the future of society. I didn't even have to choose which classes I would take the next semester. Never again would I have to do anything. All of it would be over in three short weeks.

I carried this powerful secret with me for those weeks. I attended my classes and talked with friends and family as if everything were normal. After all, the rules are that you're not allowed to tell anyone when you're really going to commit suicide. You would only do that if you were counting on them to talk you out of it. I had made a carefully considered decision based on logic rather than mere emotion. I was going to leave the party.

This secret throbbed inside me day and night. An unfamiliar gratitude came with the shift, an appreciation for all the different flavors of experience passing through and around me. Each event looked different through my new glasses. Everything was *"the last time...."*

I also became more observant. My personal interactions carried greater depth and meaning, as I realized that I may never see the person, or *any* person, again. There was a new care for each soul I had connections with. Even strangers on the street became worthy of note. I paid attention to the little things, the skills, actions, and feelings of life. Moments mattered. Colors were brighter. The world around me became more thrilling. I was actually cheered and inspired by this new receptivity and appreciation. I could probably have changed my mind about the whole suicide thing at this point, but that would have removed the very element that was cheering me up. What a dilemma.

Finally the big day came. I was staying with my mother and stepfather during spring break. They went out for the day, leaving the yellow Dodge Dart for my use. I picked up the bottle of sleeping pills that had been in our medicine cabinet for a long time (*too* long, as I later discovered!), and drove to a nearby shopping center.

Walking through the mall, I was disappointed with its normalcy. Didn't these people realize the world was about to end, at least for me? Wasn't somebody going to throw a surprise party for me? Didn't anyone want to say goodbye? A part of me expected *something*, although, of course, this expectation was completely illogical. People passed by me, absorbed in their own worlds. I tried to make some small talk with a man who was purchasing a cappuccino machine, but he wasn't interested in chatting.

Feeling even more empty and desolate, I left the mall and began to drive north. I drove on freeways I had never heard of, following some invisible map that was being whispered to me subconsciously by … by what? I didn't know. I turned when I was moved to turn, and went straight when I wasn't. This went on for many hours. I was driving to the place of my death.

My mind became peaceful and focused in the present moment. The aspects of myself based on past and future were somewhat lifted from me. I was a soul, driving, preparing to enter a new adventure — obliteration — I knew not what. I was driving toward the very threshold of life.

At one point, I pulled over to a little roadside bar to use the restroom. There was a pinball machine there, and I thought I'd play a few games before moving on. I wanted to see what it would feel like to do something so ordinary en route to my last moments on earth.

I played for a while and won several extra games, which I left on the machine. It was starting to get darker outside. The air was chilly. As I traveled further north, patches of snow began to appear along the roadside. I turned into the driveway of a small bungalow-colony motel.

I went into the office and rented a room from the friendly desk-clerk. He came into the bungalow with me to make sure the heat was on, and then left. I was alone.

It did occur to me that it wasn't very considerate of me to kill myself on this nice man's property. He would probably be the person who would discover the body.

The Body. What a strange feeling it was to think of *my* body as *the* body. But that was how it was going to be.

I sat down and turned on the TV. "The Brady Bunch" was on. I smiled and berated myself, "You're so pathetic that you watch 'The Brady Bunch' during your last hours of life!"

But I did watch it. This was going to be a "Very Brady Suicide." While it played, I began to take the pills. One after another, I popped them all in my mouth. I didn't want to be half-baked and end up in a coma, so I took the whole bottle.

Not surprisingly, I soon felt drowsy. I turned off the television and went into the bedroom. I didn't even pull down the covers, I just lay down on top of the bed. A sleepy dullness was settling into my body, making me feel numb all over.

As I lay there, an energy field I would one day refer to as my *subtle body* started to undulate. It was moving within me, as though there was another body lying along with my physical body. My energy-body legs were moving up and down; my arms from side to side, and yet my physical body continued to lie still and unmoving.

I began to recall certain events from my life. I remember thinking at the time that the idea of one's life flashing before their eyes while they die is strangely accurate. The scenes appeared to play through like a tape-recording. The image I had at the time was of a DNA-like strand running through a playback head, as it prepares to turn off the lights. It was like a review of the whole semester before the big final exam. Death. The real final frontier.

I perceived that before one leaves this world, there seemed to be a review that happens as a natural function of the body and brain. This appeared to be just as physical and scientific as the other processes that happen to a body at the brink of death.

The idea that we can re-experience life events is not too far-fetched when you consider certain neurophysiological experiments performed several decades ago. By accident, it was discovered that touching a surgical probe to certain areas of a patient's exposed brain could elicit clear and distinct memories. With these unnatural electrical forces activating their brains, the patients would actually smell the smells, feel the feelings, and hear the sounds of their memories. It was with this vivid quality that I began to reexperience certain events from my life.

I also understood that, unlike the playing of a tape or the surgical eliciting of memories, this experience had a different flavor. It didn't seem to be bound by our rules of time or linearity. First of all, it was happening within a very compact period of time. This also is not so strange, when we remember the extensive dreams that can take place even during a short nap. Also, my impression was that somehow, while watching this show of my life, I was somehow there again. It was like a replay being replayed *while* it happened. The structures of time began to crumble. Entire bundles of memories were reexperienced in just moments. I had the sense that this was an opportunity perhaps to digest lessons I had missed along the way.

It also occurred to me that it is possible to be one's own *guardian angel*. The tangible quality of this experience made me feel that I was actually back in the original moments. It felt almost as though I was watching myself go back and clean things up. More happened that night, though some images are too vague to be properly captured here.

The next thing I knew, I woke up and opened my eyes with the freshness of a child. There was the sun, already rising in the sky. I was alive. I guess a part of me was happy to be waking up, but then my drugged mind kicked in. "Oh no! I'm going to be in so much trouble for staying out all night!" It was one thing to die, and quite another to deal with the wrath of my parents.

I staggered out to the car, and started to drive home, hoping I was going in the right direction. Maybe I could make it back before anyone noticed I was gone. But I was dazed, unable to control the car. I was weaving crazily back and forth all over the road. I think one car did pass by me and honk. Then red-and-white lights were flashing behind me. Time was warped by all the sleeping pills, and my next image was the close-up view of a policeman's face in my car window. I tried to act as though I wasn't inebriated, but I was too far gone. He brought me into his police car and I fell asleep. Not a very good demonstration of sobriety!

We arrived at the little town's court building, where I was booked — fingerprints, photos, everything. I gave the officer my family's phone number and was led into a cell. I lay down and fell back asleep, dipping back into awareness only occasionally to shift my position on the cement bench. Eight hours later, I was awakened by the sound of my parents' voices coming toward my cell. I opened my eyes as they entered. They just stood and looked at me, unable to exhibit any sort of affectionate display. My stepfather asked, "What happened?"

The lie came out of me. "I don't know. I was at the mall and, the next thing I knew, I was driving my car this morning."

I was NOT going to tell them I had done this on purpose, requiring them to drive for so many hours. I was also embarrassed to tell them I had tried to commit suicide, because these were not exactly the most sensitive people. So they didn't know if I had been kidnapped or had suddenly gone into some kind of schizophrenic fugue state. I'm sure they wondered if I was crazy. I felt bad for misleading them but couldn't really see any other choice.

I was charged with driving under the influence, but since it was a small town and everyone was related, we were offered a package deal. The policeman was the cousin of the lawyer, who was the brother-in-law of the judge. The lawyer said if we gave him $2000, the case would be closed.

For the next few months, I lived in a trance-like state. My friends at school knew nothing about what had happened. I tried to act as though everything was as normal (or perhaps in my case as not so normal) as usual.

I spent the next summer working as a waitress in a local delicatessen. The walls were covered with big bright orange spikes, intended to encourage people to eat fast and keep the tables moving. The owner ran around snapping at the waitresses all day long, "Careful, baby!" The cooks were grumpy, and the line of customers never seemed to end. Some of our guests expected me to be the mother they never had, as I attempted to satisfy all their needs and wants — with a smile, of course. Others had been mistreated at their job that day, and were looking for a minion upon whom they could release some of their pent-up frustration. Some of the men just wanted to flirt with a young woman without being snubbed. Then there were the few normal people, who were like a breath of fresh air. Unfortunately, they always seemed to be the ones who would end up with the wrong order, or the spilled coffee.

I did experience one benefit from this hectic, overly active environment. During the previous year, I had spent three hours a day dissecting reality. I had seen levels of manipulation that I felt could destroy society as we knew it, and I had tried to commit suicide. In the midst of what could have been a black hole for my personal sanity, I now had to focus on what I was doing. I would run from table to table, with carefully balanced plates and cups up and down my arms. I'd be constantly adding numbers and calculating tax. For eight hours a day, I had to smile and be friendly to all kinds of people. All this responsibility kept my mind busy, giving me an active but much needed vacation from the disturbing path I had been on.

Divine guidance often comes
when the horizon is the blackest.

—MOHANDAS GANDHI

9.

WHEN THE STUDENT IS READY

DURING MY SECOND YEAR OF COLLEGE, I enrolled in a class called "Consciousness." Having had a strong interest in the unconscious, hypnosis and Freudian theory, I thought it might be a class I'd enjoy. But it turned out the "Consciousness" in this course title referred to something quite different from the word as used in psychology. It seemed to have something to do with more metaphysical, higher consciousness issues, ideas unfamiliar to me. This class brought many new concepts to my door.

Every week there would be another bizarre reading assignment. First, we studied Carlos Castenedaʼs journeys with mescaline and his ruthless teacher, Don Juan. Then we delved into new areas of science, where quantum physics begins to merge with ancient spiritual teachings. We studied parapsychology experiments and even replicated them ourselves.

One week, I didn't buy the book for the following Consciousness class, since I was planning to skip it anyway. But after missing the class, I was overcome with guilt. What was I doing with my life? What did it say about me that I couldn't even make it to classes I enjoyed? This wasn't high school anymore. I was racking up a hefty student-loan debt. Shouldn't I at least attend my classes?

The next week, our professor handed me a photocopy of the handout from the class I had missed. The book for that week was called *Play of Consciousness*, written by an Indian swami named *Muktananda*. I felt better about having skipped the class. This was not a book I would have wanted to read anyway. New-Age physics was one thing, religious thought quite another.

I considered religion to be a crutch for those too intellectually weak to face the brutal reality that ultimately we will never understand what is really going on here. God was a pacifier, a parental substitute for adults. One little psychoactive chemical could destroy everything I have ever known. My own unconscious mind could instantly transform the entire universe as I knew it. What deity could be more powerful than that?

I looked at the handout from my professor, and read a few lines. It wasn't at all what I would have expected to find in a religious writing. The Indian swami described some of his inner experiences from decades of meditation, specifically when his *third-eye energy center* opened. His eyes rolled upward and he saw colored lights, along with a tiny, shimmering *blue pearl*, and various other "hallucinogenic" experiences. This was interesting to me. I decided to make up for the missed class by writing a scientific discussion of the chapter.

I analyzed the swami's visions from a neurophysiology viewpoint. The melatonin in his brain might have catalyzed into melanin, through the adjustment of just one atom of the molecule. This could possibly give the internal perception of a color such as blue. Also, his rolled-up eyes may have accessed dream-like functions in the occipital lobe, creating these internal visual phenomena. I had a whole list of theories, including the possibility that the swami had simply suffered a petit-mal epileptic seizure.

Soon afterwards, the whole Consciousness class took a field trip to the Ann Arbor Meditation Center, a residential, monastery-style building based on the swami's teachings. I was a little concerned about going to a Hindu commune. One woman in our class warned me that she had gone there once and received several calls inviting her to return. I decided not to give anyone my address or phone number. I was not interested in getting involved with some strange religious group.

As we walked into the meditation hall, there were pictures of Hindu swamis and strange-looking people, some half-naked, all around the walls. An American woman wearing a white Indian sari, talked to us for a few minutes, and then we started to chant. I couldn't figure out what word went where, or what the tempo was supposed to be. Still, this place was intriguing and certainly different from anything I had ever experienced. The dim lighting, candle flames, and incense created an exotic, occult-like atmosphere.

Though I continued to remember this visit to the meditation center, I didn't consider going back until several months later. One Monday morning, I was scheduled to meet with the "Consciousness" professor to go over a parapsychology experiment I was coordinating for the class. We were replicating a remote-viewing experiment that some scientists were performing at Stanford University. In this investigation, an outbound experimenter would use a random number generator to choose one of fifty folders, within which was a location somewhere in Ann Arbor. He would go to that location, while an inbound experimenter would sit alone in a room, trying to draw pictures and verbally describe what the outbound experimenter was observing at this randomly chosen location.

The purpose of this experiment was to prove or disprove the existence of telepathic perception using traditional scientific methods. In the end, we had several impressive correlations, but the fact that some were subtle or subjective made it clear to me that certain phenomena cannot really be captured statistically.

The professor walked into the room for our meeting, and I looked up. He was glowing! I don't think I had ever seen anyone glow like that before. He looked like a beautiful angel archetype of himself, with a blissed-out, benign smile on his face. I had to ask what happened. He explained that he'd just returned from a weekend visit at a monastery in upstate New York with that swami who had written about the third-eye energy center in our course book.

Well, seeing this professor glow like that definitely piqued my interest in this whole swami thing. I started to think about maybe going back to the meditation center in Ann Arbor. It took many months for me to get up the nerve.

I was too shy to ask anyone about it. What if they thought I was interested in joining the group? Finally, I got up the courage to ask a woman from our class when the programs were. She told me the main programs were on Tuesday nights at 8 pm, and gave me directions to the building. The following Tuesday, I got in my car early so I wouldn't be late.

I got totally lost.

The meditation center was in an area of Ann Arbor that I was unfamiliar with, and even though I had been there once before, there were some strange angled streets that left me totally confused. I drove around and around, getting increasingly nervous about the whole thing. I kept looking at my watch: 7:45, 7:49, 7:54.... I didn't want to be late. Maybe they had some big rule about being punctual. I certainly did not want to get in trouble in such a bizarre place!

It was becoming clear that I probably wasn't going to find the center in time. I made a decision that if I didn't get there by 8:00 sharp, I would turn around, go home, and try again the following week. This was upsetting because I had really been looking forward to finally getting there after so many months of being too shy to ask. But that was my firm decision.

My watch said 7:58, and then 7:59. I turned around to go home, thinking I would have to get more specific directions before the next week. Then, just moments after I had looked at the watch display which showed 7:59, I looked down at it again, just to confirm the closure of this deal I had made about the 8:00 deadline.

The watch was dead. 00:00. No time. No 8:00, only 00:00. I turned a corner and rushed back to the address block of the center. This time I found it right away and went inside.

The evening was awesome. I laughed, I cried, I was emotionally moved and intellectually stimulated. As we started to chant, a strong sentiment built up inside of me. I didn't know if it was related to the stopped-watch incident or because I was in such a strange environment, but I found myself weeping through most of the chant. This was unlike me. I rarely cried, certainly not without good reason. And I was feeling perfectly fine.

After the chant, there was a reading from one of the swami's books. His words were brilliant and wise. They echoed my own deepest insights and answered questions I had long pondered. There was a quality about this exotic place that made me feel at home.

I looked up at the big picture of the swami in front of the hall. It was an extremely striking photo of him, with deep, intense eyes. I silently thanked him, and was sure I saw him wink.

> *A tree as big around as you can reach*
> *starts with a small seed;*
> *a journey of a thousand miles begins*
> *with a single step.*
>
> —*LAO-TZU*

Fare forward, you who think you are voyaging.
You are not those who saw the harbor receding,
or those who will disembark.

— *T. S. ELIOT*

10.

MAGICAL MEETING

A FEW MONTHS LATER came an opportunity for me to meet the swami in person. There was going to be a Health and Healing workshop in the upstate New York monastery, and I was going. Still, beneath my lighthearted excitement played a soft note of apprehension. I had been going to chants and programs at the Ann Arbor meditation center for several months. During that time, I'd developed quite a friendly relationship with this teacher through the big bright picture in front of the hall. It is one thing to relate to somebody through a photo, and quite another to meet them in person.

But mainly, I was thrilled and excited. Once again I was moving into the unknown, taking a leap off the cliff of the ordinary. Who would ever have thought I would be making a pilgrimage to meet an Indian guru?

It was a twelve-hour drive to New York. I went with my professor, his wife, and another student. We spoke a bit here and there about when to stop for gas or change drivers, but for the most part we drove quietly. It was a very yogic way to begin the pilgrimage, sitting still for twelve hours in silence. I don't know if I had ever done that before in my life!

We arrived just in time for the evening program. I dropped my suitcase off in the dorm room, and made my way to the meditation hall. My professor and his wife were going to introduce me to the teacher in what was called a *darshan* line of greeting. I became more excited as the moment of meeting came near. I expected that the swami would be happy to see me. After all, I had come from so far to see him, and had heard about how he was filled with pure, unconditional love.

We moved forward slowly in the line of greeting, until finally I could see his face. He looked very different, not quite as handsome as the photo I had come to relate to. I thought he looked better with the beard. Yet, there was a brilliant glow around him, an intense visual and kinesthetic brightness that went beyond what I had perceived from his photo.

The swami was seated in a slightly elevated chair. People would bow their heads in front of him, and he would brush them on the head or back with a big wand of peacock feathers. He was interacting with four to five people at any given time. We knelt down in front of him. My professor introduced me as a student from Ann Arbor.

A beautiful Indian woman translated the words into Hindi. The swami looked at me with a very serious face, and grunted. No smile, no hug, no "Where have you been,

O great disciple?" Just a serious look and a grunt. My professor and his wife got up to leave, and I realized that the meeting was over.

I began to walk away disappointed, when a bolt of energy shot through my body. At first, I thought I was angry. "How could he snub me like that!" I had never felt this kind of force in my body before. The closest label my mind could create for the sensation was the adrenaline rush of being really angry, and so it pinned that fabricated anger on the most obvious target.

I ran out of the hall and practically flew up to my room. Nobody else was there. I jumped onto an empty bunk and lay down on my stomach. My consciousness became immediately focused inside, and there I broke through into a new kind of awareness.

These inner spaces were different from the places I had tapped into during my previous self-hypnosis-style explorations. They were more active, more colorful. A series of visual images surfaced in my awareness. It was like dreaming, except I was wide awake. This was a new experience for me. I had never hallucinated with visions, even when taking drugs as a teenager.

At one point, I was shocked by images of lizards with big scary teeth, glaring at me. With this came another big rush of energy. Lying there on my stomach, my arms and legs jerked up, totally out of my control. It was like the reflex action when a doctor hits your knee. My arms and legs continued to fly up and then come back down, filled with more energy each time.

You might think I would have been frightened by these bizarre experiences, but it seems my endorphins had kicked in. I was witnessing it all from a soothing, peaceful state. My brain's consistency-making mechanisms had stepped in to save the day.

Our minds have a latticework of defense mechanisms to keep them from having to confront the discomfort of new information that might disrupt our ever-nebulous sense of personal control. When an event happens for which we have no pre-established context of understanding, our mind will often flip into "make it okay" mode. My body was doing things it had never done before, and I didn't even think anything was strange. My mind made the experience seem more or less ordinary, just as the woman in my hypnosis class had convinced herself that jumping up and down like a gorilla was normal behavior.

After a half-hour of this inner carnival ride, I went back downstairs to the meditation hall to hear the swami's lecture. I no longer felt angry or snubbed. Instead, I wanted to know more about this man who's energy had affected me so strongly.

The swami's voice was melodic, his manner jovial. Every now and then he would break into a deep, growling chuckle. I couldn't help but smile. He was so wonderfully animated. As he spoke, my attention was drawn to his hand movements. There was something about the way he moved his hands that intrigued me. He appeared so graceful and free. It was almost as though his hands were dancing. Sitting there amidst hundreds of people, I began to imitate his hand movements. It's not that I thought about it or intended to imitate the swami. In fact, I was feeling a little embarrassed about my strange behavior. Fortunately, the audience around me was focused on watching him, or I'm sure they would have thought I was odd. I became puppet-like, spontaneously reflecting the swami's movements. My arms were moving as though I was in the middle of an animated conversation.

Finally, I thought, "This is ridiculous. What am I doing?" I made myself stop imitating him and put my hands in my lap.

He put his hands in his lap.

I quickly moved my hands out to the sides. He moved his hands out to the sides. I was shocked. He wasn't even looking in my direction! For the next ten seconds or so, he imitated everything I did with my hands. First I felt confused, then amused. The swami was playing with me!

The next evening I had an idea. I would make him interact with me by asking for a *spiritual name*. Most of the people involved with this path had received Indian names from him. It was considered a gift to be named by this great saint. There was also a psychic element. What would this supposedly omniscient person name you? I thought a name request might start us off on some friendly conversation, hopefully more than a grunt!

I arrived at the front of the *darshan* line, and asked the swami for a name. He looked into my eyes for a moment, reached over to a little business card holder on his side table, and handed me the top card. It said, "*Kumuda.*"

I was disappointed that this teacher had just pulled a card at random. I'd expected him to take a good, careful look at my *karmas* or whatever and come up with a special, perfectly appropriate name on his own. Even *I* could have picked a card from the top of a stack! I had not yet developed the understanding that universal perfection can express even through apparently random circumstances. Later I looked up the name and discovered several meanings for the word *Kumuda.* Two of my favorites were "one who gladdens the earth" and "a lotus flower that grows in mud without being sullied."

I thanked him for the card and went back to my seat. As I sat down, the strangest thing happened. It was as though someone had inserted a big straw into me, blowing me up like a helium balloon. I felt my body getting bigger and bigger, really fast, and really big. I expanded to fill the whole room. I kept expanding and growing, until I seemed to encompass the whole city, and then more. I knew this was impossible, yet I was experiencing it clearly, not in a dream state, but right here in the supposedly trustworthy waking state. The sensation felt normal and strange at the same time. I seemed to be in the wrong dimension. We're not supposed to do things like that here.

But again, I wasn't scared. Rather, the experience was ecstatic. It was extremely pleasurable to have so much energy inside me that I had to expand to contain it all.

It was interesting to see how quickly I was able to let go of everything I held dear, my very conceptual structures of reality, as soon as this new experience came into the picture. No longer was I just a person sitting there in this meditation hall. I was now an energy field, expanding far beyond my body. Thus ended day two of my visit.

On the third and final night, I went up to see the swami one last time. Ever the optimist, I hoped we would be old friends by now. Surely, he would be aware of all the breakthroughs I had just experienced. Clearly, they were a consequence of being in his presence. I reached his seat, knelt, bowed my head, and looked up. The swami was looking everywhere but at me. I waited for a few moments, then gave up. I walked away, disappointed by the lack of attention, but still feeling a tangible, warm vibration invigorating my body.

With each step, I was getting more upset. We were scheduled to leave the next morning. This might be the last time I would ever see the swami in my life. Why hadn't he said good-bye?

I sat down near the back of the hall and felt *bad*. Not as an adjective, but a noun. I felt myself feeling bad, without actually feeling bad. I experienced the whole set of electrochemical and hormonal patterns that creates the sensation of feeling abandoned. I was able to watch objectively as my body synthesized the necessary ingredients for this "rejection soup" that I had cooked up so many times before. I watched myself preparing to, and then feeling *bad*. It took the subjective experience to a completely new level, where I was witnessing the emotions without being stuck in them. The psychophysical factory was synthesizing this recipe of rejection, while I watched from an inner balcony.

A strong force then began to spiral up my body. From my detached perspective, I could see that this energy was the pattern of rejection emotion. It was the archetype itself, the root from which so many painful branches had flowered and faded away, year after year.

Through the swirling energy, I began to see face after face of people who had abandoned or rejected me throughout my life. A series of images moved across the screen of my mind, opening old pockets of repressed emotional energy that had been trapped inside the memories. I must have gone through years of psychotherapy in ten minutes, becoming aware of people and painful experiences that I had long ago forgotten. Some individual faces were prominent, but the experience was essentially an indistinguishable mass of associated images and feelings spiraling up my body. I was shaking with deep emotion. It felt as though every system in my body had been activated.

Had I not been in a room with hundreds of people, I might have burst out sobbing with the intensity of grief and energy that was moving through me. Yet I sat quietly, streams and rivers of tears pouring out of my eyes. Not a few drops here and there, but the holy bath of deep hearted tears.

It was as though a "karmic Roto-Rooter" had been sent to purge my system of this mass of psychic tissue that had grown inside me through the years. The vine of childhood rejection had wrapped itself around the events of my life, coloring them with its painful flowers. Now it was being pulled out by the root.

Eventually, the emotional force began to subside, and I opened my eyes. There was the swami, still seated in his chair at the front of the hall, a long line of people waiting to greet him. I felt myself yelling to him with my mind, "What are you doing to me!?!"

To my utter amazement, he began to disappear. I could see the lines of the chair's upholstery through the image of his body. My eyes opened wide. As the swami completely disappeared, a blue circular flame began to form in his place. It became a big, swirling, bright blue ball of flame. It was such a bright blue, that it almost looked like a cartoon. I watched this extraordinary sight for some time.

The program ended and I walked back to my room. All night long my body and mind were pulsing with the powerful vibrations of all that had just happened.

The next morning, my car-mates and I met in front of the main entrance. As we began to put our suitcases into the trunk, I looked up and saw the swami walking directly toward us from across the street. What a surprise! His orange robes shimmered in the rising sunlight as he returned from his morning walk. One woman who had just arrived flew into his arms with a big hug. I felt a twinge of sadness that I could never hug him like that. I was way too shy.

The swami continued walking toward us and stopped as he reached the front of our car. He stood right in front of me and looked into my eyes. I looked back at him with a breathless innocence. Right there, he gave me the big, beautiful smile of recognition I had been longing for, and he waved at me. From two feet away, he waved! I smiled shyly and waved back.

Though the interaction only lasted a few moments, there was a sense that we had met one another on a deeper level. With this simple gesture, I felt that we silently accepted the respective roles of teacher and student. It was like a handshake. He agreed to guide me, and I agreed to learn. I would continue my journey on this path.

My teacher turned to go into the front doors, leaving me with a big, goofy smile on my face. As we began the drive home, my eyes gently closed. It felt as though I was dragged into a deep pool of consciousness. It was like taking a bath in golden light, but this light was more than just visual. It was like waves of golden bliss, folding me under as they caressed and hugged me. The smile remained on my face throughout the twelve-hour drive. Every now and then, I would come up for air, becoming aware of the car and the external world for a few moments through a thick molasses of peace. Then I'd be pulled under again into this pool of shimmering sweetness.

Across the aeons of time,
irresistibly, undauntedly,
by some uncanny internal forward thrust,
the consciousness of the creature
in its advance through evolution
strives to touch the absolute,
to soar into further dimensions.

—PIR VILAYAT KHAN

11.

TOWARD THE ONE

I CONTINUED TO ATTEND programs and chants at the Ann Arbor meditation center, and drove back to the New York monastery twice more that year. During my third visit, I attended a two-day initiation workshop with my teacher. This was another experience-filled weekend, when I received his physical touch in the space between my eyebrows and was carried into a tender but emotionally intense feeling of being loved by the divine.

The person seated behind me was having an intense experience herself, and was basically screaming her head off, right into my ear. I managed to stay fairly centered in my own inner space, even with the loud disruption. I especially didn't mind when my teacher came back to our row to calm the woman down, because he gave me one more touch on top of my head. He also brushed his wand of feathers against my back, leaving his enticing scent on my sweater.

Back in Ann Arbor, I discovered a fascinating book, *Toward the One*, written by Sufi master, Pir Vilayat Khan. With every page, this book challenged and then expanded the limits of my understanding.

One day, I heard the author was going to be giving a lecture in Detroit the following Friday. For a moment, I wondered if it was okay to see two different teachers. I couldn't imagine why this would be a problem and drove up for the program.

Pir was a thin man with long gray hair and beard, wearing a white woolen robe with a hood. He looked like Gandalf from the *Hobbit* books, like one of the great wizards of medieval times.

After Pir's wonderful talk, the whole room sang a song together, the word "Hallelujah," sung to the various melodies of what I later learned to be Pachelbel's Canon. I had never heard the tune before. The melody and harmonies affected me strongly. I thought that Pir or one of his followers had written the song, and was extremely impressed and taken with its magic. Each section of the room was given a different harmony to sing, and when it all came together, the sound was celestial. We were a choir of angels singing the music of the spheres. My soul was lifted high by the power of this song.

As the program ended, someone announced that people wishing to be initiated by Pir should go to a specific location. I wanted to at least meet this man, and waited in the designated area. One of Pir's assistants escorted me into a dimly lit room behind the sanctuary where the program had been held.

At first, the room appeared to be empty. It took a moment before I saw Pir standing there. I walked up to him, feeling surprisingly bold. Though I was in awe of this man whose writings had carried me to such elevated levels of consciousness, still I was feeling quite comfortable.

Pir opened his arms and took my hands, as he greeted me with a soft smile. I looked at him and said, "I want to know the Truth." I hadn't planned on saying anything like that, but this was too important a moment to waste on small talk.

Pir looked into my eyes and pronounced, "You will." Then he smiled informally and asked, "Do you want to be initiated?"

I did, but I had a conflict. I knew it was important to be honest and forthcoming, especially with a great spiritual being such as Pir. I told him I would like to receive his blessing, but that I had already been initiated by Swami Muktananda. I didn't know if there was a rule about not being initiated by more than one guru.

Pir's eyes lit up with a big smile. "Muktananda is a wonderful teacher! Once I saw him speaking, and in the middle of a sentence he turned into an ecstatic *dervish!* (lover of God). Pir exclaimed, "We're all one, aren't we!?!"

I nodded as he led me into a short dance together. My heart was happy. What amazing turn was my life taking?

Then Pir looked into my eyes. "You should stay with Muktananda as much as possible. Learn his teachings."

I bowed my head in gratitude for the guidance and blessings, and smiled, "I will."

I returned to Ann Arbor and floated through the night. The next morning, I woke up bright and early to go to the morning devotional chant at the meditation center.

In my head, I began to hear the melody of the previous night's "Hallelujah" song, playing over and through the

Sanskrit verses. Even though the two melodies were quite different, still they blended together to create a new, beautifully balanced piece of music. I stopped chanting and allowed myself to be swept away by the beauty of this intoxicating, symphonic blend.

After the chant, I went to the meditation center's snack bar. Although I had been going to programs for nearly a year, I hadn't spoken with most of the people there or participated in any of their social discourse. They seemed like wonderful people; yet I was in a seriously introverted phase, where words did not flow readily.

There everybody was, laughing and eating, having fun with one another. There was a lot of activity, because some of the fellows were putting a new stereo system into the small room. I ordered a cup of tea and sat down, taken aback by the brightness and chatter. Every now and then, I would close my eyes and touch once again the peaceful state inside myself. Through it all, I continued to hear that beautiful melody resounding through my heart, hallelujah, hallelujah.

The stereo installers finished plugging in the last speaker and announced that they were going to check the new sound system.

Out came, blaring at full volume from the speakers, *that melody!!!*

I nearly dropped my cup of tea.

I had no idea this was a famous piece of music. I thought Pir had composed the melody. And here was a full orchestra playing all of the harmonies and melodies we had been singing the night before, full volume!

A part of me dissolved in that moment. It had nothing left to hold on to. Although I later found out that Pachelbel's

Canon was a well known composition, still the awe and gratitude I experienced from this seeming *miracle* had already done its job.

I am neither the conscious
nor the unconscious mind,
neither intelligence nor ego,
neither the ears nor the tongue
nor the senses of smell and sight,
neither ether nor air
nor fire nor water nor earth.
I am consciousness and bliss.
I am Shiva! I am Shiva!

— SHANKARACHARYA

12.

WHO IS SHIVA?

IT WAS MARCH, 1980, and I had been going to the meditation center in Ann Arbor for nearly a year. By this time, I'd moved into a large house owned by one of the local devotees. He wanted to make it into a kind of annex, where people could live with others who were also on the spiritual path, without having to follow the strict schedule of the meditation center itself. We called it "Mike's House."

There were four or five people staying in the house at a time. The owner lived in the basement, and rarely came upstairs. He was a complete recluse. I hardly ever saw him, even though we were living in the same house. Mike was quiet, pale, and unemotional, with an odd sense of humor to boot. He reminded me of my sister's old nerdy boyfriend from high school, who had once developed a plan to take over the world by blowing up Australia with anti-matter. I couldn't figure out if Mike was a potential psychopath or just a good yogi, spending his time in silence and contemplation. He was always respectful and friendly to me though, so I wasn't too uneasy about it.

Then there was Hari, who lived there for a while during my stay. I had never met anyone quite like Hari. He was thin and had a very flexible, yogic body. You could tell he practiced hatha yoga, the physical exercises, because when he sat in the lotus posture, which is like crossing your legs with your feet on top, he seemed to do it perfectly.

This guy was passionate in an unusual way. He may have been a contemporary version of the archetypal "mad lover of God," or possibly, he was just totally nuts. I guess I think of him as a little of both.

Hari was always falling in love. His heart was so open that he would walk through the woods nearby, weeping as he hugged each tree. He would feel love-energy flowing into him from the leaves and would lie on the ground embracing Mother Earth.

Hari used to tell me about this *clear, blue light*, the light of consciousness in the space of the head. He explained that the bones in his skull were somehow blocking his flow of *kundalini*, the powerful force that is said to move up through the nerve centers along the spine. I had not yet learned about the ancient science of *kundalini*, and so this all sounded a little far-fetched to me. While we were meditating or chanting at the center, I'd occasionally look over and see him undulating with his hips, as though a spigot there turned on a flow of energy that seemed to move up his spine and into his head.

Hari fell in love with a different woman every week. He would become totally obsessed with each one, worshipping them as manifestations of the Divine Mother. When I moved out of the annex, he fell down to the floor and grabbed my ankles, shouting, "Goddess! Don't leave me!" I guess you could say I was flattered. I had certainly never thought of myself as the goddess type, and this was my first experience of being worshipped! I couldn't imagine that he wasn't faking this whole divine love thing to some degree, but looking back on it now, I can't imagine that he was. For him, the experience was very real. Maybe it had something to do with drugs.

I never saw Hari take drugs, but occasionally we spoke about them. By age seventeen, I had stopped taking anything more than an occasional pipeful of pot. And now even that had fallen away. Drugs did not seem to be necessary or acceptable on this spiritual path.

One day, it was announced at the center that a holiday called *Shivaratri* was coming up in two weeks. *Shivaratri* means the "Night of the Lord," and is a widely celebrated holy day in India. The meditation center was going to celebrate with an all-night chant of the mantra, *Om Namah Shivaya*, which means "I honor Shiva, the source of the universe."

I thought to myself, "I can hardly stay conscious for ten minutes during the evening programs when we chant *Om Namah Shivaya*. How on earth am I going to chant all night!"

Along came Hari with a suggestion: peyote, hallucinogenic cactus. I had never taken peyote, but felt it would be a challenge and adventure. I accepted his offer. Hari bought eight grams of peyote for me, and meticulously cleaned it all, He then boiled the cactus for six hours, so I could drink the drug without getting sick from the plant fibers. Peyote was known for its side effect of nausea. We hoped this process would protect me from a potential puke-fest, which would have been really out of place in the meditation hall.

I was a little nervous while drinking the nasty-tasting brew. After all, once it's in, it's in. Each sip made my body convulse, as if someone were shaking me violently. Finally, I managed to choke it all down, and went to the chant.

As I sat in the meditation hall, my vision became more acute. I could see the colors in the picture at the front of the room glowing brightly. Through the dim lighting, it was still possible to see some faces. I began to see a yellowish glow emanating from some of the people sitting around me.

Then, for the first time, I experienced my personal power in a tangible way. There was a wonderfully strong, bright, deep golden radiance surrounding me like a big ball. My personal power. My will-power. My aura. I could see it in my mind's eye as a bright golden light. My focus changed from that of the physical body to this explosion of power that was also there. I could feel the energy pulsing through me so vividly. It seemed to be a new perception of a force that had always existed inside and around me, though perhaps not always as powerfully as in this moment.

I perceived the same kind of glow around other people, and noticed a few lines of light-energy stretching across the room from one person to another. My intuitive understanding was that these represented the strands of relationship. I saw some particularly strong energy lines connecting from one of the married people sitting up front to a woman who was not his wife, and wondered if there was a deeper relationship going on between them that I wasn't supposed to know about. The thought made me smile. I thought, "This must be what it is like to be psychic — watching people pretend to be one thing while you can see through to who they really are or what they are really thinking."

The chant began at 8 pm. and continued until morning. In the deep dark hours of this holy night, I had the most subjectively REAL experience of my life.

I closed my eyes, and the inner show began. I saw myself as a white bird with large, expansive wings. I could feel myself flying, becoming aware of how familiar it was to soar so freely.

The sensation awakened memories from my childhood. I used to fly every night in my dreams. I'd fly to distant lands, gliding through the sky. This had been one of my main modes of transportation in dreamland. But as I began to get older, I had found myself unable to go as high. My flying abilities declined like an elderly person's ability to run. I kept going lower and lower, slower and slower. At one point, I was unable to soar at all. I could only hover above the ground. One night at age eight, while floating from my bedroom down the stairs, my feet touched the ground, and I had to walk down the rest of the steps. After that, I couldn't fly anymore. Even in the dream state, I grieved for the loss. And here I was after all these years, soaring through this expansive space of personal consciousness with huge, white wings. It was breathtaking.

I saw amazing things that night.

There was a scene from what I assumed was a previous lifetime. I was a young, bald monk wearing light blue, silky robes. A man who seemed to be my teacher at that time was in the vision as well. He was oriental, and quite old and thin. I can still see his kind face in my mind's eye.

This was interesting to me, because I had been recently having thoughts about being a monk. Right after I started going to the meditation center, they had showed a video about the rites of passage involved with becoming a monk, a *swami*. I had never, ever had any thought, in any way, shape or form, about monkhood before this. They would have had to call me "Swami Atheistananda!" Yet while watching this video, I had been surprised to find a deep longing inside myself to renounce the materialistic world in favor of a contemplative, monastic lifestyle.

After this inner vision, I became aware of the chant that had been moving through me. Even without any kind of drug, chanting can be totally intoxicating. The powerful rhythms, deep breath cycles, and open-hearted devotion, put the mind in a uniquely fertile state.

On this night, we were chanting the mantra *Om Namah Shivaya*, over and over. I started to contemplate. Who were we really singing to? Who was *Shiva*? Was he just a Hindu deity, or was this Shiva an integral part of my universe in some way? Who's name was I chanting? The peyote had created a more intense focus on my actions. I was no longer content to sit and simply sing this phrase. I was filled with a determination to know what it really meant.

In my mind, I began to repeat my own mantra along with the chant.

Who is *Shiva…*?
Who is *Shiva…*?
Who is *Shiva…*?

My lips continued to chant *Om Namah Shivaya*, but my mind was splitting its attention between the two lines.

Om Namah Shivaya…
Who is *Shiva…*?
Om Namah Shivaya…
Who is *Shiva…*?

After several hours of this focus, I experienced a new shift. With my eyes closed, I could see and feel the world around me. It began to fold in on itself, as one might fold in all the flaps of a box to flatten it. I perceived a large area of the world and my various points of interaction with it, which kept bending and folding in. Flap after flap of this *reality* I had been living in, moved from being multidimensional into flat, two-dimensional, compact forms.

Within the folding process, I began to see faces of people from my life. Some stood out for a while; others passed by in large groups. Some manifested symbolically as a particular type of person or relationship. I acknowledged each one with a silent *Om Namah Shivaya*, as they appeared and then folded in with everything else.

I was emotionally moved to see many faces that had been forgotten long ago. They still had a place in my heart. I saw people I liked, people I loved, and people I'd had a hard time with. But in this space, I loved them all. Each one was precious, a special part of my experience of life on this planet. I repeated the mantra with as much care and intention as I could for each person, each face that appeared before me. Every one received a well-wishing repetition of *Om Namah Shivaya*, as they dissolved into the psychic void. I knew something powerful was taking place, and participated with full attention.

Now there were several things going on in my mind at once. Externally, I was chanting the mantra; inside, I was repeating "Who is *Shiva*?" and, in my vision, I was saying the mantra to all these faces from my past. It was my way of thanking them for whatever role they played in this life and universe that now seemed to be undergoing a massive transformation and collapse into itself. It was as though a black hole had appeared in reality, drawing in everything that was familiar to me.

I wondered if this was *it*, if this was the end of the world as I knew it. I wondered if I would ever be able to — or even *want* to — recreate that construct of reality again. Even if I desired to put all the boxes back together again, would it be possible? This was new territory, and by now it was profoundly out of my hands. There was no congressman to write to, no friend to confide in. There was no turning back, because the land I had come from no longer existed.

It had been stripped away, folded up and dissolved into the ether. It was obvious to me, watching this reality folding in on itself, that none of it could have ever been real. It was like seeing a sideshow disassemble after the carnival; watching the tattooed man washing off the ink, and the sword swallower reset all the retractile devices in his swords. I had been fooled. I had been so gullible and naive. I had fallen for the illusion of this world. I thought things were important and they didn't even exist! I should have known better. How could I have fallen for all this *again*!

As soon as the idea of *again* popped up, I slipped into the awareness that this had all happened many times before. Then, the final folding of the universe took place, to the farthest reaches of anything I had ever conceived. It all folded in, until there was flat, infinite darkness.

But right in the middle of this vast darkness was a point of consciousness represented by a still light. It was like a star or a small flame with no flickering at all. It was more peaceful than anything I had ever known. I knew this was the seed from which had sprouted the entire world, including who I thought I was and every thought and idea I'd ever had. Everything originated from that point, and had now folded back into it. So *this* was *Shiva*, the source of the universe!

For a moment, I wondered if this point of light existed in me or if I existed in it. But then it was so obvious. Both were true. In this place, even opposites coexisted perfectly.

I remember thinking that, for many people, this experience is available consciously only after they leave the physical world. I knew without a doubt that I had been there before. In fact, this space was absolutely the most familiar place I had ever known. It was familiar in a deep way that nothing else had ever come close to.

> *At the still point of the turning world.*
> *Neither flesh nor fleshless;*
> *Neither from nor towards; at the still point,*
> *there the dance is,*
> *But neither arrest nor movement.*
> *And do not call it fixity,*
> *Where past and future are gathered.*
> *Neither movement from nor towards,*
> *Neither ascent nor decline.*
> *Except for the point, the still point,*
> *There would be no dance, and there is only the dance.*
> *I can only say, there we have been;*
> *but I cannot say where.*
> *And I cannot say how long,*
> *for that is to place it in time.*
>
> —*T. S. ELIOT*

I was suspended in a space between *me* and *not me*. There was just awareness. I was somewhat conscious of the personality and circumstances I had been living in, but I was not them.

I wondered if I would ever go back to the illusion. It didn't seem possible to return to things as they had been, because it was clear when everything folded in on itself that it would never reappear in exactly the same configuration. If the seed sprouted again, it would be a whole new illusion, a new life-dream, though I might not realize it from within the mirage. What a play!

I hoped I would not be fooled again. I wanted to stay with this peaceful light and not jump back into the mirage. Well, not only did the mirage reappear in new forms, but it has reappeared in new and different manifestations again and again throughout this dance I call "my life."

It was after this experience that I could no longer consider myself an atheist.

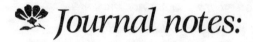 *Journal notes:*

A tribute to that point of Supreme Consciousness, written after this experience on Shivaratri

How can the Ultimate be described?
The mind always tries to categorize and organize,
Yet when it turns toward That
and ceases to manufacture its intellectual illusions,
it is shattered, dissolved,
or deflected by defenses arising from

...a distorted sense of self-preservation
...a fear
...a passive submission to the sleep state
...a bright silver toy, dangled above

To distract one's attention
and re-crystallize,
re-solidify,
re-move one's awareness
from the process of dissolution,
turning one back - again -
thus maintaining the underlying,
fundamental process of pulsation.
The continuous oscillation of contraction
and expansion, being manifest through
infinite dimensions
 of cycles and frequencies,
     Patterns upon patterns
       upon patterns.

The highest, most infinite states of expansion
and the most compact states of contraction,
being (not becoming!) one,
in a simultaneous, eternal...
Symphony?
Void?

Bringing into one's awareness the highest truths
whose very being form a total lack of knowledge,
a lack of mind.
A state of awareness far beyond the world
and universe.

Not beyond in space,
but right under, or under-lying,
in an all-pervasive, enfolded kind of way.
Yet it is really not enfolded...

IT IS
And nothing else is.

It's not that this array of worlds and universes is not,
but only that point of infinite space,
time, knowledge, love and emptiness IS

Manifest as the point of light
Shimmering in the darkness,
A symbol of a state of transcendence
over the illusions
that bind one in so many ways,
and on so many levels,
to contraction...
or to the cycles of expansion and contraction,
as these cycles underlie and maintain
the qualities into which they crystallize.

Thus all of these qualities,
and their underlying cycles,
and the time flow that sustains them,
and the infinite other dimensions of pattern,
are all contained within this point...
yet they're not really there at all,
for the point contains nothing,
perhaps like a channel of unlimited potential
that is always manifesting, pulsating, creating,
yet which never moves or changes at all.
It is we, who by interacting with this potential,
manifest or create these patterns
of world or universe.

And yet we ourselves are,
at our most fundamental level,
completely one with both that potential
and its manifestation
or lack of manifestation.

The mind has logic systems
which reflect back in the form of our thoughts.
They want reasons and explanations
for all of this illusion.
The closest they can come to conceiving
of a "Divine Motive" behind this universe,
is in the metaphor of enjoyment through creation,
one of the least distorted or contracted
modes of experience
which the mind has access to.

This joy - the merging with one's own creation -
experienced by the daydreaming child,
the artist, the lover, and the mother,
are contracted forms of that limitless joy.

Thus the mind uses a contracted concept of desire
for these states of bliss, love and enjoyment -
states which require manifestation and duality -
to explain the need for contraction and multiplicity,
absorption in one's own creation.

But it's not that the expanded "Shiva" state
is just the underlying of the contraction, "Shakti."
The two create, maintain, and destroy one another,
or itself

and neither aspect is more true or real,
because when seen through the point, it all just IS.
And yet, only the point IS.
And not even the point really is,
because it, like all else, is symbol.

ALL MANIFESTATION IS SYMBOL

The point is simultaneously more contracted
and more expanded than the worlds it creates.
It is infinitely compact and infinitely all-pervasive,
as they say "smaller than the smallest,
yet greater than the greatest",
and yet it is still only symbol.

And nothing else IS except symbol.
And not even symbol really is
because as much as it is,
it is not.
And it neither is nor is not, really.
For the cycle of is and is not
is itself symbolic manifestation.

Om Namah Shivaya
I honor Shiva, the source of the Universe.

Two roads diverged in a wood, and I —
I took the one less traveled by,
and that has made all the difference.

— ROBERT FROST

13.

DESTINY CALLS

URING THE WINTERS, our swami would travel to various locations, giving programs and workshops. The winter after our first meeting, he was living in a Miami Beach hotel that had been transformed into a meditation center. I drove there with one of the Ann Arbor devotees for a two-week visit. I was sitting outside one evening, enjoying the ocean breeze, when my car-mate came by and gave me some shocking news. He didn't think his car would make it back to Michigan, and he was going to stay in Miami through the spring. I looked at him in disbelief. I only had enough money to stay for two weeks.

Somehow, I felt surprisingly calm in spite of this new twist. Even though it seemed to be bad news, my warrior spirit surfaced. Here was a challenge presenting itself before me. I felt empowered by the hefty schedule of spiritual practices of the previous week, and could sense that this may be the brink of another breakthrough. I had to be courageous and meet my destiny head on. There was no use getting upset with this fellow. There was no use crying about my fate. Why not stay for a while? I went out the next morning and found a waitress job at one of the local hotels. The wages paid my room and board, with enough left over for the eventual trip back to Ann Arbor. My two-week visit expanded into two months.

During this period, I experienced an intense contrast between the two worlds. My days were spent in a frenzied environment, serving food at a Miami Beach hotel. All day long I was dealing with friendly people, grumpy people, and flirtatious people. Then I'd return to the monastery, just in time for the evening program. Walking through the front doors of this oceanside monastery was like stepping from the harsh desert heat into a cool breeze of sweet smells and refreshing energy. The contrast gave me a new appreciation for the palpable purity of this place.

One morning, I stood on the sundeck with several other devotees as we watched the sun rising over the ocean on one side, and our teacher standing on the roof on the other. The monastery's video crew was trying to capture all of this beauty with their cameras, but their tape deck wouldn't roll. I had worked a bit with video in my college classes, but was no expert to be sure. However, I had learned a term: *capstan servo*. I knew it had something to do with the tape's turning in the deck.

I don't know what made me walk over to the camera crew and ask them whether there might be a problem with the capstan servo. If I had tried to come up with my motivation at the time, maybe I would have said I was trying to show off. But I really wasn't. Maybe I was genuinely trying to help them fix the equipment. That's a nice thought, but I'm sure they were far more capable of dealing with the problem than me with my two-bit vocabulary word.

No, it was destiny. The winds of karma blew through me in that moment and wafted through the video crew as well. The department head looked up with a surprised expression. Perhaps he was impressed that a girl could use such a technical phrase. It probably made him think I knew more about video than I really did. When he asked about my experience, I was honest about what I had and hadn't done. Regardless of my lack of qualifications, he invited me to come to the New York monastery and work in the video department during the upcoming summer retreat.

My mind stopped when I heard his offer. He said that if I could afford to stay for at least two months, I would be able to work with them. This didn't seem possible, since I was still living from week to week on my restaurant wages, and had no savings whatsoever.

About to explain my situation, I happened to glance up toward the roof. Our teacher was standing in the distance as before, but now his finger was pointed directly toward us. In his gesture I saw the metaphorical finger of fate, and immediately said, "I'll be there!" I walked away, wondering how I was going to manage financially, but sensing a benevolent force propelling my commitment. It's not that I was expecting some miraculous boon or that I could think of any way to be able to fulfill these conditions. And yet, a soft note of faith was playing beneath my concerns.

That note turned into a symphony back in Ann Arbor. Somebody I didn't even know offered me an incredible job,

out of the blue. The job title was "consultant for City Hall."
My task was to take a list of all the businesses in Ann Arbor
and to make sure they were still there. I was given a shiny
new Caprice Classic to drive, along with keys to the city's gas
pumps. I had my own office in City Hall with a wooden desk
and swivel leather chair and was allowed to hire one of my
friends as an assistant. The job ended three days before the
summer retreat was to begin, and paid exactly what I needed
for my travel and lodging expenses.

Actually, something strange happened during this job.
After receiving the list of businesses, I was able to check
many of them off right at my desk, since I lived in the
college town. Then my friend and I began to drive around
with the lists, carefully checking all the remaining
businesses, and looking for new ones to add. We found the
job surprisingly easy and quick. Within a few days, we were
finished with nearly a third of the list. This was odd because
the man who hired me said that it had taken three people
three months to do this job the previous year. We would
only have a month and a half, which would give me exactly
the amount of money I'd need to spend the summer at the
New York monastery, and it would end three days before
the first day of the retreat.

But there was one problem with this otherwise perfect
scenario. My assistant and I were too fast at this job. It made
me wonder at what pace the three employees the previous year
had worked. Maybe they stopped to chat with each business,
or maybe there had been extra elements involved with their
project. Either way, I needed this job and so did my assistant.
We tried to slow down, but it was getting ridiculous. We were
just wasting time. We were young and full of energy. Neither
of us felt right about *trying* to be lazy.

So we decided to paint the new building at the Ann Arbor center. It was a fairly large building with six rooms. We spent a full week prepping the walls and doing all the painting. Of course, we'd have to quickly clean up before returning back to City Hall with our business lists. We felt a little guilty for putting on a facade, but not enough to give up this blessed job. And now we felt extra good, because we were using the time to provide service to our spiritual community. When grace descends, there is a natural desire to give back something in return, which of course then creates more good karma and brings more grace, inspiring even more gratitude and good karma. Now, that is a great machine to get on!

Instead of hiding ourselves away, we became outlandish and flamboyant. We started coming to work wearing straw hats and shorts, and requested a big wall map of the city from the city hall office supplier. Every afternoon we would hold these incredible, pseudo meetings. The walls separating all the offices were open at the top, so everybody could hear about our great and tedious progress through this difficult task. We discussed all the streets we would hit the next day, and generally gave a really good impression of what phenomenal workers we were. Without even seeing a page of our work, the other office staff began to praise our great dedication and work ethics. I think mostly they were amused to see us kids hopping around with our straw hats and big smiles. Our work was "miraculously" completed on the very last day of the month-and-a-half time period. Now it was time to take my next step on this amazing, unfolding journey.

I arrived at the monastery two days before the summer was to officially begin. Someone told me the video crew was doing an out-of-town shoot for two days, and suggested that I sign up for another service assignment until they returned.

To be honest, I wasn't crazy about the idea of working for free. I didn't really understand the practice of selfless service, and especially didn't want to be given an unpleasant task to do. And here I was supposed to walk up to the service assignment desk and be given some random work to do. It was one thing to help out in the video department, and quite another to do things like housekeeping. What if they asked me to clean toilets?

Before the service time, there was an optional midmorning chant called the *Rudram*. Thinking this would be a good way to postpone my fate, I went. The text was from the ancient Sanskrit Vedas, and the syllables, melody and pacing were so fast and complex that I don't think I managed to get a single word out right. It went on for nearly an hour, and about ten minutes into the chant, I put down the book and closed my eyes.

I tried to calm down and prepare myself for the unknown work ahead of me. It may sound ridiculous to have been so worried about a few hours of work, but for some reason the situation had pushed some old buttons. My emotional responses were magnified out of proportion to the problem. I'd heard quite a few spiritual lectures by this time, and started to mentally file through the teachings about *surrender.*

I comforted myself, "Don't worry about what service you get. This place is a conscious field of energy. Whatever assignment you receive will be perfect for your spiritual growth. It will contain a significant message for you. It will be like a big fortune cookie. They say the entire monastery is the body of the guru. Nothing here happens by chance."

Feeling inspired and rejuvenated, I set off somewhat enthusiastically to the assignment desk.

On the other side of this karma play was the woman working at the desk who had a difficult project on her hands. There was an unpleasant job that needed to be done, but whenever someone came up, she just couldn't bring herself to give it to them. Finally, out of desperation, she decided that whoever came up next would be the one for this task, no matter who it was.

Up walked the newly inspired and surrendered Kumuda, ready to find out what great message her service assignment would reveal. The woman at the desk asked me and the next fellow in line to wait for the project supervisor. In came a man carrying two buckets with mops. He walked up and greeted us. "So you're the shit crew."

Our assignment was to go to a basement area right next to where our teacher lived. All of the monastic sewage had backed up into three rooms and a hallway. There were inches of raw, smelly slime all over the floor, including several large, soaked pieces of carpeting. The three of us were to clean all of this disgusting mess using the most primitive of tools: mops with not enough strands and a jug of bleach. I couldn't believe my eyes. I couldn't believe my nose.

I burst out laughing. What a funny cosmic joke. What part of the guru's body was this? Here I was awaiting a profound message about my life and I get rooms filled with shit? And I had been worried that I might have to clean a few toilet seats!

I was also bubbling with unexpected joy, because there was a perceptible, pulsating energy in these rooms. After all, they were right next to where our teacher lived. He had raised his personal energy through decades of intense spiritual and yogic practices, as was obvious whenever I was in his presence. Even here, in the general vicinity of his house, I could feel a distinct vibration strumming through the air.

I became totally ecstatic, giggling inwardly. *Somebody* was playing with me again! It was such an obvious punchline after my big lecture and my worries about the possibility of having to clean bathrooms. It just had to have been scripted by a higher intelligence. In this moment, a bond of friendship was established between the monastery and myself. I cleaned and cleaned with great love, wearing the only pair of shoes I had, not even worried that they were being destroyed by the mucky mess. Even the stench didn't bother me. "I guess this is one way to learn to be detached from the senses!" I thought, chuckling to myself in bliss. I couldn't recall when I had felt so free and giddy, and I certainly wouldn't have imagined the circumstances under which I would be feeling so light and happy. The three of us cleaned for hours, scooping up the sludge, rolling up soaked carpeting, scrubbing the walls, and finally polishing the floors. Soon, the rooms were sparkling clean, and I had tasted the secret nectar of selfless service.

On this day, there was an extra service shift in the evening to prepare for a big workshop the next day. I went back to the desk for my next assignment. The woman apologized for having given me such a yukky task to do, and asked me if I liked to paint. "Oh yes," I replied, "I love to paint."

"Great," she said, "you'll like this assignment. Go across the street to the children's playhouse where they'll be painting the rooms tonight."

I skipped across the street. But as I arrived, the workers told me they would not be ready to paint until much later. "But we'd appreciate if you could help us with another project until we're ready," one of the supervisors requested. "There are several dogs living in this area, and there is dog doo all over the ground outside the children's house. Would you please go around with this tin can and collect all the mess?"

What could I do but smile and pick up all the doggie-doo with great gusto? I couldn't keep from chuckling while speaking mentally to this invisible consciousness that had suddenly become quite apparent through the events unfolding around me. "Okay, friend, I think I got the message!" On this day, my idea about what activities were and were not pleasurable was shattered.

This experience also helped to prepare me for the great surrender essential to monastic life. It cleared away a thick layer of my ego and concepts, giving me a taste of the divine as a conscious and even comedic being.

For the rest of the summer, I enjoyed an interesting job as a general assistant in the video department. I typed scripts, labeled tapes, researched quotes, and even had a chance to assist the editor every now and then. The first time I worked with him, Luc was editing a talk by our teacher. The tape decks were failing to line up properly for the edit, and for nearly an hour we heard the exact same five-second pre-roll line over and over again. "Know the one who knows the mind. That one is true and that is the Self." It would play forwards, then backwards; fast-speed, slow-speed, normal-speed. I felt as though I was taking a bath in "Know the one who knows the mind. That one is true and that is the Self." As Luc became more and more frustrated with the broken equipment, I smiled to myself, wondering if the machine was planning to keep replaying the line until I finally got it!

I thought, "This would be the best job in the world,

editing videos of our guru and his teachings. You couldn't help but get it!" In that moment I made my first big wish within the walls of the monastery. I prayed and asked that I might have the opportunity to edit videos of our guru one day, even though I didn't really know how to edit yet.

The summer continued, with challenges and blessings around every corner. The predictability of the daily schedule created a rhythm of days that I was able to ride like waves of the ocean, flowing out with one wave and back in with the next — moving effortlessly with the breath of God, with the rising and setting of the sun, with the easy times and the difficult tests. There was a sense of fitting into myself and this lifestyle, as if I were wearing clothes that fit perfectly, not too loose or too tight. The video department staff were a fun bunch, and we shared many light moments while reveling in this wonderful work of capturing our teacher's words and image on film.

As the summer began to wind down, it was nearly time for me to leave and return to college. My teacher and his staff were going to be traveling to Los Angeles for the winter. I thought about how wonderful it would be to join them there.

At this point, I was just about out of money. As it was, I was going to have to work hard and take out another student loan to pay for my fall semester of classes. In truth, my heart was no longer enthusiastic about going to college. I was confused, at a major crossroads, and didn't know which way to turn. I needed guidance.

Well, isn't that what a spiritual *guide* is for?

I finally got up the nerve to ask my teacher's secretary if I could have a private meeting with him, explaining that I wanted to discuss my alternatives and ask for his blessings and guidance. She was very kind and open at the time, and said that if I composed a letter describing my situation, she would present it to him. I painstakingly wrote a three-page letter detailing the entire situation, clearly and concisely. Over the next few days I waited, excited to think I would be receiving a personal directive from my guru at any moment.

Finally, the call came. The secretary asked me to come down to her room. My heart was pounding with anticipation as I made my way to her office.

She opened the door and handed my letter back to me with a somewhat serious face. There were several red lines scribbled across the page. "I've decided not to show your letter to Baba. I've highlighted the main points you made. You can just ask your question during the public *darshan*."

I was appalled. I could have done that long ago! The reason I had gone through all of this trouble was because the situation was too complicated to be expressed in one or two sentences, in the midst of hundreds of people.

I tried to argue with her, but she was much tougher than I, a real hard-nose. She had no compassion or concern for my situation. I could see on her desk a stack of letters from other people like me. I was just a name on the list, a letter in the pile. Didn't she understand this was my *life*? Didn't she realize this was an important decision for me?

The secretary looked at me, impatient to get on with her work. I stormed away from her room and walked down the hall toward the stairway. I wasn't just mad at the way this woman treated me, I was mad at my teacher. I was furious with God. "Here I am ready to surrender and do whatever you say, and you won't even take five minutes to see me!"

Right by the stairway, there was a curtain which separated our teacher's living quarters from the rest of the building. He would sometimes stand behind the curtain, looking through a peekhole to see what was going on in the lobby. As I stormed past the thick blue curtains, I saw that they were parted in the middle. There, standing all alone, was my teacher, looking at me.

I was so angry, that even the shock of seeing him there wasn't enough to jar me out of my fury. I glared fiercely into his eyes thinking, "Why won't you let me see you!?!" I didn't say anything since I didn't think he spoke English. But I stared into his eyes, fiercely.

He glared back, and won the staring contest immediately.

The bolt of energy that came through his eyes hit me so strongly that I turned and practically flew up the stairs. Before I hit even the tenth step, I cracked up. My insides filled with pure humor and joy. The energy pushed into my head, my eyes, my face, and my heart. There was a deep laughter bubbling through me that would have been *extremely* loud if I let it escape. I couldn't make so much noise in this peaceful, meditative atmosphere, and managed to hold in the sound. My body was physically doubled over, as I hugged my chest in an attempt to contain all the laughter energy. In the midst of this explosive dance, I thought, "You won the staring contest!" and laughed some more.

I decided to return to college, including a Sanskrit class in my schedule to give myself some enthusiasm. Nevertheless, it had become evident that this kind of school was not teaching what I most wanted to learn.

On the third day of the semester, I went to the Art School for my new film class. We were going to learn how to cut film using a 16 millimeter editing flatbed. While the professor demonstrated the equipment, I stood against the door, thinking. I had returned to school, but was still unclear about my career goals. I had been registered as a double major in film/video and neurophysiology, and now wondered, "Where should I focus my energy? Should I become a scientist or an artist?"

On the intellectual path, my goal was to become a research scientist, to use all the information learned from age seven on, to help move myself and society toward a bigger view of the mind and the nature of reality. Specifically, I wanted to explore the processes involved with multiple personality disorder. I believed this dysfunction could be a great doorway through which to explore the foundations of human personality in general. First, however, I'd probably have to spend at least a decade injecting frogs with some pharmaceutical drug before being trusted with a grant to fund my own research.

Then there was the artistic side. My creative work had always been very important to me. I stood there, watching the film professor go on about the mechanics of this editing flatbed, and made a decision. The people in my film classes were definitely more fun than the pre-med students. There was more laughter and enthusiasm, along with an inherent respect for the soul, the spark of creativity, and one's personal emotions and expressions. In that moment, I decided that the rest of my life would be more fun if I became a filmmaker. Suddenly, bright splotches filled my visual screen, and I passed out.

Right there in class, I fell completely unconscious, for no apparent reason. My classmates didn't know whether to laugh or be concerned, because a strange thing happened when I blacked out. I had been leaning against the door, wearing a student's backpack. As I slid to the floor, the little piece of canvas sewed into the top of the pack hung itself neatly over the doorknob. I basically ended up hanging on the door. Most of the classmates didn't know me yet, and must have wondered if I was one of those kooky film students trying to be funny. We definitely had a few strange birds in the film department. I regained consciousness, went downstairs to the student cafe for some juice, and soon felt well enough to go home.

Still dazed, I checked my mailbox, and was surprised to find a letter from the video department in the New York monastery. At first, I was touched that they would think to write and let me know they remembered me. But when I opened the envelope, there was a letter asking me to move into the upstate New York monastery for the winter.

The fellow who had previously agreed to take care of video distribution for a second year decided, at the last minute, that he couldn't bear the idea of another freezing, desolate winter out in the boonies. My teacher was going to be leaving in a few weeks, and if the video people didn't find *someone* willing to stay in this deserted, snowed-in building in the middle of the Catskill Mountains, then one of them would have to stay behind, missing all of the tour excitement of sunny southern California.

I was already in a state of shock from having passed out in class, and now this. I thought it was compassionate of the video crew to find a way for me to come back. They knew I hadn't wanted to leave. Of course, they had made a bit of an error in satisfying my desire. I wanted to go *traveling* with our teacher to Los Angeles, not stay in a freezing, desolate place in the Catskill Mountains, stuck with twenty-five people I didn't know!

Still, it was remarkable to get such a letter. I took it to a friend's house and showed it to him. His response was, "It's nice to be needed."

For my friend, this was a simple statement. For me, it was

the universe speaking through his lips. It hadn't even occurred to me that anyone actually *needed* me to do this work. I assumed they were offering it to do me a favor. This shifted things considerably. I was needed. It was time to take a leap, and I decided to do it. There was no logic behind this decision. I just knew I had to go. My warrior-spirit rose up to help me through the complex transition, as I canceled classes, informed my family and friends, and arranged the many details involved with the big move. It all went surprisingly smoothly.

We must be willing to get rid of the life we've planned,
so as to have the life that is awaiting us…
The old skin has to be shed
before the new one is to come.

—JOSEPH CAMPBELL

A happy life must be to a great extent a quiet life,
for it is only in an atmosphere of quiet
that true joy can live.

—BERTRAND RUSSELL

14.

WINTER WONDERLAND

MY MAIN WORK IN THE MONASTERY was to make video copies of all of our teacher's magnificent talks. He had studied many different branches of Indian philosophy, was able to explain each of them in a way that made sense to me, and was humorous and entertaining to boot. Only a small portion of the building was open for the winter staff, and my video room was tucked away with its little wall-heater between two meditation halls that had been filled with the energy of spiritual practices all summer long. I had a whole half of this huge building to myself. What more could a loner ask for?

I worked alone in a room with several hundred videotapes of my teacher giving talks, traveling around the world, and visiting the holy shrines of India. I decorated the office with pictures of various sages and saints, and it became my temple. Once again, I began to reconnect with the inner spaces.

This time I had powerful chants, mantras and spiritual teachings to help guide me into a deeper level. Last time I had gotten caught on my inward explorations by a snag that made life unbearable for me. But now I felt protected in accessing new areas of consciousness. I was no longer on my own. I had a friend on the path, someone who knew the turf. For the first time in my life, I didn't feel alone.

I could never have imagined finding a place whose primary purpose was to support inner growth. Just two years after trying to leave this world in despair, I had discovered what I hadn't even dared to hope for: a place dedicated to inner growth, deeper knowledge, and the exploration of life.

None of the twenty-five winter staff knew how to play either the harmonium organ or drums for the chants. So I decided to learn the basics. With no real musical background, I played an instrument for every chant during that winter, usually three times each day. That also meant I had to attend every chant. It was time for this aloof teenager to learn some discipline.

Every morning, I would play a hand-pumped organ called a *harmonium* for the hour-and-a-half chanting session. One hand would pump the accordion-like bellows while the other fingered the keys. Both were moving constantly for the entire hour-and-a-half, and any attempt to remove either hand would make a noticeable glitch in the chant. Every single morning, I would sit cross-legged on the ground, both hands attached to this instrument. It was a definite lesson in self-control. Itchy nose? Forget it. Legs starting to fall asleep? Tough. Sleepy this morning? You can't sleep through this one.

Actually, that's not quite true.

Soon after beginning to play for these morning chants, came a strange new occurrence. I would be sitting there playing the instrument and chanting the words, and I'd start to lose conscious awareness. I would relax deeply into the sounds, movements, rhythms and vibrations of the chant, yet my fingers would continue to play, almost on their own.

When I was able to remain alert during the chant, I would enjoy reading the translation of the text. This scripture, called the *Guru Gita*, revealed many secret teachings about the nature of the universe and the deeper significance of the *guru*, which is not considered as just a person or teacher by this scripture, but as the grace-bestowing power that flows through the outer, physical guru and penetrates all of creation, lifting souls upward through the power of grace.

From my inner explorations I knew that our belief systems cannot be separated from the world as we see it. These teachings opened my mind into a much higher view of life. No longer was the universe just a mundane place I had to put up with until I died. It was as magical as anything I had ever imagined. I couldn't believe such wonderful philosophy was so easily available, and yet so unrecognized in the society I had been living in.

One day, our manager came in during the morning chant. The managers were notorious for rarely coming to chants, even though they were devotees as well. But this morning, the manager not only came in, but began pulling the chanters, one by one, out of the room. He'd walk up to each person and whisper in their ear. The person would pick up their sitting pillow and chanting book and leave the hall. I was certainly curious to know what was going on!

However, I couldn't ask anybody anything, because I was playing the harmonium and had to keep the chant going. By now, I was quite alert as everybody in the room except the drummer and me was mysteriously led away. I couldn't even imagine what was going on! Was I missing something special? Were we at war? Was the building on fire? What was *so* important to call *everyone* out of the chant, but not important enough to have *me* stop playing?

Finally, the text ended, and I found out what happened. A roofing crew had been hired to do some work on one of the residential wings of the building. On the previous day, they had peeled away the surface roof layers and put a simple plastic tarp over it for the night, as there was no sign of rain. Well, while we were chanting that morning, it didn't just rain. It rained like hell. It was pouring so hard that the rain not only collapsed the entire roof of the third floor, but some of the second-floor ceilings as well.

Everyone had been led out of the chant to help keep the flood at bay. There were only about twenty-five people available to help, the winter maintenance crew. We set up bucket brigades. We'd catch water in some buckets and shovel gray gunk into others. Everyone left whatever work they normally did to help clean up this mess. We were all completely wet and filthy, as we shoveled away. It was actually great exercise for me to be doing this kind of work after spending so much of my time sitting. It also forced a certain surrender, because I'd waited until the last minute to send out some videotapes that "had" to go out that day.

At one point, the security guard asked me to bring a tool to the manager, who was in our teacher's house. This would give me a chance to see where my teacher lived! I tiptoed into this holy space, and found the manager.

He said, "Look, I need for you to stay here and keep changing all of these buckets throughout Baba's living quarters. There are a lot of leaks in the roof and we have to make sure his rooms remain dry. Just stay here until I come back."

He didn't come back for sixteen hours.

At first, I was very shy about being there, and was careful not to touch anything. I just stood in the middle of the room, watching the buckets fill up slowly and changing them when they were full. Eventually, I got up the nerve to walk through his kitchen and dining areas, and even peeked into his ever-so-cool bathroom, with pictures of his favorite saints molded into some of the tiles. The energy in the area was tangible and sweet. You could feel a charge of purity in the air. It was like a scent, but an electrified scent you could also feel.

Well, the hours ticked by. Sixteen hours alone in this magical wonderland, my teacher's house. I sat on the lush carpeting between bucket changes, and experienced many delightful and peaceful meditations. It felt as though I had somehow become his friend. I was hanging out in this private room, in his personal energy. And, of course, that bathroom which I had tiptoed into so reverently during the first couple of hours, eventually became *my* bathroom. After all, I had been told not to leave the premises, and a person does have to go.

By the time I missed both lunch and dinner, it became clear the manager had forgotten I was there. I could have left to find him, but why do that? I was quite happy in my new quarters. Sitting in this pure environment for so long, I felt as though my entire being was being bathed clean.

What is contentment?
To renounce all craving
for what is not obtained unsought
and to be satisfied with what comes unsought,
without being elated or depressed ever by them —
this is contentment.

—Yoga Vasishta

15.

The Happy Pauper

Having care and respect for all things was part of the discipline practiced in this monastic place. Every corner was kept spotless and each penny was accounted for. But inevitably, there were a few fanatics. Freddie, the office-supply guy, was one.

Freddie carried the practice of budgeting to new and absurd heights. He once proclaimed that Post-It notes and Sharpie pens were going to bankrupt the entire monastery. He used to get upset when our teacher used only one side of a sheet of paper. Freddie and my father could have had a great time together in Europe with the $5-a-day book!

One day, my friend went to Freddie to get a new tape dispenser. She was in charge of all the mailing needs at the time, and the plastic wheel that fit inside the tape roll had broken. She assumed it was simply time for a new dispenser, or at least a new plastic wheel. Freddie asked her to go back to her office and bring the broken dispenser to him. When she handed it to him, he said, "Look, you don't need a new dispenser *or* a new wheel. You can put a paperclip inside of the tape reel, and use this small piece of pencil to balance it in the dispenser." He put the flimsy configuration together for her. My friend was not thrilled, but had an extremely amicable nature. She quietly thanked him and turned to leave.

"Hey wait!" called Freddie. "Don't you have your own paperclips down in the mailroom?" And with that, he removed the paperclip and handed the rest back to her. She just smiled and walked away, without even getting angry with him. I think she must have been well on her way to becoming a saint.

In spite of the occasional extremist, this idea of respect was prevalent throughout the monastery. In my upbringing there had been little respect, not just for me, but for the world, for life itself. This idea of honoring the universe as a form of divinity was very new to me. I had to learn many new rules quickly. During my youth, for example, if we didn't want to finish some food, we would simply throw it away. Here, there was a focus on respecting the meals we were given. We would try to only take what we could eat. Before putting the first bite in our mouths, we would close our eyes and offer thanks in our own way for this benevolent sustenance.

The scriptures of India are chock full of rituals and rules. Some didn't seem necessary, many seemed odd to me. I came to realize that it wasn't so much that each specific rule must be followed dogmatically. For example, when entering a holy place, it is considered auspicious to put your right foot down first. I don't believe some bad thing would have happened if I stepped over the temple threshold with my left foot. Rather, these rules were there to inspire us to live more consciously. Becoming more conscious is, after all, an important element in spiritual evolution.

At times I might be preoccupied and walk into the meditation hall or temple quickly, rushing to get my seat. However, when I did remember to follow that rule about putting the right foot first, it would make me immediately aware of where I was and what I was entering. I would slow down and focus on the present moment. I would move more gracefully while positioning my steps so the proper foot would enter with a smooth stride. Although this "right foot first" decree seems like an eccentric rule, in truth it was a tool, a spiritual practice in and of itself. The monastery was filled with these kinds of tools.

During my first six months of monastic life, I lived without spending a single cent. After paying all the necessary fees and costs of leaving school, I had arrived with only a few dollars in my pocket. There was enough toothpaste and soap to last for a while, and my room and board were covered. I experienced another surprising shift during that first year. I learned to love poverty.

I loved not needing anything and not having anything. After all, three times a day I was served a delicious, home-cooked vegetarian meal. I had marvelous videos and teachings to imbibe, and a wonderful service to perform.

I've since learned about an amazing woman named Peace Pilgrim. She was deliberately penniless for twenty-eight years, as she walked back and forth across the country in the name of peace. Even if someone offered her money, she would not accept it. She would never ask for food or shelter. If someone offered food, she would eat. If nobody offered shelter, she would sleep under a tree or on a bench, covering herself with newspapers during the cold months. Yet she never caught so much as a cold, or encountered any significant trouble.

Through poverty, she actually achieved the great treasure of inner freedom. Peace used to joke that it would be crazy for anyone to mug her when she didn't have a penny to her name.

> *Who am I? It matters not that you know who I am;*
> *it is of little importance.*
> *This clay garment is one of a penniless pilgrim*
> *journeying in the name of peace.*
> *It is what you cannot see that is so very important.*
> *I am one who is propelled by the power of faith;*
> *I bathe in the light of eternal wisdom;*
> *I am sustained by the unending energy of the universe;*
> *this is who I really am.*
>
> —PEACE PILGRIM

In this wondrous environment, I had the opportunity to taste a drop of the freedom she attained. It's as though our souls become swathed in all these layers that have been created by our society, our families, and the media. One of these layers is that of material desire. This entire layer was simply and painlessly removed from me. There was no sense wanting to buy anything, because there was no money. Yet I was more content than I had ever been. I would happily hand-wash my clothes in the bathtub. I never even thought about buying the pastries and cookies available in the snack bar. I ate what was given to me, and lived with whatever I had. I learned that happiness is definitely not dependent on money.

I did go through some external hardships due to my poverty, but didn't experience them as hardships. I felt I was being challenged to rise above my previous limitations.

At one point during that first winter, my glasses broke. I could have gone to the manager and asked for help, but chose not to. I had worn glasses since age five, and wondered what it would be like to just let them go.

Here I was doing these visual jobs of video duplication and bookkeeping, and I could hardly see a thing. I had to put my face right up to the monitor to check the tapes, and stick my nose down into the ledgers and invoice books. I couldn't help but chuckle when someone would phone to complain that their tape quality wasn't quite right. I felt like saying, "What do you expect? The person making the copies is practically blind!"

I would see the fuzzy shapes of people passing me in the hallway. Sometimes I could tell who they were and sometimes I couldn't. It's likely that some of my fellow residents may have felt snubbed when I didn't return their smiles, but I couldn't see them! This went on for nearly two months. It was very powerful for me. I felt two things: my aloneness, and the faceless quality of humanity. This situation really gave me a chance to focus my attention inside. The visual distractions of the outside world were reduced to a minimum, and my other senses, thoughts and feelings were given a higher priority in the experiential realm.

The most striking part of the experience came when our manager realized my plight and sent me out to get a pair of glasses. All of a sudden, I could see people's faces. It was almost painful to look into people's eyes, because they carried so much power. I could literally see and feel the dazzling consciousness that poured out through each person's eyes.

Another challenge was to remain comfortable in spite of the cold weather. Here we were in the Catskill Mountains of upstate New York in the dead of winter, and I didn't even bring a sweater or winter coat with me. And within a few months of taking off my shoes to enter the meditation hall, my socks were full of holes. Eventually, I stopped wearing them. I would run to the outside temple in my bare feet, skipping over the icy ground in my version of a fire-walk. Nonetheless, instead of feeling scarcity or need, each of these experiences carried me to a new sense of freedom. I didn't even experience the discomfort of being cold. My pampered nature had been replaced by the serenity of contentment.

> *Poverty is not there for the sake of hardship.*
> *No, it is there because nothing exists but God.*
>
> —*Rumi*

16.

THIS KARMIC DANCE

IN THE RICH ENVIRONMENT of this monastery, I encountered all kinds of new ideas. When my teacher was in residence, he gave an extraordinary lecture almost every evening. In his natural manner, he would discourse on the most brilliant philosophies I had ever encountered. I was grateful to have an opportunity to watch these talks again and again while duplicating the videotapes. After watching the same tape hundreds of times, I'd inevitably glean deeper understandings from his words.

The monastery guests and residents were stimulating as well. In my home town, people seemed to fit more or less into fairly consistent, suburban parameters. However, the thousands of people who attended these summer retreats came from all over the world. Being open-minded enough to spend time with an Indian guru, they were some of the most interesting, colorful, and uniquely quirky people around. Some were knowledgeable about esoteric topics such as tarot card reading, astrology, and various healing and energy fields. Each one added a new note to my symphony of experience. Some were sweet and loving, while others were tense and harsh. Yet in this environment, even the most obnoxious people provided fertile ground for interaction and contemplation.

Once someone asked my teacher how he was able to work on so many people's egos and purify so many karmas all at once. He answered that he didn't have to do anything. He just brought everyone together, and they worked on each other. We used to pass this line around in a humorous way, usually when someone was getting on our nerves. Nevertheless, this is what was really happening. Our teacher didn't have to tell *this* person to be difficult with *that* person, to purify *that* person's authority issues. We were so many pieces of this puzzle, this group trek toward eternal Truth.

It is noteworthy that my most memorable lessons from these years often came through the steepest challenges or the most difficult people. As the correlation between challenges and inner breakthroughs became clear to me, I gained a new respect for difficult circumstances. I discovered that grace was hidden within every challenge. It's not that I sought out uncomfortable situations, but when they arose, I didn't despise them either. In the midst of even my most painful states of anger, frustration or grief there would be a soft whisper: "Go through this time… Learn from it… Welcome these flames of grace… "

It was becoming clear to me that many of society's ideas about the goals of life are formed through a very limited perspective. A new awareness was growing within me. The dualities of "good" and "bad," "attachment" and "aversion," were starting to look more like illusions. Something much bigger was going on here.

Purification would burst forth in explosion after explosion, outbursts of ecstasy and anger, pride and self-doubt. Lessons showered down on all our heads. Amazing synchronicities abounded. New insights lurked around every corner. Karmas were flying back and forth. People were acting out, being sensitive, forceful, benevolent, difficult, energized, exhausted, or filled with divine love.

You might imagine that people living in a spiritual place like this would all be very peaceful and friendly. This was not necessarily the case. It seemed as though spiritual growth wasn't always a linear movement into increasingly sweeter and higher places. Each of us carries countless layers of experience within our personality structures. Some of these layers involve deepseated emotions and belief systems. Before we can reach the space where there is true love and respect, we may first have to clear out the accumulated garbage. And having these patterns of anger, rejection, frustration, pride, and insecurity rooted out could be deeply distressing, both for us and the equally activated souls around us.

In this monastic environment, there was no escape from tension through drink, drugs, or even television. We had to process whatever came up. With thousands of people going through this intense, personal transformation at once, there was always a whirlwind of drama and growth. We had to learn to be *in the flow*, or we would encounter snags at every turn.

During my ten years in the monastery, I had several run-ins

with various people in charge. Some were security guards. Although most of the guards were friendly and barely noticeable, some of them seemed to think their purpose in life was to keep everyone else in their place. One job of the security department was to keep overzealous devotees from lunging at our teacher's feet begging for initiation, although amusingly, the chief of security had done just that upon meeting him.

I think some of the security guards may have taken their jobs so seriously so they could clear up some karmas, or work out specific psychological issues that may have required a subjective experience of personal authority. One guard used to sit during the programs, looking out over his chanting book to eye the other devotees suspiciously. We were singing God's name, for goodness sake! Did he think we were going to steal the photos? Fake the words? Such silly, unnecessary behavior. And yet, I had an intuition that this man somehow needed to really get into that "security guard" mentality, to feel those feelings and think those thoughts, so his soul could finally learn certain lessons about the nature of power and paranoia. Under normal circumstances, he might have had to spend his entire adult life developing a career path that could have ignited these particular issues for him. However in the monastery, we had the opportunity to live many lifestyles in one lifetime.

Here, we could be a secretary one day and our boss's boss the next. We might find ourselves planting flowers in the garden, hauling trash, milking cows, supervising crews, organizing records, managing departments, taking care of a room full of children, studying sacred texts, washing dishes, or answering people's questions at the information desk. It was even possible to find oneself doing several kinds of work with distinctly different groups of people in one day. Then you would go back to your six roommates. Then you would assume the role of a disciple, bowing down before the great master. Then you would sit during the chant, cringing with impatience at someone singing way off key next to you. Then your soul would be lifted to unimaginable vistas of bliss and ecstasy. There was never a dull moment in this place.

I had two particularly memorable security-guard experiences. The first took place in Miami.

One day, I found a mysterious key in my suitcase, right under my clothes. I decided to imagine it as a key to my heart, and offer it to my teacher as a symbolic, devotional gesture.

That evening we had the *darshan* line, where each person could come up to be in the guru's presence for a moment. I handed him the key. He held it in his hand for a moment and looked at me. Maybe he was wondering what the key was for. Was there a new car waiting behind curtain number three? More likely, he could see the meaning of the gesture in my eyes.

Unable to bear the intensity of his glance, I bowed my head and was brushed powerfully with the wand of peacock feathers he'd use to bless people. I felt an influx of warm energy enter my upper back and fill my body.

I started to stand up, but realized I was completely intoxicated. In this drunken state, I was barely able to stagger back to my seat. I sat down and closed my eyes. An exquisite energy swirled around inside my body. It felt as though my aura was being bathed in brilliant light. As the *darshan* line ended, my teacher began to deliver his lecture.

He spoke about how young people are so hot-blooded and rebellious. I was touched by his words, because I'd been that way myself. I didn't listen to my parents or to other figures of authority. I was protecting something inside myself from the opinions of others, yet this *something inside* was subtle and difficult to capture. Listening to my teacher's words, I moved into an emotional state, and began to weep. At the same time, I was witnessing the emotions moving through my body. I wasn't sad or upset at all, yet tears flowed freely.

Toward the end of the program, we all meditated together for fifteen minutes. My mind was filled with beautiful inner visions, thoughts and feelings. I was lifted out of myself by these exciting and intoxicating sensations. As the musical chords brought us out of meditation, I was still feeling euphoric. My service assignment at the time was to wash the dinner dishes. I was supposed to leave the hall as soon as meditation ended, to have a quick dinner before my shift. I began to walk slowly to the door. My glasses were so stained with tears that I took them off. Also, the lighting in the hall was dim. Between the intoxication and my inability to see, I was focused intently on my path to avoid stepping on anyone.

As I neared the door, a security guard grabbed my arm and held me back, barking, "Wait!" At first, I didn't know why, but as I looked up, I saw that my teacher was also heading toward the door through a different aisle. In truth, he wasn't *that* close. I could have made it out the door well before he arrived. Who knows what karmic scenario this guard must have been playing out with such an assertive attitude? And who could have imagined how perfectly his lesson was orchestrated with my own.

I wasn't angry, just shocked. Still in a daze from the sweet energy that was moving inside me, reveling in an inner innocence, I watched as my teacher continued to walk toward the door.

But he did not step out the door. Instead, he turned to the side and strolled over to where I was standing. He gently took my arm, and walked with me toward the exit. He leaned on my shoulder while putting on his shoes, and then guided me out the door in front of him. It was a beautiful and completely unexpected gesture.

Clearly, it had been grace that had ultimately motivated the security guard's apparently aggressive actions. Maybe the guard had unknowingly been holding me back not to keep me *from* my teacher, but specifically *for* him.

It was notable that I hadn't become angry with the security guard. Whatever happened while I knelt before my teacher in *darshan* had left me clean and empty of ego distortions, at least for a while. There was nothing and nobody left to fight. Maybe my teacher's respectful gesture was his way of acknowledging that an important personal shift had occurred within me this day. Perhaps he had already used the symbolic key to my heart.

A similar event took place the following summer in New York. I walked into one of the meditation rooms and was pleased to see my teacher walking right toward me. He was going to exit through the double doors behind me. I stood back against the wall to give him plenty of room to pass. Nevertheless, one of the security guards ran up and pulled me out of the way, hissing, "Baba doesn't want you to get so close to him!" My teacher walked through the doors and I was left in a state of confusion.

I wasn't really angry at the guard, though I certainly thought he had overreacted. But his statement concerned me, "Baba doesn't want you to get so close to him." During this time, I was exploring a space where the Consciousness I thought of as God and the manifestation of the world around me were no longer two separate arenas. I understood that the same quality that gives our dream worlds their rich depth of meaning was also present in my waking state. I recognized that events were symbolic and intertwined, that there was no such thing as meaningless experience.

By focusing on the teachings and practices of this path, I had developed a simple reverence for whatever appeared before me, no matter through whom it came. Its mere appearance on the screen of my consciousness gave it significance. If it was there, it was worthy of note. And here this security guard was telling me that my image of divinity didn't want me to get close to him.

What did it mean? Was it a message from my teacher? I contemplated this question all afternoon. The old rejection sentries from my past were standing at attention on the horizon of the present moment, waiting to have an unruly party in my mind and heart. These old tendencies pressured me to take the words at face value, hoping for the opportunity to play the "feel bad" game again. I tried to hold them at bay, focusing instead on what meaning might be hidden beneath the surface words. Maybe the deeper meaning was that I shouldn't get too close in terms of *dependence* on my teacher. Or maybe it was a message that I should keep a distance in my external relationship with him, so our subtle communion could remain unsullied by mundane expectations. I really didn't know what to make of these words. Regardless, I made an effort to feel less attached to my teacher, just in case that was the intended message behind this event.

At 5:00 pm, I went back to the same meditation hall for the afternoon chant. I played a big drum, while one of the monks waved a lamp of flames to the statue of our teacher's teacher. After putting the drum away, I stood near the back of the hall, chanting loudly. I had a resounding voice anyway, but the music people had specifically asked me to chant extra loud to help maintain the pace of this acappella chant.

I closed my eyes and focused completely on the pronunciation of each Sanskrit syllable. A few minutes into the chant, I felt someone brush up against me. That was no big deal, but they just stood right next to me, with their shoulder touching mine. I became disturbed by this. Why did this person have to stand so close to me? There was plenty of room in the hall. I kept my eyes closed, and tried to maintain my focus on the chant. I wasn't quite upset enough to move away from the person angrily, but it was irritating to have someone practically leaning against me. I've always liked to have a reasonable amount of personal space, and this person was definitely invading it.

After a while, I couldn't help but open my eyes a bit to see who could be so unconscious that they didn't even notice they were actually touching someone. I saw a flash of orange.

Was it one of the monks?

No.

It was my teacher!

This was the first time I had ever seen him come to this particular chant. It was *he* who was standing so close to me! I lost my concentration and stumbled on the next few words. I was absolutely shocked. My teacher looked at me with a mischievous half-smile, and then turned and walked away.

I thanked my lucky stars that I hadn't abruptly pulled myself from this "oblivious person" who had dared stand so close to me! If I hadn't been so humbled by the security guard's chastisement earlier that day, I might have responded in a way I would have later regretted. And the intricate dance played on.

We are not human beings having a spiritual experience.
We are spiritual beings having a human experience.

—*TEILHARD DE CHARDIN*

17.

STOKING
THE INNER FIRE

EVERY MORNING, WE WOULD have an hour-and-a-half chanting program. Most of the words were in ancient Sanskrit. I began to fall in love with the pronunciation of these syllables. Sanskrit syllables are said to have a unique potency, as do most root languages. According to the yoga scriptures, every sound has its own vibrational resonance. The spiritual science of energy centers gives intricate details about exactly where in the physical and subtle bodies each sound lies. It's like the analogy of two violins. If a particular string is plucked on one violin, the corresponding string on a nearby violin will begin to vibrate. Our energy bodies seem to have similar tendencies.

Now I was going to learn how to tune *my* instrument, and

the monastery schedule was devoted to this task. We chanted for hours every day, singing repetitive mantras, long-form scriptures, and devotional poetry. I took time to study the proper lengths and expressions of each sound. Working in the video department, I had access to video and audio tapes of the singing and speaking of these syllables by various singers and scholars. I listened carefully to the subtle nuances of pronunciation on the various tapes, and began to experiment with them during the morning chants.

After all, we were chanting for an hour and a half every morning. I had to find ways to entertain myself. Since I was already chanting, this seemed to be a good time to explore the subtleties of mantra recitation. As I focused intently on the intonation of each syllable, I would fall into a space that surely explains why some Brahman priests from India spend their entire lives memorizing and reciting Sanskrit passages. While chanting the rhythmic verses, I would enter into an eternal, person-less realm, far beyond the superficial level of my external surroundings.

The text would be recited, line by line, alternating between men and women. While the men sang their line, I would have a chance to read the translation and take a slow, deep breath in. Then we women would sing our line, and I would shift my attention to the sounds, the syllables, and the regulation of my breath. I didn't want to have to stop midline to take another gasp of air, so I'd ration the sound escaping through my lips. When I sang the syllables properly, they would burst forth, increasing the energy inside me. It was as though these syllables and my breath were sticks being rubbed together, creating friction, heat and energy.

One of the first things to arise was a sensation of hot fire, blazing from just above my groin area to the middle of my stomach. It was real, tangible heat. It was not like I was visualizing some flames and interpreting them as energy. It was hot. It was fire. Sometimes the sensation would last for as long as five minutes. I would just close my eyes and bask in this inner glow. It was intense but not quite uncomfortable. In a way, the heat was also pleasurable. I had this experience mainly during my first two years of chanting.

Then, for many years afterward, I had a different experience of the energy. While chanting away, all of a sudden I would get an inner signal that *the pot* was full. I didn't know quite what this container was or where it existed. There was just a sense that the energy had built up somewhere in my midsection, in a subtle energy co-body. Sitting cross-legged, I would put the chanting book down, hold on to both of my knees, and pull up, hunching my back slightly. My head would be facing downward, as the explosion took place. The energy would shoot up into my head, and out to my fingers and toes. My entire body would be ablaze. As it lit up my head, I would be consumed by a deep, throbbing vibration, and move into *nothing nowhere-ness*. My mind would become intoxicated with bliss, and *I* would disappear.

The experience would last anywhere from twenty seconds to several minutes. I could tell how long it had been by how many pages I had to turn to catch up after I returned. I would come back so refreshed and clean. It was as though a big bath of healing energy had flushed through my entire being, clearing away all the debris with it. Perhaps this force somehow moved into the physical structures of my body and cleared out all the chemical and hormonal residues from present and past stresses.

This went on for years and years. Every morning, I would be treated to at least one of these baths. Sometimes the flow was subtle, other times dramatic. Sometimes it was sweet and loving, other times it was like a fire hose blasting through my body and into my head. Sometimes I would sit very still, other times my body would be moved, vibrating and shaking with the powerful force. I tried to maintain some composure so as not to draw attention to myself during the chanting sessions. But there was a point when my self-conscious mind had to let go into this delicious rush of energy. A few times, I even fell forward, surprising the unsuspecting chanter in front of me.

During this time, I discovered another intriguing concept, *urdhvaretas.* This was a practice of celibacy, in which the subtle, potentially sexual life essence is transformed into higher energies of creativity or spirituality. I wondered if this was related to my daily energy surges.

It might seem surprising that I wouldn't have jumped into sexual activity during my teens, especially considering the wild lifestyle of my family and friends. Maybe their lack of fulfillment was a lesson to me that sex did not necessarily bring happiness. Also, I had made the decision to wait when one of my friends confided to me the regret she felt about having broken her virginity with a fellow who worked in a traveling carnival. Within two days, the show had moved on, and he with it. I decided not to make the same mistake. I would wait until I fell in love. Who knew I would be spending my twenties in a monastery!

Even so, it wasn't an issue. Just as my maternal instincts hadn't kicked in at age seven when I opted for a chemistry set over dolls, so my internal energy was not manifesting as a desire to be sexual with another human being. Instead, it was bursting forth through my drum-playing and flowing through each creative moment in this rich environment. And early every morning, it would shoot up my body with a thrill that was as ecstatic as any sensual pleasure I'd ever known.

I didn't miss a morning chant for more than ten years. Every day, I would wake up at four or five a.m. to go to the hour-and-a-half chant. For the most part, my dedication was based on a desire to become disciplined and on my enjoyment of the spiritual experiences that were coming to me through this practice. But after a few years, there was also an element of ego in my discipline. I had a record going! So I became somewhat fanatical about it. Even after working late into the night, I would pull myself out of bed while the world still lay in dark silence, ready to sing God's name.

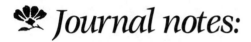 *Journal notes:*

A poem to express that blissful awareness

The Sweet
Its presence more real than my own
Under, under everything
and always there -
here, right here
Inside of me
I Am
Inside the Sweet.
The precious
Love beyond love
Experience beyond experience
Memory beyond memory.
How can I forget it
again and again?

Is it only for the bliss of rediscovery?
the longing and its fulfillment
Returning to the Eternal real
that exists within itself
Alone, containing nothing
and perfectly full
as it always has been.
To taste this state is so important
beyond importance.
To taste the Sweet.
There is nothing else to do
but taste the Sweet.

*In the external universe
there is ceaseless turmoil, change, and unrest;
at the heart of all things there is undisturbed repose;
in this deep silence dwelleth the Eternal.*

—*James Allen*

18.

The Fruits of Surrender

IT WAS THE SUMMER OF 1981. The outer sheathes of my body, mind and heart were being whittled away by the intensity of each day. This was my first summer as the head of video distribution. VCRs were quickly becoming the hottest new household commodity, and our output expanded from a few tapes per week to at least 200. I was suddenly swamped with all of the duplication, bookkeeping, labeling and packing of videotapes.

Not only was I busy, but the summer was in full swing. My teacher was in town and had brought thousands of visitors with him. There were programs nearly every evening and long lines to wait in for meals. My video room *temple* was now filled with grungy piles of equipment and way too many people. My teacher had decided to spice things up by putting three people in charge of the video department at once. A swarm of scriptwriters, cameramen, technicians, engineers, and other peripheral workers assembled in one medium-sized office and a few small cubbyholes. There was often a line of people outside the video door, waiting to introduce themselves to me and ask questions.

So much for my peaceful solitude.

All of the video decks were connected together in the main office, where the system was now being used to record the daily programs and courses. These were the five decks upon which I was meant to duplicate 200 tapes a week, and now they were constantly being used for other purposes. If a situation like this had occurred anywhere else, I would have declared it to be *impossible*. But that was not a word used lightly in this place.

I came up with a plan. I would copy tapes all night long. That would also give me some space to get my work done while everyone else was asleep. When I became tired, I'd set up a thirty-minute tape to be duplicated and go into the small meditation hall next to the video room. I'd set a timer for thirty minutes, and curl up next to the statue of our guru's guru to fall into a well-earned sleep.

Often, I would awaken just before the timer was to go off. The most wonderful, blissful thing started to happen. I began to hear music. I was listening to unbelievable symphonies in my sleep. I would hear them echo out while moving through the tunnel into waking consciousness. It was like legions of angels singing in full, rich harmonies. Sometimes, they seemed to be singing specific chants, other times there was just a thunderous symphony of sound that would shock me as the *speakers* were suddenly unplugged during my passage back into conscious awareness.

Awakening in a state of happy awe, I'd change the tapes, lie back down, and do it all again.

Two of the security guards were upset that I was sleeping in this public area, like some homeless person finding a place to crash. They woke me up and told me to leave. Even when I explained the situation, they said I couldn't sleep there. But fortunately, we had *people in charge*. One could only hope the people in charge had enough common sense to do the right thing. It was always a gamble. The fact that there was no other way to get the tapes duplicated made my phone call to the manager's office quite easy. It was either let me sleep there, or buy $10,000 worth of new equipment, or close down the entire video distribution department for the summer. An easy choice.

One of many lessons I learned during this period was the value of living in the present moment. In the present moment, everything is always fine. All the work could get done as long as I stayed completely focused on each moment. Whenever my mind wandered to the past or future, the flow would be distorted and interrupted, and I would feel an enormous burden on my shoulders. This gave me a chance to receive immediate feedback whenever my mind strayed away from living in the present. If I could keep all my energy directed to whomever was stepping into my office or whatever tape needed to be labeled at that moment, a great deal of productivity was able to move through me.

Toward the end of the summer, it was announced that we were going to have a 7-day, nonstop chant. Only eight drum players were available to play for all these long hours of chanting.

I was assigned to play three drum shifts each day, one in the morning, one in the late afternoon, and one in the middle of the night. I was also scheduled to play the harmonium organ for one hour each day, in the midafternoon. *Plus* I still had a line of people outside my door, waiting to talk with me and order videos. *And* I had hundreds of videotapes to duplicate and send out each week. The demands became greater. The exhaustion and discipline necessary to keep doing what needed to be done from moment to moment had a strong effect on my psyche. It simplified me. Whatever energy I had was needed for the work at hand. I was thrust into living in the NOW.

Then there was the physical offering involved. My hands soon became raw from so much drum-playing. Within two days, all the drummers were walking around with gauze and tape on their hands, even the experienced ones who had built up calluses over the years. When you hit your hand against leather fairly hard and constantly for three hours a day (with occasional bumping against the metal rims that hold the leather in place), it causes pain, rawness, blisters, and even bleeding.

What a strange situation. Here I was with sores all over my hands, and I would voluntarily sit for hours and bash them against the surface that caused the wounds in the first place. I say voluntarily, because I could have refused to continue playing. However, then the other drummers would have had to pick up the slack.

The strange juxtaposition was the happiness I'd feel while playing drums for this wonderful seven-day chant. The energy in the room was so strong and fragrant that even the pain would begin to taste sweet.

I was playing in front of 50 to 800 devotees, each savoring their own inner experience. And every time I hit the drum, there was pain. The constant question was how much to sacrifice the musical quality of the chant to lessen my personal discomfort. Each beat carried this dilemma. Every time I went to strike the drum, in that expanded space between the beats, I would balance these two issues. Usually, I played the drum with a very strong hand because a loud *boom* tends to increase the excitement of the chant. Perhaps, I thought, it would be a good time to learn to play with a gentler touch.

And yet, at times the chant cried out for some passion. I would do whatever I had to do inside my being to allow me to play with vigor, regardless of the physical pain. Such a simple task, playing drums for a chant; yet the issues that arose were so significant. This apparently minor conflict brought up important lessons about surrender, courage, sacrifice, faith, and transcendence.

This, again, was one of the most valuable elements about living in this magical place. Even apparently minor considerations, such as whether a particular moment of the chant was as powerful as it could be, became important and significant. Powerful lessons could be learned without our having to descend into more dramatic or threatening circumstances.

I wanted the chants to be exquisite and intended to play my role well. It was such an honor to be able to play for so many people, especially with my teacher still in residence. Usually when he was there, only the main musicians would get to play. So this was a special opportunity, important enough that I was willing to suffer for it. I knew my hands would have a chance to heal, and that I would once again get a full night's sleep in just a few weeks. The tour was going to move on to India, and I had agreed, once again, to remain at the upstate New York monastery.

Four days into the chant, I went to the hall a few minutes before my harmonium shift was to begin. It was wonderful to close my eyes and rest in this holy space. Chanting is said to create energy. When one is internally repeating a *mantra,* the energy is created within one's own psycho-physical system. But when a group of people are chanting out loud, that energy is said to be released into the room. I sat down and fell into a deep relaxation.

While mulling over how much work I had left to do, I thought, "Why do I have this harmonium shift anyway?" There were plenty of other players who could have taken the time slot. I enjoyed playing the harmonium, and had offered to play a daily shift, but that was before I realized how intense the drum schedule would be. As I listened to the music of the chant, I thought, "I'm not such a great harmonium player anyway. There are a lot of people who play better than me."

Regardless, it was too late to change anything now. I had to surrender to playing for the next hour, but made a mental note to remove myself from the harmonium schedule for the last few days of the chant.

I sat down and began to play. As the rhythm of the chant was established, I started to lose my grip on *me.* There was just the playing of the chant. Falling into the blissful rest of deep consciousness, I started playing all kinds of riffs and trills that I could hear inside myself. While singing or playing the chants, I would often hear various harmonies and decorative frills around the basic melody. Sometimes, I'd include a taste of them in my harmonium-playing, but this time my filtering mind stepped aside, allowing all these dramatic flourishes to be more fully integrated with the chant. My hands were moving all over the keyboard, dancing around the more simple, basic melody being sung by everyone else in the hall.

In this deep peace, I was no longer fatigued. I was residing in the boundless expanse of pure mind, while the playing moved effortlessly through me. This was the sweet fruit of my surrender.

The exhaustion had taken over my body, and yet my will to fulfill this commitment kept the music going. I rested my head on my arm, and let go. . .

I was awakened by a tap on my shoulder.

"Oh no!" I thought, "I must have played the wrong notes!"

I opened my eyes in a state of confusion, watching as my hands continued to play the chant. The hall monitor leaned over and whispered in my ear. She told me that my teacher's translator had phoned to send a message that "Baba really loves the way you are playing."

I would have laughed if I wasn't so shocked.

How exactly *was* I playing? I watched as my hands continued to move across the keys. In my mind's eye, I could imagine my teacher sitting in his room, listening carefully to what my hands were doing. Fingers, don't fail me now!

Suddenly, what had been so easy as to be practically unconscious now required effort. At the same time, my subjective sense of time seemed to slow down. Although I was playing 1-3 notes per second, I found myself with ample time to have an internal discussion between each one, debating which note to hit next, and then watching as my fingers played it. It felt as though I was watching processes that always existed on other levels of my psyche.

Though surprised, I was delighted. What a phone call! Nevertheless, I couldn't indulge too much in the ego-pleasure.

I was still on the hot-seat. If I hit the wrong notes, my teacher would know that a little praise could blow my state.

Eventually, my hour was up, and I moved on to the next task at hand. Things were so busy in video distribution that I had all but forgotten the entire event by evening. Fortunately, my teacher's translator came by the video room to express, once again, how much he had liked the way I was playing. I decided not to cancel my future shifts, after all.

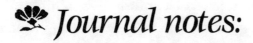 *Journal notes:*

A poem expressing the longing for union and eternal freedom, written during this summer

I always hope and feel
That one day there will be that moment
of merging with the Beloved
On all levels. . .
That moment together
Without veils
The moment of recognition
Which would crystallize into eternity
Where no "other" would even exist, or have ever existed
Just that Oneness everywhere, at all times.

We are but shadows:
we are not endowed with real life,
and all that seems most real about us
is but the thinnest substance of a dream –
till the heart be touched.
That touch creates us –
then we begin to be –
thereby we are beings of reality
and inheritors of eternity.

—*NATHANIEL HAWTHORNE*

19.

THAT
GRACIOUS GLANCE

MY TEACHER WAS LEAVING for India after three years in the United States. A final chanting session with him had been scheduled, and I was asked to play the harmonium. This was going to be my first opportunity to play an instrument right in front of my teacher. Little did I know what was about to happen.

Initiation is a central tenet of the guru/disciple relationship in many traditions. There is said to be a transference of energy, a kind of deep bond that is earned by the disciple, and solidified by the intention of the master. In most traditions, this gift is given only after the sincerity and strength of a disciple have been tested. With spiritual power, you are given keys to the stuff from which reality is constructed. You have to be ready.

However, my teacher had a different theory. He wanted to create what he called a "meditation revolution." He wanted to give initiation to anybody and everybody. He wanted to awaken the entire earth with the flame of spiritual energy. So he held programs around the world, giving an initiation he called *shaktipat*, which translates as *the descent of grace*.

To be honest, I wasn't expecting or waiting for another initiation. Many of the experiences I'd already had would be considered signs of initiation. Those special moments seemed to reveal what lay ahead, allowing me the taste of a more enlightened perspective before my time. After rising into more lofty states of consciousness, even when I'd find myself back in the petty day-to-day events of life, the vibration of that space would be singing beneath the surface, urging me onward and upward in my journey.

I sat in front of the harmonium, before my teacher's empty chair. Nobody was sure how long the chant would go, or how it would end. I was told to begin with the slow recitation of our mantra. Several hundred people sat in the dimly lit hall, waiting to see my teacher off. After a few verses, I felt him brush by me and watched as he bowed to the chair of his spiritual lineage and sat down. I was a little nervous, but felt a certain confidence due to his praise for my harmonium playing just three weeks earlier.

We were singing the mantra in call-and-response format. I would sing a verse into the microphone, and the rest of the group repeated it back. My teacher sat completely still, with his eyes closed. I realized at one point that he was listening to my voice. This created a mixture of emotions. I was nervous, thrilled, focused, devoted, and surrendered to the inner intelligence that could do everything right as long as *I* stayed out of the way. I had to remain centered in a space beyond ego.

Suddenly, he opened his eyes.

My heart stopped.

He was looking directly into my eyes, and I froze. Not outwardly. No, I continued to play the harmonium and chant the mantra. But inside I froze with his glance. Time stopped. My false, limited identity slithered off like the skin of a snake, and it was just me, the me that I've always been, even before becoming this personality. With that one glance, I was ripped open to the soul.

Now it was my soul sitting before the master. And he was, in essence, the same soul. It wasn't *me* playing for *him*, or *me* trying to learn from *him*, or *me* trying to please *him*. It was just my soul and his soul, two projections of the same one light.

We began to chat. It was as though we were sitting together, sipping coffee at a café. There was that kind of informal one-on-one, or more accurately one-*as*-one, talk. Where was this conversation taking place? In my head? In the ether? On an astral plane? There was no room for such questions in that moment.

I was the first to *speak*. "I know I'm never going to see you again."

Where this idea came from, I didn't know. It was not based on anything I had ever consciously thought. It was as though an intelligence inside me was having this conversation with him while *I* eavesdropped.

He replied, "It's okay — you've received what you were supposed to receive from me."

"But what will happen to my *sadhana* (spiritual practice) after you leave this world?"

"The seed I have given you will continue to grow and blossom. Just keep doing your *sadhana*."

The conversation went on for nearly half an hour. It was an intensified talk about my journey and the work I was to do, both in the context of my spiritual path and the world. For that half hour, I had access to a space of understanding that had previously been beyond my reach, though it had clearly always existed inside of what I had come to refer to as "me."

"The seed I have given you will continue to grow and blossom."

I understood in that moment that this is what the guru does. He is the universal gardener, planting seeds of realization into our soil of inner understanding. Then it is up to many factors as to when and how these seeds will sprout.

All this was happening inside me. On the outside I was sitting there, my gaze completely locked onto his. It seemed as though neither of us blinked for the whole time. This was the first time I had experienced more than a few moments of direct eye-contact with my teacher. When all the devotees came up to meet him in the evening *darshan* line, he would often look into people's eyes for a moment. Many times I had relished the uplifting force I felt from his eyes. The intensity was so strong, I would often have to avert my eyes or look down. But now our eyes were completely locked, and I was not about to turn away.

May the guru's gracious glance ever dwell upon me.
It creates all worlds, and yields all nourishment.
It bestows the viewpoint of all holy scriptures.
It regards wealth as useless, and removes faults.

Always focused on the Ultimate,
It is sovereign over all universal qualities.
This glance confers the path of liberation.
It is the central pillar
supporting the stage of this world.
It showers the nectar of compassion,
and reveals all principles of creation.
It is the creator of time;
pure existence, consciousness and bliss.

—THE GURU GITA

My teacher finished a verse of *Om Namah Shivaya*, and sang a phrase that would normally have signalled the end of the chant. But the chant didn't end. Instead, he began to sing a fairly complex song from our morning services. Fortunately, I had played many morning chants on the harmonium, and was able to play by ear. I played the melody without breaking our gaze for even a moment. I had to focus completely. I had to step out of the way and allow my subconscious mind to hit the right notes.

After this five-minute chant, my teacher began chanting other complicated mantras, which I also was able to play without looking down. It felt as though he was playing with me, directing this very unusual combination of chants, perhaps to test my focus. Because in that moment, nothing was going to make me break the eye-to-eye union with him. He could have started a Bach concerto and somehow I would have followed. My fingers took care of the playing, while our silent communion continued.

There's prayer, and a step up from that is meditation,
and a step up from that is conversation.

—*A Sufi saying*

My guru sang the final mantras and sat up for a moment. Breaking our gaze, he stood up and briskly left the hall. Everyone else followed him, hoping to catch one last glimpse before he left for India.

I closed my eyes.

Felt the energy still moving inside me.

What blessing had just been bestowed on me?

It helped that everyone had run out of the hall. This gave me a chance to just sit quietly and absorb what had been given. I began to come back from the depths of my inner being, into a new, improved waking consciousness.

As I sat in this holy space relishing all the teachings he had shared, they began to slip from my conscious mind. I tried to hold on to them, but to no avail. It was similar to what sometimes happens when we awaken in the middle of a dream. We lie there remembering events that have just unfolded within our consciousness. Even while we see them so clearly, the images sometimes slip right from our memory. Though we try to hold on to them, they dissolve from our grasp.

And so I sat empty-minded now, yet still basking in the powerful presence. My teacher and I had met one another in what felt like the closest way possible. I had never experienced this depth of intimacy before.

I didn't really want to come back to the outer world, with all its people, concepts and experiences. Yet I knew I must. Having savored this taste, I now had to find my way back there in my own time, and through the circumstances and dilemmas of my own journey.

🌺 *Journal notes:*

A *poem written during this time to express the wellspring of spiritual knowledge revealed by grace*

My Light of Truth
You are always right here.
When I can see you, I know you so well.
Awakening to that freedom,
The knowledge far beyond knowledge.
Beyond even the regret of previous ignorance.
For in the light of that knowledge,
Ignorance never was,
Or could be.
How could it be?

And how could I ever dislike this world?
It's my world,
My very form,
My own creation.
What can I do but enjoy and love it?
And understand it as an artistic piece
That is erased and recreated,
Erased and recreated over and over again;
Molded from Consciousness,
As a dream is molded from consciousness.

What is a dream made of?
You pick up a solid object in a dream.

What is it made of?
What is your hand made of?
Look at your hand now.
What is it made of?
Who is the One who is watching this dream?
Just as you watch dreams while sleeping,
Not moving yourself —
But with yourself moving on you, or in you.
And not really moving at all, because it's just a story,
An illusion or fantasy.

Freud suggested the dream's function to be
The acting out of unfulfilled desires.
Look at your own life, your dream.
What desires have you had in the past?
Watch them play before you now.

What are you doing here?
Why are you here
If you're not doing anything really worthwhile?
And what action really is worthwhile?

So why don't you leave for good?
Why continue to leave and then come back?
Going and returning,
Creating and then forgetting;
Becoming lost in your own dream,
And then remembering that you never really were lost,
And then forgetting again — so quickly.
As day follows night follows day,
Revolving and oscillating continuously
In time,

In the mind, the ego,
In the sense of limitation,
The sense that includes all physical and subtle senses.

Close that sense
As you would plug your ears
Or shut your eyes.
What will you see?
Who are you without that sense of limitation,
of separateness?
Do you have the courage to face it?
If you need more courage,
then you haven't let go enough —
The limitation and separateness are still there.

How can we become totally free of that sense of limitation?
Only through Grace.
Through the Grace of the One who is dreaming this dream,
The One far beyond even our highest concepts and ideas
Of God, of Consciousness.
Beyond any construct of the mind at all.

Use your will to reach that Will.
Desire and pray only for liberation,
true freedom and bliss.
Think of nothing else.
Let your next dream be an acting-out
Of only a pure desire for liberation;
A desire to know that which is so incredibly
beyond even God,
How could we possibly call it anything less than God?
It's everything that's inside, outside, and everywhere else,

It's the only One
I mean, what can a person really say about That?

So if you can't desire and pray for only That,
Then desire and pray for the ability
to desire and pray for only That.
Be tricky.
After all, it's a game
That you've already won,
And your intellect is a wild card.
It can turn even the poorest hand into a winner
Instantly,
Without changing anything.
Through a shift of knowledge,
A new sense of understanding,
A change of focus - waking up.
That pure intellect is the Grace.
It is that intellect which creates the world,
And also takes you past it.
It remains with you there as pure awareness,
And then contracts with you back into limited memory.

It's very difficult to even think about,
Much less describe.
How can I think about it?
When it is that which is thinking,
How can I serve it?
When only That can act,
How can I love it?
When That itself is love.
What then can I do,
but stop all thoughts, and bow with reverence.

The soul is never born,
nor does it die at any time.
Nor, having been, will it ever cease to exist.
It is unborn, eternal, indestructible and everlasting.

—*THE BHAGAVAD GITA*

20.

HOW COULD HE BE GONE?

OCTOBER 2ND, 1982, was one of those days when I woke up thinking it was going to be just another day, but instead it became a day I will never forget.

My teacher had been in India for nearly a year and was expected back in New York the following summer. The manager and I had been having an ongoing battle. Joe wanted to show movies to the residents, while I felt it was not appropriate. If someone wanted to see a movie, they could watch it at a theater in the nearby town. To me, this monastery was a place to focus on the eternal, to break free of illusion. And what was a movie if not illusion? Joe and I had gone back and forth on this many times, always ending with no movie being shown. Admittedly, I was a little smug about my victory.

However, one week earlier Joe had called and told me that on this day, I was to show the movie "Harold and Maude" after lunch. "Don't argue about it. Don't try to discuss it. We are showing the movie, and that is final."

"Harold and Maude" was a strange choice for a monastery movie, since it is a dark comedy dealing with a young man's obsession with death. He keeps faking his own gory death, and then falls in love with a 70-year-old woman. This was the only movie we had in the video department. I don't remember how we had acquired the copy, but somehow it was there, alone on the movie shelf.

I had no choice but to show it. Joe was the manager, after all, and he was pulling rank on me. So after lunch, I asked Mark, a fellow who helped out in the video department, to help me set up the big screen projector. It was a particularly beautiful day outside. The next six months would be filled with freezing temperatures, snow, sleet and ice. Why show a movie after lunch, when this may be the last day we'd have to enjoy the outdoors? I grumbled on while setting up the screen.

Then, something hit me. I was overcome by a feeling of exhaustion so overpowering that I literally could not go on. I had to go to my room and lie down. I told Mark that we were not going to show the movie.

"But Joe said. . . ."

"It doesn't matter," I told him. "We are not going to show it, and I have to go lie down right now."

I went to bed and felt myself being carried into swirling waves of consciousness that spun my being around in circles, like water moving down a drain. I remained semiconscious for a while, watching the visual energy patterns. Then the whirlpool overtook my conscious awareness, and poured me into deeper spaces, from which I could no longer maintain memory-based awareness. I stayed in this sleeplike state for two hours.

Upon awakening, I went to the video room to continue my work. Clearly, I was going to get in trouble for having refused, once again, to show the movie. But I was still in a groggy and dazed space, not yet worried about the repercussions ahead. As I entered the alcove outside my office, there was music coming from one of the meditation halls. This confused me, because it was the middle of the afternoon. We never had chants during that time. I listened closely. People were chanting our teacher's name.

I froze.

Several months earlier, we had asked for permission to sing our teacher's name during chants. He had been in India for nearly a year, and we missed him. But the reply came back that we were not to sing our teacher's name as a chant until he *leaves his body*. It was only to be sung after his death.

As I walked into the alcove, still woozy after the strange experience of having my consciousness sucked into that deep, unconscious space, I heard the words of the chant being sung in the meditation hall. It was his name.

I sat down on the floor as the implication hit me. Tears welled up, and my heart broke open. My teacher had left this world. I would never see him again. I remembered our communion as he left one year before. It truly was the last time I would ever see him.

Shocked, I went into my office and played one of his videotapes. There he was, alive as ever on the screen, talking and laughing, walking and singing. How could I be so sad when he was still right in front of me? It was only the thought that he'd left that was making me feel a loss. Nothing else had changed. Today was the same as yesterday. I could still feel him in the air.

> *You will feel my presence much stronger after I am gone.*
> *The Shakti (energy) of the Guru*
> *has nothing to do with his physical presence.*
> *It is always there.*
> *By constant and regular meditation*
> *you place yourselves in tune with the Guru,*
> *and you will receive messages from within.*
>
> —SWAMI MUKTANANDA

I pondered what had happened during those two hours while I slept. What was that strange swirling mass of consciousness? Where did I go? I wondered if I had been given a glimpse into the death experience itself, this flow into another dimension. Or maybe there had been a bon voyage party on an astral plane. I really didn't know, but I do know one thing. I will be forever grateful that we didn't show "Harold and Maude" on that holy day.

The Heart is the hub of all sacred places.

—BHAGAVAN NITYANANDA

21.

FROM HEART
TO HEART

AFTER MY TEACHER'S PASSING, I wanted to spend some time in solitude, to keep myself centered amidst all the potential confusion. I moved into a little room behind the main meditation hall. Sitting there, contemplating all this great being had given to me, I was moved to make an offering in honor of his presence and memory.

Several months earlier, my teacher had taught a powerful selection of mantras to his close disciples in India. At the time, I was overseeing the audio department, and had access to a tape of this half-hour arrangement of hymns and mantras. I thought about how he had made these mantras available just before his passing, and I decided to memorize them as an offering to him. For eight days, I lived in this little room, fasting and singing his special mantras over and over until I could do them without looking at the pages.

One thing I noticed in the monastery was that whenever I made an effort solely for the sake of offering or for the purpose of spiritual growth, it would often bear unexpected, pleasant fruit. It was to be so with this offering of mantras.

Several monks arrived from India a few months after my teacher's passing. They had learned these special mantras from him, and wished to continue practicing them. Every day at four o'clock in the afternoon, the monks would gather in our teacher's bedroom to chant for a half an hour. But none of them really knew the intricate melodies very well, and the only tape available was slow and difficult to follow. Even though I wasn't a monk, they invited me to join them, since I knew how to chant the mantras.

And so it was that every afternoon, at the magical hour of four o'clock, I would leave my daily work to enter the wonderland of my teacher's holy room. It was like having a chance to go to heaven for half an hour every day. Feelings of reverence and gratitude would leap up inside me as I walked through the entrance into his quarters.

One day, the woman who prepared his room for these daily chants was unable to make it. She asked me to set up the room in her place, and I readily accepted. One hour before the chant was to begin, I entered my teacher's room. At first, I just stood there, soaking up the pure vibrations. Then I put together the silver tray with a flame to wave before the pictures on the wall. This practice is called *puja*, and is a form of devotional worship.

As I stood before each image of these great saints, I would try to erase my ego personality and become a clear channel of reverence. Slowly, I would wave the flame in clockwise circles around each photo. It created a wonderful, intimate connection with each representation of divinity. Finally, I walked over to the large picture of my teacher's teacher, the grandfather guru. I had a special connection with him, and invoked even more care for his image.

While moving the flame down toward his feet, my glance fell upon the shelf below his photo.

There was my heart.

I immediately recalled a time several years earlier, when I was about to spend my first winter in the monastery. As I exited the morning chanting session, one of the managers invited me to attend a farewell meeting with our teacher in two hours. He had almost forgotten to tell me, because I was only a recent addition to the winter staff list.

In India, it is traditional to bring an offering to one's spiritual master. I looked in the snack shop for a beautiful piece of fruit, but found only mediocre oranges. That was not the quality of gift I wanted to give to my sweet guru during this special meeting. A friend had loaned me her bicycle for the winter, and I decided to ride it into town to find a more appropriate offering.

It was pretty cold outside, and I didn't quite know the route. I rode up and down hills for several miles before I finally found my way into the small town. It was Sunday, and most of the stores were closed. But there was a small shop that sold Indian goods, and it was open.

My financial resources were rather limited. After making all the arrangements to leave school and travel to New York, I only had ten dollars to my name. This narrowed my options, yet I still considered each potential gift carefully. Finally, I selected a beautiful, heart-shaped container made of stone, which cost seven dollars. The heart was embellished with intricate carvings, its cover decorated with inlaid mother-of-pearl lotuses. In the monastery this kind of container was often used to hold *kum kum*, the red powder many Indians wear as a dot on their foreheads. My teacher nearly always wore one of these dots as a symbol of his commitment to God, and to honor the spiritual-energy center between the eyebrows.

I had somewhat identified myself with this *kum kum* powder, because the word was so similar to my guru-given name, Kumuda. I asked the shopkeeper if he had any *kum kum*, but he apologized and explained they had recently run out.

While riding back to the monastery, I came up with a symbolic interpretation for the gift. I was offering my empty heart to the guru, and asking him to fill it. This made me feel better about not having any *kum kum* to put in the heart.

I rode as hard as I could, but still arrived a few minutes late. I took a quick hot shower, and went down to the small hall. Fifty or so devotees were already seated, waiting for our teacher to arrive. I sat next to the aisle in the back.

Our teacher walked past me, and sat in his chair. He gave a wonderful talk that touched on a wide variety of topics, from his dogs, to marriage, to *Shiva* and *Shakti*, the male and female energy forces that are said to create the entire universe. A beautiful woman from Holland began to sing Indian devotional songs, while our teacher explained the meaning of each verse.

Within moments, I began to feel waves of energy moving up my body. They were as tangible as any physical sensation I'd ever known. The pulses would start at my feet and move to the top of my head. It felt as though each wave would pick up my scalp and hold it high above my head.

These rushes were so dramatically delicious; the music was so beautiful; everyone around me was shining with happiness; and my teacher was right there. I wanted the moment to go on forever.

Eventually, it was time for each of us to come up and greet him personally. As I knelt before him, he said something to his translator in Hindi. She asked me, "You're working in video, aren't you?"

I said, "Yes."

She spoke again to our teacher, and he replied, "*Bahut acchha,*" which means, "Very good."

I handed him the heart. He opened it and looked inside. Then he asked, "No *kum kum?*"

I softly replied, "No."

He put the top back on and handed the heart back to me. "You should keep this and fill it with *kum kum.*"

I returned to my seat with an immediate appreciation for his symbolic gesture. I had wanted to give my empty heart to him, and he was commanding me to fill it with myself. I closed my eyes and savored this interaction.

After the last person sat back down, our teacher stood up to leave. He began to walk down the aisle toward the back door. I bowed my head as he passed by, but then he stopped. As I looked up, he smacked his hand down on top of my head, and moved it around for what felt like a very long time. It was probably only a few seconds.

He left the room, and everyone else slowly filtered out as well. However, there was no way I could move. The funny part is that my mind was still lucid and commenting to myself about all had just happened, yet my body was completely numb and immovable for nearly a half an hour. It was a very pleasant and peaceful experience.

After the meeting, I managed to find some *kum kum* to put into the heart. Instead of the usual dark red color, it was more of a bright orange. But I wanted to follow his instruction as soon as possible, and filled the heart with this unusual orange *kum kum*. For the next year, the heart sat on my bedside altar.

> *Fill yourselves first and then only*
> *will you be able to give to others.*
>
> —*AUGUSTINE*

One year later, I was invited to see my teacher in his quarters at six o'clock in the morning. Two other staff members and I were having birthdays that week, and we were going to have a special meeting with him, called a *birthday darshan*. Again, I contemplated what gift to give.

I smiled as the thought struck. My heart! I would continue our symbolic dance by having filled the stone heart (my heart) with *kum kum* (myself), and still offering it to him (God).

Seated before my teacher in his room, I was too shy and awestruck to hand the heart to him. Instead, I left it on the floor next to where I had been sitting. That was the end of the metaphorical heart game, or so I thought.

Coming back to the present moment just months after my teacher's passing, there I was in his bedroom, waving lights before the photo of his guru in preparation for our daily mantra recitation. I looked down and saw my heart on his altar.

It sat upon a delicate, heart-shaped, lace doily. I opened the top and saw that there was only a small amount of that bright orange *kum kum* left. He must have applied the rest to his forehead in his own offering to God.

When love beckons to you, follow him,
Though his ways are hard and steep.
And when his wings enfold you, yield to him,
Though the sword hidden among his pinions may wound you.
And when he speaks to you, believe in him,
Though his voice may shatter your dreams
as the north wind lays waste the garden.

—Kahlil Gibran

22.

Get a Job

EIGHT MONTHS LATER, our new teacher arrived for the summer retreat. For many years, she had been our first teacher's translator, and was installed as guru after his passing. This woman was exquisitely beautiful, though this did not account for the effect she had on me. I had met many beautiful people before. None of them affected me like this.

I was surprised at how shy I became around this new teacher. If I saw her heading toward me down a hallway, I would try to take a different route. Looking back, perhaps there was a sense of foreboding about the depth of commitment and the level of spiritual work that was waiting for me around the corner. This woman touched my heart in a way that was unfamiliar and uncomfortable. Although I had experienced great affection for my first teacher, somehow she moved me on a more personal level. It was like having a huge crush on someone with no sexual connotations, just falling deeply in love with her soul.

Until this point, I had never fallen in love. I'd met my first boyfriend in summer camp at age 8, and dated sporadically from age 12. But nobody I had ever met affected my heart like either of these two masters. The first had entered the deepest recesses of my soul, but now this woman was affecting me as a person. Me, who grew up without really knowing love or affection. Me, who was free of attachment to any human being. I didn't know what it was about this woman, but she seemed to break into territories of my heart that I preferred to keep locked. I didn't want to feel so much for her. I didn't want to be attached to anybody. I didn't want to expect her to notice me, and I didn't want to be disappointed when she didn't. Something about this woman ripped through all my locks. I could hardly even bear to look at her.

With her entrance, my rational intellect crumbled, my heart awakened, and life once again broke into a new series of lessons. Until this time, my quest had been on a path the Indian scriptures call *jnana yoga*, the attainment of inner freedom through knowledge and understanding. Now I was entering the road of *bhakti yoga*, union with the Supreme through one-pointed devotion. This was way out of my league.

She would sit in the main lobby every day before lunch time. Gregorian chanting played over the sound system, and the residents and visitors would gather around for the practice of *darshan* — being in the presence of a saint or sage.

Several hundred people gathered each day before lunch. Sometimes, our new teacher would just sit quietly; other times she would conduct business or chat with devotees. I knew this mainly from the reports of others, because I never went to these gatherings. That is how apprehensive I was in the presence of this teacher. And, conveniently enough, a daily chanting session had been scheduled in the meditation hall that very hour. We were singing the special mantras my first teacher used to sing privately with his close disciples; the ones I had memorized during the week after his passing.

One day, I decided to go to the lobby just to see what was going on there. There she was, our new teacher, seated with a large group of devotees gathered around her. There were two levels in the area, and I sat far away on the second level. Our teacher was wearing a big pair of sunglasses, so I couldn't really see where she was looking. Every now and then, she would turn and speak with the people sitting next to her, but I was too far away to hear or lip-read what she was saying. I was starting to get bored, just sitting there watching a group of other people also sit there. I had a lot of work to do back at the office.

In the midst of this thought, I *felt* her look at me. My entire body got palpably hot. I couldn't see her eyes at all. I could only assume she looked at me, but I didn't really know what was happening.

My video-department boss was sitting right next to our teacher. Gail stood up and pointed in my direction, signaling for me to come up to the front. At first, I remained seated. Why would she be calling me to come up there? She kept gesturing, and I finally gave in and motioned to ask, "Me?" She nodded "Yes."

I walked up to my teacher, swimming in a sea of sensations. I was quite reclusive at the time, and it was a shock to be publicly marched down this aisle, in front of hundreds of onlookers.

With the Gregorian music drifting through the air, I shifted into a more primordial level of what was happening. I was now the symbolic disciple kneeling before the Master, awaiting her command. The experience elicited memories of service and devotion from pre-*me* history, recorded deep within my psyche, in what Carl Jung referred to as the collective unconscious. In an indescribable way, *I* dissolved, leaving only the archetype. She could ask me to slay demons or rescue her land from an enemy kingdom. She could ask me to pierce my heart with a sword. As if in slow motion, the master turned to me and spoke.

"You should go out and earn money."

I looked at her.

She looked back.

Inside, I smiled and felt that I had gotten off easy.

I asked, "Should I stay here or go somewhere else?"

Now *she* melted! I saw it in her eyes. But I didn't know what was happening. My heart understood what was unfolding before me, but my mind could not figure it out.

She spoke with tenderness, "No, you should stay here but work outside for a few months, so you can have some spending money." With her nod, I bowed my head and walked away. I decided that instead of going to eat lunch, I would find a job.

I went to the corner store, and bought a newspaper for the first time in three years. Looking through the Help Wanted section, I circled a few possibilities. Some acquaintances walked by, and I mentioned that I was looking for work. One of them told me of an opening they had just heard about. A local resident owned a bungalow colony and was looking for housekeepers. In this area of the Catskill Mountains, there were several Hassidic bungalow colonies.

Most of the occupants came up from New York City for the summer. This work entailed preparing the bungalows for their arrival, and providing maid service once they arrived.

I applied, and got the job. The owner asked me if I would like to do a bit of cleaning in his house that afternoon. I cleaned for just over an hour, and received six dollars in pay.

Relieved at having found this work, I returned home. While heading toward the meditation hall to prepare for the late-afternoon chant, I ran into my video-department boss. I told her that my new job would begin the next day. She took the news well, considering it would be nearly impossible for anybody to walk in and take over all of my complex bookkeeping, duplicating, labeling, invoicing and mailing duties. I shared with her my desire to give our teacher the six dollars I had just earned, as a way of offering her the fruits of my labor. But we both knew I would probably be too shy to do it.

After the chant, my teacher was sitting right outside the doorway, in front of the outdoor temple. As people exited the meditation hall, they moved outside to join her there. I was carried with this flow, and somehow stepped right into the spot directly to the left of our teacher's chair. I sat down, as if the place had been reserved for me. Normally, I would not have been so bold, but at this point I was being moved by forces beyond my control.

I hoped to be able to muster up the courage to give her my first income. Even though it was only six dollars, I really wanted to offer it to her. But as I sat there, it became clear that I would not be able to fulfill this inner prompting. I was simply too shy to hand her the six bucks.

As I realized this, my teacher looked at me and said,

"You'll have to find a job." She was giving me an opening, but I wasn't able to take it. With the words painfully lodged in my throat, I was frustrated and disappointed with myself.

She turned to Gail and said, "You'll have to get two people to replace her."

I looked up with hope. Gail was anything but shy, and seeing my plight, she shot back quickly, "Well, we'll have to find them soon, since she's already found a job."

My teacher asked, "She found a job?" and turned toward me. "You found a job?"

The excitement in my heart swelled. I lowered my eyes with a hesitant smile, and whispered, "Yes." I reached into my pocket and pulled out the six dollars, and with all the courage I could muster, handed them to her. "I'd like for you to have this. It's my first income."

She accepted my offering with a surprised smile. I had come back less than five hours after her instructions, with not only a job but some first income as well. I didn't think of this as anything extraordinary at the time. She had told me to get a job, and I did. No big deal.

My teacher asked about the work I had found. When I told her I would be cleaning bungalows, she observed, "You must be very strong from playing drums. Let me feel your muscle."

This made me smile, because I was proud of my strong arms and loved to show them off. I made a muscle, and she reached to feel my arm, but then pulled me down into her lap. She held my head and lovingly stroked my hair for a few moments. This was perhaps one of the strongest expressions of affection I had ever known. But there, with the Divine Mother caressing my soul, all I could think of was the red *kum kum* dot on my forehead. I didn't want to stain her robes.

She began to praise me, how hard I worked. To my surprise, the onlookers began to chime in. "And she plays the drum and harmonium for so many chants." "And she stayed here for three cold winters." "And she studies Sanskrit in her free time." "And she's so nice to everyone."

Blushing at the attention, I was transported into a trance-like state. It was neither pleasant nor unpleasant, uncomfortable yet nourishing at the same time. Beneath my surprise was the sweet bliss of being recognized and appreciated. There was so much energy moving through me, it was all I could do to maintain my composure.

She handed the six dollars back to me. "You should wrap this in plastic and keep it forever. It's a good omen."

While walking away from this breathtaking event, I ran into a friend who was not aware of what had just taken place. She asked me if I could loan her a few bucks for dinner. Without thinking, I began to reach into my pocket, and in my stunned state, almost handed her those blessed bills. Fortunately, I caught myself in time.

The next morning, I went to work. The bungalows were filthy. They required a lot of heavy-duty cleaning. As we began scrubbing, some of the cleaners who had done the job before told horror stories about the previous year. As bad as it was cleaning the mess before us, they recalled, it was much worse once the families arrived. Some of the housekeepers had been forced to scrub the linoleum floor until the ink came off. The kids would run around dropping and spilling things right and left as if the cleaners were their personal servants. This did not sound like my cup of tea!

I considered that maybe this was not the right job for me, after all. At lunchtime, I told the supervisor that I might not be back that afternoon or ever. I thought it would be a good idea to check the Help Wanted section for something better. There was a twinge of anxiety over the fact that I had just been praised for finding a job so quickly. But, after all, who would even know if I quit and looked for different work? Who would care? What I didn't realize was that while finishing off the morning's work of scrubbing, I was being made famous during the noon *darshan*.

I slid into the monastery through one of the back doors, and headed toward the dining hall. The gathering had just disbanded, and everyone was getting ready for lunch. Several people stopped to mention that I had been the topic of discussion. I had been praised again. This time, instead of feeling elation and joy, my heart began to sink. Our teacher had told the whole story about how she sent me out to work, and how I'd found a job and offered her my first income that very afternoon. It did sound pretty good!

But I had sadly demonstrated the truth of "easy come, easy go." I found the job in a couple of hours and had quit in just about as long. I was a sorry specimen of a human being. And here, as I wallowed in my lack of fortitude, were these people looking at me with admiration, expressing their respect for the great surrender I had revealed. Each person who praised me thought they were making me feel really good about myself. But every look of admiration was like another arrow being fired into my ego.

I realized with a flash of relief that I could still return to my job that afternoon. I hadn't really, officially quit.

During the following week, I'd return home from my job each day to find that I had been praised again. One day, the manager came up to me and said, "She praised you three different times today." This left me in a sea of mixed emotions.

It was wonderful that this new teacher thought I was a good person, but I really didn't feel my actions deserved such lavish praise. Nevertheless, the ripples of my act continued to reverberate, day after day. Maybe she could see that this was the kind of ego work I needed right now. Maybe she was trying to build whatever structures of confidence I had missed out on during my childhood. At the time, I had no idea why she was praising me so profusely.

A week later, we had a celebration for our teacher's birthday. A small group of us got together to perform devotional songs for her and the several thousand people who had gathered. This was going to be another special moment, singing the Hindi songs I had learned during the previous winters in front of our new teacher.

It seemed that wonderful times in this place were never 100% pleasant or easy, just as difficult times were never 100% unpleasant. During the most wonderful moments, there always seemed to be an unexpected challenge. You'd be in the middle of the most magical moment, and the crown would fall off your tooth. Or you'd have a chance to sing devotional songs to your teacher and the musical instrument would break. That is exactly what happened on her birthday.

After our first song, the harmonium organ broke. We had to switch to another that could not be adjusted to the same lower key I was used to. This meant my solos would be four notes higher than my planned key, which had already been at the absolute limit of my vocal range. There was no way out, except to cancel my songs. But to me that was not even an option. I had to let go of my concepts. It was not a question of *if* I could do it, or *how* I could do it; I was simply *going* to do it.

Somehow, I did manage to hit even the highest notes. I was thrust into a mental state of witness-consciousness and watched as the singing moved through me. Maybe my subconscious mind went in and opened up my vocal cords a little more. Perhaps the magic of surrender allowed my body to extend itself on my behalf. I wasn't even nervous. In fact, I was probably less nervous than I would have been if the harmonium hadn't broken.

The audience applauded, and my teacher prepared to begin her talk. Before speaking, she stopped for a moment and glanced toward me.

"Kumuda? Do you go to the *Shiva Arati*?"

I nodded. The *Shiva Arati* was a chant sung every evening in the temple.

She smiled and gestured, "Come."

Once again, I had to stand up in front of so many people. I walked up to her seat, and she handed me a set of large Tibetan cymbals as a gift. I was already in an energy-filled, surrendered space from the singing, and now this dramatic, public presentation. My mind was in shocked stillness as I sat back down.

She gave a wonderful lecture about birthdays, grace, and her experiences with our first teacher. I started to relax and enjoy the discourse, relieved that she was not going to praise me publicly again. But then she said, "It's good if you resist. Because in my life I resisted him (our first teacher). So if you don't resist, I won't really like you." The entire week of praise was instantly overshadowed by these new words. "Oh no," I thought, "Now she won't like me because I didn't resist her!"

A few minutes later, my teacher's glance brushed past me once again, as she began to speak about what had occurred the previous week. "A very fresh incident happened, and I'm totally overwhelmed by this." I held my breath as she continued, "And I won't mention the person's name because I don't want the person to turn red. I don't want you to spot the person. She has been working in the video department for many years now, a very, very fine girl."

By this time, I was relieved to hear her praising me again. She told the whole story, placing me in a very flattering light, then looked up to the picture of our first teacher and continued, "Why did this happen? Because she's totally one with *him*."

O my. Now things had gone too far. What did she mean by that? The idea of being one with our first teacher, this great realized being, insinuated that maybe I was up there too. But I knew I wasn't! When my teacher said this, two things happened inside me.

First, I had to stop ignoring the good qualities I had cultivated through all those years of dedication and grace. I gained a new respect for myself and the process I had been through. If she could even say such a thing without bursting out laughing, I must have attained something from my efforts. A new self-respect established itself in my mind and heart.

At the same time, however, I feared that self-esteem was only a hop away from egotistical pride. This led to the second effect of her talk. I wondered, "Why would she be trying to build up my ego? She's supposed to be eradicating it!" I had heard that the job of the guru was to dissolve your limited egocentricity so the inner Self could shine forth unobstructed. At the time I often mistook self-respect for ego, thinking a truly humble person would never speak or think too well of himself.

As my teacher continued to praise my actions, I remembered a talk she had once given about the methods a guru can use to work on a disciple. She had shared with us that whenever our first teacher was really tough on her, she knew it heralded an upcoming positive breakthrough. But when he was especially nice, it was often a set-up for a difficult test. For example, he would often puff up someone's ego so it would make a louder, more efficient pop with the inevitable burst. As I put all this together, my delight in being praised became mixed with apprehension. I suspected that there was a less enjoyable counterbalance to this event, waiting for the right moment to snap itself around my karmic neck.

His exterior is an idol,
but his interior is an idol-breaker.

—*RUMI*

23.

SMASH THE IDOL

SPIRITUAL PATHS THROUGHOUT history have incorporated representational images of divinity into their faith. Many Western churches have statues and paintings of Jesus and various saints. Temples in the East often house holy figures, from golden Buddhas through a pantheon of Hindu gods and goddesses. These icons are not merely admired; they are worshipped as manifestations of the Divine. They are looked upon as portholes to the heavens, placed amidst our earthly surroundings; the formless *Absolute*, assuming form for the sake of its devotees. At one time, this idea seemed strange to me. Yet in the wake of my first teacher's death, I began to transfer the devotional relationship I'd had with him to the statue of his teacher, which sat atop a large marble pedestal in the small meditation hall.

Sitting quietly before his image, I would hear the answers to my questions being revealed inside myself. I'd feel as though I were in the presence of a living saint. Was the statue actually alive with the consciousness of the great being it represented? I had no means to measure this objectively. To me, it felt conscious. Standing in front of his image I found guidance, which seemed to be coming from him. Perhaps I was not yet able to tap sufficiently into my own inner wisdom, and his form was a mirror through which could reflect what I really wanted to give myself. Regardless, what mattered was that it worked.

I'd had an ongoing relationship with the statue for several years. During my first winter, more than half the monastery had been closed down, including the smaller meditation hall he was in. The only inhabited section in that whole area was my little video room, tucked behind the hall. Being the only person walking past the statue during those months, I felt obliged to pay him some special attention. He was, after all, an image of my guru's guru.

There had also been a couple of times when I'd passed through the small hall during my first two summers, to find our teacher sitting all alone, looking upon the statue of his beloved master. Both times, I sat down and joined him in sweet, devotional silence.

During the winter after my teacher's passing, the statue took on more importance in my spiritual life. Every morning, I would perform a special worship of him, lighting incense sticks, waving a flame, and singing songs of worship. Engulfed by devotion, I would often be moved to tears. While staring into the eyes of the statue, I felt I was looking into the eyes of God.

He wasn't all that well made, to be honest. One of the devotees who was a pretty good artist had made him out of plaster. The previous year, a new, improved bronze statue of the same "grandfather" guru was placed in the recently constructed outdoor temple. So now we had two; the classy new one and the older, funkier one. I was partial to my friend in the meditation hall.

One of the traditional ceremonies I'd perform was to bathe him and change his shawl once a week. This is called an *abhishek* in India. I didn't necessarily follow all the scriptural rules about the practice, but enjoyed it nevertheless. I was able to hop up on the marble pedestal with this great guru statue and express my devotion in a more personal way, bathing him and even kissing him on the top of the head as I finished.

How did I get so hung up on idolatry? Who would have ever imagined I would be relating to a carved block of plaster as though it were a great spiritual being? This did not sound like logical old me. And yet, the statue became very important to me after the passing of my first teacher.

The relationship I'd had with the Divine through my teacher was transferred to this statue, which became *alive* for me. Through this process, I was learning to believe in what was not quite believable, knowing that from the viewpoint of the ultimate, all our beliefs are inaccurate, or at least incomplete. If the adoption of a particular belief system allows us to open up to new depths of consciousness and divinity, then it is useful, it is worth believing. There may be an inherent potential in certain symbols or objects, which our society does not yet understand.

Even if we don't know all the chemical complexities of

water, we can still drink it. We just have to accept that it is there and available. Whether we think the water appeared through magic or through scientific processes, the important thing is that we have a belief system that allows us to recognize the water and drink it.

Spiritual power may be similar to the water in this analogy. Because it is not understood by science or society at large, we may need to access this elusive force through faith, intention, willpower, or through an external image. It can be useful to project an image of greatness into this symbolism-laden universe. If divinity exists in and through all things, why not choose an image that is familiar and comforting to us?

If triangles had a God, he'd have three sides.

—OLD YIDDISH PROVERB

I had only spent one month with our new teacher, and already my entire world was turned upside-down. After cleaning bungalows for several weeks, I was hired by one of the local residents to help him write a book. Now, instead of living a peaceful, monastic life, I was spending my days with this elderly man. He was writing a very negative book about how screwed up the world was, and I became the copy-editor. Beneath this external job was the fact that the man was lonely. He really just wanted to have intelligent discussions with someone. It was a cushy job, but after three years spent in near silence within the walls of a monastery, I found it disconcerting to have to deal so closely with someone else's convoluted thoughts.

During this time, my statue guru became even more

important to me. He was an emotional anchor I could depend upon to keep me centered through all the changes and excitement. One week into the job, I came back home with a smile and a light step. Today was Thursday, and that meant I would be giving my statue his *abhishek* bath.

I hopped up the back stairway, past the video rooms. My boss was in her office chatting on the phone, and I waved a quick *hello*, not wanting to be sidetracked from the task before me. I walked into the hall, and he was gone.

Gone! *GONE!!!!!*

How could he be gone? He was bigger than life-size. He was made out of heavy plaster. And he had been sitting on top of a huge, heavy marble pedestal, which was also gone.

I still can see the image in my mind, the bright pink square in the middle of the old, faded, dull carpeting. This untouched spot, where the carpeting had been covered for so many years by the statue. I couldn't figure out what had happened. No theory made sense. Where was he???? He was too heavy to have been stolen. There was no reason to move him out of the room. I couldn't think of any possible reason. I just sat down in kind of a stupor, and stared into the empty space.

As I sat, two people walked through the hall talking about how the statue had been sent, as a permanent gift, to the meditation center in Philadelphia.

I was devastated. I sat there and wept silently, wondering why nobody had told me about this. After all, I was the one who took care of him. I couldn't believe it was true. My rock of Gibraltar, torn out from under me without the slightest warning. My image of God — gone.

I think I felt more grief in that moment than when my teacher passed away. This was final. Now they were both gone.

Eventually, I stood up and walked toward the stairway.

214 · *Never to Return*

This time my boss, Gail, called me into her office. She saw from my face that something was amiss. "What's wrong?"

"He's gone," I whispered.

Immediately, she knew who I was talking about and apologized, "Oops, I'm sorry. I forgot to tell you."

It turned out that a week earlier, my teacher had been sitting out for one of the lunchtime gatherings, when she told everyone that the statue was going to be given away. We now had this new bronze statue, and she wanted the Philadelphia center to have the benefit of the older one. While explaining this to those gathered, our teacher had also mentioned that some of the winter residents had become too attached to the statue.

She turned to Gail and asked, "Do you know anyone who is too attached to him?

Gail said, "No." Actually, I had never told her about all of my responsibilities with the statue. It was my personal practice, my private spiritual relationship.

As I was told later, my teacher had asked her, "Isn't Kumuda attached to the statue?"

Gail replied, "Probably."

"Well, you should tell anyone who is attached to the statue that it will be gone in one week."

She had forgotten to tell me.

So here, one month after praising me in front of everybody, my teacher had taken away the one thing that was most important to me, the image that represented my relationship to God.

From this side of the event, I can see how important it was that my dependence on this object be broken. A living spiritual master was back in town, and the next path on my journey was about to unfold.

Nevertheless, this image had served an important purpose for me. Just as the square of pink carpeting stayed clean and unworn under the protection of the statue and pedestal, so a part of my heart had been kept unsullied by this statue as well. *He* had been there for me during a time when it might have been easy to lose faith, when the physical form of my master was removed.

I was not yet ready to expand into the state of knowing the divine in its all-pervasive formlessness, and so my first teacher's role of *divinity in form* had been transferred to the statue, giving me the support I needed to be carried through that time.

And now it had been removed by that which was to take his place. It is said that when God enters a heart, He removes all that is not Himself. So it was with my second teacher. Once the connection was made, she took me into herself and pulled off even the sweet pacifiers that had kept me comfortable and steady through the previous year. And like a mother pulling off a Band-Aid that has served its purpose, she pulled it off fast and clean — and with a sting.

A few days later, one of the monks came to my office to give me a gift from my teacher. It was a photo that had been taken of the statue before it was moved. It's just a poorly lit Polaroid, but every time I look at it, I am once again touched by the compassion that came through this gesture so many years ago.

> *When one door of happiness closes, another opens;*
> *but often we look so long at the closed door,*
> *that we do not see the one which has opened for us.*
>
> *—HELEN KELLER*

One word frees us of all the weight and pain of life:
that word is love.

—SOPHOCLES

24.

CLOTHED
IN DEVOTION

A FTER MY SUMMER JOB, I returned to the video
department, now as the editor. My wish from three
years ago had finally blossomed. All day long I
watched tapes, read transcripts, researched quotes, and created video expressions of all the transformations occurring
inside me.

As time went on, my devotion to our new teacher
increased. She became the mother I'd never had, but in a
more spiritual, *divine motherly* sense. I decided to really trust
her with my heart, and jumped headlong into the yogic practice called *bhakti* — devotion. Devotion consumed my entire
being, and inspired new breakthroughs on my journey.
Through devotion I was willing to change, to suffer the pain

of breaking out of old habits and comfort zones. My entire consciousness was absorbed in the contemplation of this person who represented divinity for me. Her every flowing movement seemed to indicate the gracefulness of God. Her smile would burst forth in my heart like a dramatic rising sun. Her tender words melted my sharp edges, and her harsh reprimands moved me beyond egotistical identification. Through her, I was able to have a continuous and constant interaction with universal grace, divine consciousness. Everything I did was an offering to God through her. In *bhakti yoga*, we worship all the highest qualities that we are not yet able to see in ourselves through the form of another. We can love this image, this reflection in the mirror of consciousness, as we could never love ourselves.

The end result comes when a merging takes place between lover and beloved. Through one-pointed focus, this intimacy is created and nurtured, until it breaks through the imaginary walls that separate "I" from "Thou."

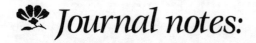 *Journal notes:*

A poem written during this time, in praise of Divine Love

O Love, See what You've done to this life!
With Your wild, churning throb
Exploding beneath every instant.

So obvious, O Love, yet at times very subtle,
Always there just under the surface,
Below the words, the ideas, the feelings.

You, O Love, are the feeling behind all my feelings,
The impulse of my life,
The only reality in this crazy, scattered world.

Even if I am not able to hold on to You at all times,
O My Love, You have enveloped me within Yourself.
No fault of mine can upset You at all.

It's not that You belong to me,
Or even that I belong to You, O Love,
Nor is Your Truth to be understood by my clouded eyes.

Yet, O Love, You are there at all times.
This is not a fact to be proved; but accepted.
No sadness, no grief — not even joy can touch You.

Perhaps You are not the Highest Essence of this world.
But who is there who can say that You're not?
You are within Everything, and far beyond Everything.

Even now that You have spread throughout my being,
So many images continue to play on so many channels —
Good feelings, bad feelings, sportings of the mind.

Still, O Love, how wonderful that we watch together,
Like a contented couple watching TV on Saturday night,
Flipping the stations and laughing at the play.

O But Love, You are a Beast! What have you done?
You have ignited a restlessness in my Soul,
Which can never be fulfilled.

As the One whose Glance slaughters me
twelve times over,
You have chosen a being who is beyond this world.
How will I ever be able to reach Her?

You've stolen every pain I could have kept
To hide myself from You, O Love,
And you've left me with only Your Sweet Pain.

May I always drink of Your Divine Essence,
While laughing and while weeping,
Drowning myself in your mad waves.

Let the mind lose its petty control.
Why should the intellect always have to have its say?
O Love, My fear and greed can just jump overboard.

But let this boat glide through Your Sweet Nectar,
Flowing from the Heart into the Light of the Sky,
Your Sweet and Devastating Elixir of Love.

Wherever Your glance is cast through Her Eyes,
Every particle is destroyed, O My Love,
Where is room for existence before Her Smile?

When You speak my name through Her Lips, O Love,
There is no one left to claim that name!
How I Love You, O My Love.
How I Love Your Sweet Love.

My wardrobe seemed to be a fertile ground for new lessons of surrender. Most of the residents dressed very nicely. Part of the teaching of this path was that the body is the temple of God. Therefore, we wouldn't just worship external images but, as my teacher used to say, we would *"Kneel to your own Self, worship your own Self, honor your own Self, because God dwells within you as you."*

I got the idea, but still didn't like to dress up. I had sported the *grunge* look long before the term was coined. Also, with my limited finances it wasn't as though I could run out and buy a fancy new wardrobe even if I had wanted to.

My teacher once described me as someone who "gets all her clothes from the free box." In the basement area of the monastery there was a "free box," where people could place garments they no longer needed. Much of my wardrobe did, indeed, come from there. Most of the items were in fine shape. I was quite content with my simple but adequate wardrobe; however, my teacher seemed to prefer that I didn't have to sort through other people's discards for my clothes. Soon after her comment, I was given a special allowance so I could purchase some new clothes. Too bad the money didn't also come with good taste in clothes!

First, I went out and bought a white sweater with a hood. I thought it was a great article of clothing though, upon reflection, it was pretty funky. Nevertheless, I wore it proudly one day, walking through the lobby. My teacher was passing by with a large group of devotees. She came up to me and began to speak harshly in Hindi. One of the Indian monks translated. He was kind enough to whisper so the entire throng of people couldn't hear the words.

"Look at you! Even if a ghost were to see a person dressed like you, he would run away." He hissed, "Even a ghost! He would run away!" At first, I was confused. Wouldn't that be a good thing? Who wants to have ghosts around anyway? But the tone of my teacher's voice made it clear that this was definitely not a compliment. As everyone moved by, I walked over to the basement area to make my own contribution to the free box.

Another time, my teacher was sitting with a small group of us in the video room, watching a program that was taking place in the meditation hall. A friend of mine, Cora, was giving a talk, sharing some of her experiences. She spoke of the time she had missed the shuttle bus to her building. Our teacher's car had pulled up to where she was standing, and my teacher rolled down her window and offered Cora a ride in her car. Having just come from a *hatha yoga* exercise class, Cora was wearing sweat pants and a T-shirt. While relating this story, Cora mentioned that she had felt uncomfortable being dressed so informally in front of our teacher.

As we watched this talk on the video screen, my teacher looked at me and teased, "You always dress like that!" Then she repeated the statement to the other people sitting in the room. "Kumuda always dresses like that!" She looked at me again with a piercing but twinkling glance and repeated, "You always dress like that!"

I realized at this point that clothing had become an unavoidable issue. I was going to have to surrender to wearing nice clothes. I certainly wanted to follow the divine instructions of my guru, even though I wasn't sure why she would care about what clothes I was wearing.

Upon reflection, I can imagine her motivations for pressuring me. My desire to wear funky clothes probably reflected a lack of self-esteem, born during my childhood. Being a spiritual teacher, she had a knack for picking up on these kinds of things. I had never learned to put together acceptable combinations of clothes, and would constantly break the rules. Maybe she saw that the ability to assemble an acceptable outfit would be valuable for me in the future. Clearly, nobody had ever bothered to teach me how to dress nicely before.

I didn't look for clothes in the free box anymore, but one day I happened to walk by and noticed a great pair of wool pants lying right on top. They fit perfectly. That night, I decided to wear them to the evening program with a nice blouse and jacket. The outfit looked fine to me, though I suspect it may have been seriously mismatched in terms of texture and color.

While walking through the lobby the following day, I was called to the phone. My nemesis, Ralph, was on the other end. He was speaking to me very sweetly, because *guess who* was in the room with him. He seemed to be repeating into the phone what my teacher was saying. "From now on, you should only wear skirts. No more pants."

I had already surrendered to wearing skirts to the evening program, and now I had to wear them *all the time?*

I got up the nerve to mention that I only had two skirts and that one had a broken zipper. He then asked another girl to give me some clothes. She had a lot of money and tons of clothes. She was only too happy to have been asked by our teacher to help me out. We went up to her room, and she gave me the first really classy clothes I had ever owned. Beautiful clothes. I was quite grateful.

But I was also in a quandary. Recently, I had started working in the garden for an hour a day, to get some sun and exercise in the midst of all my video-editing work. I wondered if it would be all right for me to wear pants in the garden. I really didn't know. I debated this for days. I could have worn a skirt to the garden, but that seemed ridiculous. Yet if I wore pants in the garden and was spotted going back to my room, my teacher might not realize that I was coming from the garden. I had been told specifically to wear skirts "all the time."

After a few days, I finally decided that it would be okay to wear pants in the garden. I would just be careful not to be seen in the building with pants on. I was planning to go out that afternoon for an hour or so after lunch. While eating, I heard my name called over the loudspeaker. When I phoned the switchboard, they told me that my teacher wanted me to meet her in the outdoor pavilion. I walked there with excitement and trepidation, not knowing why I had been called.

As I entered the large outdoor hall, my teacher was standing there alone. I respectfully bowed my head down to her feet, and was so clumsy that I wondered if I hurt her toes by bumping my head on them. But she didn't seem bothered in the least. She smiled sweetly and pointed to a large, neatly folded pile of clothes on the bench next to her. "These are for you."

With relish, she took each piece of clothing and showed it to me. These were really elegant clothes. There was a woven silk magenta sweater, a silk dress from France, another exquisite pink sweater, and a bathrobe. Then she handed me a pair of Ted Lapidus red gabardine wool *pants*.

Pants?

Not just pants, but really expensive pants. And this, just a week or so after giving me a very clear instruction to wear only skirts. I often became tongue-tied in my teacher's presence. Sometimes, I couldn't speak at all. What I meant to say at this point was, "Oh, I guess that means it would be okay for me to wear pants in the garden."

What came out was, "Oh, in the garden."

She looked at me with a surprised face, and very compassionately explained, "No, these are expensive pants. You can't wear them in the garden."

The twist at the end of this wardrobe lesson showed me that instructions were not to be followed in a fanatical way. Her command had been more about respecting and honoring myself than about whether I was wearing a skirt or pants. It is very easy to take a command at face value and make a hard and fast rule of it. Through this surprise gift, she was guiding me to understand the deeper teaching behind a surface directive. This process is very important if a disciple is to develop the inner intuitive understanding that will allow them to eventually receive guidance from within.

❧ *Journal notes:*

A poem composed from the absorption of devotion

*My eyes have become intoxicated
drinking, drinking, drinking You.
This is no ordinary thirst,
The more these eyes drink of Your form,
the thirstier they become.*

*Who can care about ordinary food or drink?
Your presence is the nourishment for my life.*

Who can care about philosophy or knowledge?
You are my philosophy.

I can hardly even see myself anymore,
But O Guru!
With my eyes open or closed, I see Your face before me.
Your voice resounds throughout my being.

Somewhere along the way, this cup spilled over.
Now it sits waiting to be filled with Your sweet nectar.
I would gladly wait a thousand years
for one loving glance.
And the moment it is revealed,
I'll begin waiting for another.

This is the mission of my life, the value of my life.
If I can serve You even once, my life will be justified.

I may never be able to understand You
or appreciate You as I should,
Yet my entire being is filled with You.

The play is enlivened by the presence of trouble-makers.
They are necessary to lend zest to the play —
there is no fun without them.

—RAMAKRISHNA

25.

NEMESIS

DURING MY FIRST WINTER in the monastery, a man came from Los Angeles to help prepare for the upcoming summer retreat. He was the kind of guy who wore Armani leather jackets and dark sunglasses, very stylish and clearly a VIP. I was taking care of all of the mailing needs at the time, and he asked me to package and send a box of chocolates to his wife for Valentine's Day.

Ralph seemed like a friendly enough guy, and even offered me a little sampler box with four Godiva chocolate hearts for myself. At the time, I had no money to buy sweets, and was especially appreciative of his delicious gift.

Who would have known he was to become my nemesis? The chocolate hearts, unbeknownst to him or to me, were like the ceremonial bow one takes before moving in to destroy one's opponent.

Ralph was from the Middle East, and had been through some heavy-duty war experiences there. His mentality was different from any I had known in my life. This guy could be the most charming man in the world one moment, but in a flash he'd bare his teeth and attack. Through his presence in my life, I gained a lot of inner strength and learned many difficult but important lessons.

This was what I had come to this school for. I wanted to be transformed. I wanted to learn to respond to the universe in a new way. I wanted to rise above pettiness and get rid of all the garbage that had accumulated on top of my pure soul. I wanted desperately to grow into that great being I knew was inside myself. Ralph probably had similar goals, but seemed to require different lessons to get there. His abrasive behavior gave new challenges to many of the people living in the monastery.

On the road to freedom, adversity is grist for the mill, the sandpaper smoothing our rough edges. The choices we make in responding to life-situations is what the Indian scriptures call *sadhana*: our efforts to consciously participate in the personal evolution of our soul through this journey of human experience.

The importance of challenging experiences became clear to me as I contemplated my most valuable experiences from this time. During these years in the monastery, many wonderful people had come into my life. There had been sweet, light moments, so many amazing, powerful blessings. But somehow, when I look at the life lessons that transformed me and created the greatest leaps of understanding and inner strength, most came from people like Ralph, or circumstances that might be viewed as harsh. While they were occurring, I couldn't often see the positive effects of such difficulties, however upon reflection, with an objective eye focused beyond surface comforts, these challenges and breakthroughs are some of my most treasured moments.

Early on, I learned what might happen if I talked back to Ralph. In 1984, we were traveling through India with my teacher and a small group of devotees. My job was to shoot super-8 film of the tour. One day, she was talking to a maharaj whose house we were using for programs. I filmed a few shots of them together, and then noticed her hands. Behind her back she was fingering her rosary-type beads, called a *japa mala*. It was beautiful to see my teacher engaged in silent focus on the highest, even during this mundane conversation with a royal figure. I thought this would make a beautiful image, and moved in to get a close-up of her hands. At that moment, Ralph came up behind me and sneered, "Why do you always shoot stupid things?"

I turned around and was so surprised by his lack of politeness that I took a quick shot of his face. "There. Now I've got another one."

Within a few days, I was mysteriously sent back to the United States, because, "They need you for editing." I don't know if this decision had anything to do with him specifically, but the timing was strangely synchronistic.

Another memorable experience with Ralph occurred the following year during an evening program in Los Angeles. Our teacher was giving programs there for several months, and she had brought me out to take some video classes at UCLA. I would also direct the cameras for my teacher's programs whenever I wasn't busy attending evening classes.

My task as director was to tell our three cameramen what to shoot through our audio headsets. On the first day, my teacher came out and sat in her chair. As she spoke, I directed one of the cameras to shoot some *cutaway* shots of the audience watching, reacting, and laughing. Here was my teacher espousing profound spiritual teachings, yet I could no longer let myself become absorbed in what she was saying. Instead, I had to pay attention to the cameras. It was fun to have this new responsibility, though I couldn't help but notice I might be missing some valuable teachings at the same time.

The program was held in a huge theater, filled with thousands of people. And they were all completely silent and still, listening with full attention to her words. It sounded almost as though my teacher was giving her talk in an empty room; that is how still everyone had become. And there we were, the cameramen and me, gabbing away.

"OK, camera 2, go in for a close-up; 3, get some medium-wide shots of the audience."

"Well, should I get that same group we shot before?"

"No, maybe do a pan of the men's section right behind you."

On we went, throughout the lecture.

The phone next to me began to blink. I answered it, and heard a terse voice say, "Hey you, director. Why do you always shoot ugly people? They all look like you!" It was Ralph.

Not since my childhood had anyone insulted me so blatantly. I had a choice. I could let it get to me and respond with anger or victimization, or I could stay focused on the task in front of me, directing the three cameras as carefully and lovingly as I could.

Because of my desire to serve, I just let it go. I didn't think, "Oh no, I must be ugly," nor did I think, "No, I'm not!" I simply put the phone down and continued to perform the task before me. It took all my focus to surmount the other potential responses waiting to bring me down.

These new challenges were digging deeply into forgotten pockets of my psyche. Perhaps my growing spiritual foundation was now strong enough to support transformation of some limiting personality patterns I had accumulated during this — and perhaps other — lifetimes. With my difficult childhood, being mistreated was certainly one of my more troublesome patterns.

This is why I didn't storm out the door when this man gave me a hard time. Even though I might get upset or frustrated on one level, from a higher perspective, I saw that this challenge was just the right medicine for my spiritual growth. It pushed me into a new strength, a more dependable emotional steadiness.

There were times when Ralph would lie and tell our teacher I had done something I hadn't. Most of the time, I wouldn't even stick up for myself; I just let him say whatever he wanted to. Once Ralph told her that I had erased a batch of tapes of our first teacher, which I would never have done. When she questioned me somewhat harshly about it, I finally explained that I had not erased any tapes. At the time, she said to me, "You never stick up for yourself. You just let anyone say anything they want about you. That's why everyone thinks you're whimsical."

Because of my ideas about how a spiritual person should behave, I didn't really contemplate or take in her words. She was telling me to stick up for myself, but I really didn't know how to do this. I was also afraid that if this man became angry with me, he might cause even more trouble. Here was a test that mirrored some of the difficulties I had encountered as a child. At that vulnerable time, I'd had no option but to withstand discourteous behavior silently. And so, when this new lesson arose, I fell back into my tried and true methods. I accepted this unacceptable treatment silently.

At the same time, my lack of external response did reflect a certain peace of mind. My focus was on the states of consciousness I would enter while chanting, meditating, and watching tape after tape of elevated wisdom. Why come down from all these great experiences to get into a petty "he said, she said" argument? There was a new awareness developing in me through all these years of intense spiritual practice. Everything is as it should be, always. One of the great statements from the Indian scriptures expresses that "This is perfect, that is perfect. Even if you take some of the perfect out of the perfect, nevertheless only complete perfection remains."

Now I'm not suggesting that I always walked around in this transcendent space, but it certainly was becoming more apparent to me. When I'd find myself getting irritated by Ralph, one of my choices was always to rise above the irritation and chuckle inwardly at the strange forms our universe creates to entertain itself. Sometimes I could see that God, Consciousness, the One that is in all, was masquerading as Ralph *and* me. With this glimpse, I was able to feel deep friendliness and love for this man, even when he was giving me a hard time.

Sometimes he would tell me to do things that I would later be reprimanded for. I'd usually weather the chastisement silently. He would stand there and watch me get busted for doing exactly what he had told me to do, and wouldn't say a word on my behalf. What a good nemesis!

Nevertheless, I was aware that it was all a test, a big lesson. Because of this, even when I felt agitated, deep inside I would relish the friction and growth these challenges were creating in me. The steadiness that came from hours of chanting, meditating, serving and studying spiritual teachings allowed me to maintain a peaceful inner composure, even in the face of injustice. There was nobody inside me who wanted to fight.

Ralph was a worthy opponent. He was intelligent, creative, and fun-loving. Sometimes he was absolutely sweet and loving to me, acting like a big brother. This really required me to be flexible in my responses to him. He was as undependable as life itself.

One reason this man had so much stature around the monastery was due to his admirable dedication to our teacher and the organization. He worked tirelessly, and was often able to complete magnificent projects within seemingly miraculous deadlines.

In some ways, it was better to be on Ralph's bad side, because those who were on his good side were inevitably asked to surmount impossible challenges. During some years, I was on Ralph's good side for months at a time. The benefit was that he was able to cut through a lot of the red tape in meeting my requirements. Instead of my having to present each request to the managers and other committees, Ralph would take care of the situation, whether it was a need for new equipment or more assistants in the department.

During one winter, Ralph sent me a telex message with a list of videos he wanted to have edited in the next week. Someone would be going to India, and he wanted me to have the tapes completed in time to send with them. I picked up the message, and saw a list of twenty-five videos! This list would take a year to do! Each video had to be scripted, researched, and carefully edited, with music and narration if necessary. What kind of crazy request was this?

Obviously, I would never be able to complete twenty-five videos, but I decided to give it all I had, and accepted this new challenge head on. During the next seven days, I worked non-stop around the clock. The only exception I made to this workathon was to go to the chant each morning, which I did inevitably sleep through.

The first video was a complex, ten-minute montage of my second teacher's life, from childhood on, based on a poem she had written and recited during a recent talk. That took a day and a half.

Then came the history of the building of the monastery temple. This video required a well-researched script. Fortunately, there were two people available to help write the script for this one.

After this, I scripted and edited a video showing highlights of our teacher's recent tour to meditation centers around the country. By this time, I was beginning to hallucinate from lack of sleep.

A friend gave me some of her diet pills to help me through the last few days. By Saturday morning, I had completed six videos. The courier was leaving on Sunday afternoon. I had time for one more. The next tape on the list was an important one. The anniversary of our first teacher's passing was coming up in a few weeks. This would be a video showing highlights of his three world tours, to be sent to hundreds of meditation centers around the world. It should have taken at least a month to complete, but I somehow managed to finish the 45-minute video just in time.

After handing the package to the courier, I went back to the video room and sat down, staring blankly into space. I was too wired to go to sleep, yet my mind was completely empty. In spite of the exhaustion, I felt pretty good about myself. I had scripted and edited seven videos in just as many days. I had achieved something I would have considered to be absolutely impossible.

I could hear footsteps coming toward the video room, and looked up to see one of our managers walk into the room. I smiled and told him that the tapes were on their way. He looked a little uncomfortable, and said that he had been waiting for me to finish so he could deliver a message to me from India. "They're not going to let the video crew shoot the *yajna* (fire ceremony) this year, because your editing is so lousy."

I couldn't do anything but smile incredulously at these words. I would have expected some sort of praise for my dedicated efforts, and here I was being insulted. I didn't even feel too agitated about the message. I was just too exhausted to buy into it.

Those were the *good* times with Ralph. When Ralph was in "nemesis" mode, it was clear that arguing or talking back to him was not really a viable option. Or else, as he shouted to me once across the lobby, "With an attitude like yours, I'm not even going to let you wash toilets in this place!"

At first, my only choice to his taunting seemed to be silent acceptance, but then I managed to find another response. I would act dumb. I would look innocent and act unaware in ways that pointed out his folly.

One day, Ralph asked me what my name was. He knew my spiritual name, Kumuda, and obviously wanted to know what my American name was.

"My name? Kumuda."

He looked disgusted, "I know that! What's your other name?"

"My last name? Janis."

"No, no! What is your American name???"

"Oh, my American name." I finally surrendered, "Sharon."

He immediately shot back, "Like Sharon Tate?"

Now, I knew who Sharon Tate was, the pregnant woman who had been brutally murdered by Charles Manson's followers. But I managed to suppress my shock and looked up with an innocent look. "Who?"

He growled, "Sharon Tate! You don't know who Sharon Tate is?"

"Um, is she a devotee?"

"Forget it!!!"

He didn't know whether to be angry or bewildered at my naiveté. Inside, I was smiling.

Then came the chanting video challenge. That winter, I had been asked to make a special video for our teacher's upcoming tour, to explain the meaning and purpose of chanting. I really wanted to do a good job on this project. I had recently received several messages from my teacher, expressing her dissatisfaction with recent videos.

While receiving such messages, I was still being given projects to work on. Her words were clearly intended to inspire me to improve my abilities. One letter had expressed, "I do hope that you make good use of the skill that you've got. So far I haven't seen one video that makes me say, 'This is it! This is it!' So I'm still waiting for this video. When will it be?"

I put massive amounts of effort into contemplating how to become a better editor, how to create that one video that would make her heart sing. I prayed to God to grant me the boon of being a great editor. I meditated on how to improve my skills. Once, while editing a special winter scene, I even spent several hours walking in the snow beforehand so I could really incorporate my personal experience into the piece. I put all I could into this goal of becoming an expert editor, and my skills had indeed improved through these efforts.

I was starting to gain some confidence in my abilities, and poured my heart into this chanting video. Maybe this would be that one video she was waiting for. I spent weeks researching quotes and footage, and came up with a polished script. Then I put together a carefully crafted first edit.

Ralph was in the upstate New York monastery for a short visit, and would be in charge of approving videos. I was really excited to show him this tape, because it was by far the best video I had ever made. I thought he'd really like it. Ralph had been sweet and brotherly to me recently, and when I phoned, he told me to come right on down. I brought the tape to his office and popped it into the VCR. Ralph sat down to watch, and I hit the play button. Just before the first shot came on, some construction crew workers entered the room to talk with Ralph. He got up and walked to an entirely different section of the large office to go over some budgeting figures with them. I hit the pause key.

Ralph turned around. "I didn't tell you to stop playing it. Just keep it playing."

I rolled the tape again, and looked over to see Ralph standing far away, with his *back* to the television and me. The video played on, and eventually ended. I pressed the rewind button so he could watch it after their meeting. Ralph finished his business and came back over. He

looked me right in the eye and said, "Forget it. It's lousy.
Don't ever show it to anyone."

My jaw dropped in shock. He had been very friendly to
me lately, so I was not expecting this dramatic shift back into
combat mode. I had been caught off-guard. I could have said
"But you didn't even see it," but obviously we both knew that
he hadn't seen it. He was playing a game.

This experience was difficult and easy to take at the same
time. It was painfully difficult until I was able to let go and
experience the freedom of detachment. Detachment from all
the work and care I had put into this project; detachment
from the satisfaction of finally making a video that my
teacher might be happy with. I moved into a space of deeper
acceptance that *whatever* happened was the will of the
Supreme. At first, I was angry, and could feel the anger eating
away at me. So I had to move my experience *above* the event.
This is different from denial. It is a way to become greater
than any obstacle. We move into identification with the
conscious energy through which the circumstances themselves
were created.

All the emotional force that came with my shock, anger
and frustration would boil down, with the fire of detachment,
into energy itself. Then this "negative" energy could be used
to fuel a breakthrough into higher understanding.

The important thing was that I had performed my service
with devotion and care. I realized that it was not necessary for
my actions to achieve any more result than that. Nothing
done with love is ever wasted.

A more difficult part of this test came when I returned to
the editing room to begin the next video. How could I
maintain my enthusiasm in the face of this frustration and
disappointment? Anyone would have wanted to quit at this

point. Under normal circumstances, I would have stormed out the door. But this was not an ordinary job, and these were not normal circumstances. I packed up the chanting tapes, filed away my script, and began the next video.

I was a seeker of eternal truth. I had made a commitment to this quest. How could I turn back now? A Sufi poem says, "Not even four thorns have pricked your foot and you are ready to leave your path." I didn't want to be so weak. I wanted to be unconditionally free. I couldn't quit. I couldn't give up. I tried even harder on the next video.

Success is going from one failure to the next without a loss of enthusiasm.

—*WINSTON CHURCHILL*

Please take away my intellect, O Lord!
Take away my power to reason with clever words,
this knowledge and logic used in useless debates.
Instead, give me humility and purity.
Give me the ability to live selflessly.
Give me your love!

—AN INDIAN POET-SAINT

26.

WHO ARE YOU CALLING JAD?

IN HINDI, THERE IS A GREAT WORD — "*jad*" (pronounced jud). It is such a wonderful word that I really wish it had an English counterpart. It doesn't exactly mean *stupid*. The best translation I've heard is, "inert, like a log." When applied to a person, it is that state where you are not really aware of what is going on around you. You're not paying attention. You're not noticing connections between different things. *Jad* is that state when someone is talking to you and you're not really listening. Or an old woman may be in need of help right in front of you and you don't notice. You're just staring blank-eyed right in her direction.

Once my teacher was invited by one of the cameramen to the video department to bless one of our new cameras. Not having been invited, I went instead to the meditation hall for the evening chant.

But as fate would have it, my teacher wanted to have a *puja* performed to the camera. This is an Indian tradition where a flame and other significant items are waved in a circular motion before the person or object that is being worshipped or blessed. She told someone to find me so that I could come and wave the flame. I was more than happy to be called upon by her. Along with happiness I felt excitement, mixed with a tinge of fear.

Every interaction with either of my teachers produced some dramatic occurrence — whether just on the inside, or both on the inside and outside. The walk to enter the guru's vortex of *karmic* cleansing energy was a walk into the tides of destiny. I had come to this place to attain the highest experience. However, I knew this could mean breaking my contracted, but comfortable, notions about myself and the world. "Is it possible," I wondered, "to want and not want something at the same time?"

The experience I was about to have might manifest through my teacher's face, words, or personality; but it would be an interaction with the *Creative Force* itself. In a way, what was going to happen would have nothing to do with the guru's personal characteristics. It was the force which *moves through* the guru, that Indian scriptures referred to as "the grace-bestowing power of God."

When I walked into the video room, my teacher was looking quite serious. She instructed me to perform a *puja* to bless the new camera. For our main programs, *pujas* were performed in a very specific way, using a silver tray and a wick that had been soaked in clarified butter. Also on the tray were placed several symbolic objects, including rice, turmeric, and *kum-kum*. Usually, there was also an offering of a flower and a piece of gold jewelry or a coin on the tray to represent beauty and abundance.

I was more or less aware of this whole puja protocol. Just a few days earlier, we'd had an event called the *mahapuja*, or "big puja." All the devotees had been invited to wave their own special tray with all the goodies on it to the statue in the temple. Thousands of people participated in this event, each with his or her own specially decorated silver tray to wave in front of the statue in the temple. The women wore brightly colored saris — the garment worn by women in India.

The *mahapuja* was an exquisitely beautiful event to participate in, but I had skipped it just as I might have skipped a class in school. I never really liked wrapping myself up in a sari, beautiful though they may be. I also disliked group functions. Though I was living in this spiritual community, still my independent spirit remained strong. I wasn't one to do something just because everyone else was doing it. In fact, I was less likely to participate in anything being done as a group, even a beautiful devotional ceremony.

While the *mahapuja* was going on, I had worked for a while on a video in the editing room. Then, curious about what I was missing, I went out to the roof and watched the whole thing from that elevated view. Nearly every resident and guest was there with their fully decorated trays. There was a line of lights moving into the temple doors, and several rows of *puja* flames being waved in harmony inside the temple. You could feel the devotion and love streaming through all of these beautiful people.

So here I was two days later, preparing to perform a *puja* to the new video camera. There was no tray in the room, so I picked up a nearby candle in a nice glass holder. But as I prepared to wave it in front of the camera, my teacher spoke. "Not with a candle! How many *mahapujas* have you done? You need to wave a tray with a wick, kum-kum, turmeric, and rice. Didn't you do the *mahapuja* two days ago?"

You can't hide anything from these gurus! I mumbled, "Um, no. I was editing that night." (Well, I was!)

My teacher's glow tangibly increased as she began to berate me. "You're *jad!*" She turned to the other people in the room, "She's *jad!* She's *jad-ananda!*" (which would translate as, "the bliss of being inert like a log"), I felt bad that she had discovered my secret lack of participation, but at the same time I was filled with *shakti*, this energy that surrounded her presence. Every time my teacher said "She's *jadananda!*" another bolt of energy would hit me. I started to feel giddy from the bliss.

There was a strange juxtaposition of the discomfort of having done something wrong, and an energy that seemed to lift me high above the entire arena of right and wrong. Part of my awareness was catapulted into a state of mind that left no room for self-judgment.

Unknowingly, I did have some issues about intelligence. I had gone from being a class genius in first-grade, to the class dunce in my new school the next year. I had a very high I.Q. test score at age five, but flunked practically every grade of elementary school. I surprised myself with brilliance about as often as I embarrassed myself with dull-witted blunders. With her taunt, my teacher was clearing away both the insecurity and pride from my heart. I didn't have to be proud of my intelligence, nor embarrassed at my ignorance. There was a sanctuary beyond this pair of opposites.

The little me may have been feeling guilty, stupid, or insulted, but while it was distracted, the whole of me, including the level upon which I was feeling these emotions, was lifted up to a higher place. It was the lifting that was important, the breaking-free that was happening inside me.

"She's *jadananda!*"

Although my teacher was speaking these words with a stern demeanor, there was an unexpressed laughter beneath the surface. She had a definite sparkle in her eye. After all, the juxtaposition of the words *"jad"* (inert) and *"ananda"* (supreme bliss) is funny. It had the flavor of *ignorance is bliss.* Indian monks often add the word *ananda* to the end of their names. Maybe she was choosing a name for me just in case!

I didn't know whether to laugh or be remorseful, so I chose to mirror her play. On the outside, I appeared to be serious and repentant about having snubbed the *mahapuja*, but inside I was filled with joy.

Here was my guru, this person who I most wanted to impress, who I hoped would think of me as great, smart, and wonderful in every way, calling me *jad.* And instead of being upset by it, I was absolutely ecstatic. It was okay to be *jad*, at times. I no longer had to worry about always appearing to be smart or on top of things. I didn't have to pretend to be perfect or right. I didn't have to act like I knew what was going on even when I had no idea. I could just be *blissfully jad*, without trying to impress anybody. An immense weight was lifted from my shoulders.

Mistakes are the portholes to discovery.

—JAMES JOYCE

27.

A PERFECT MISTAKE

M Y TEACHER WOULD BE LEAVING for India in two days. Instead of saying farewell to all the staff members at one large program, she decided to meet with us in small groups, based on our departments. Everyone was looking forward to having a chance to be with her in a small group. It would certainly up our odds of having some personal interaction.

My group was scheduled for noon, but at 10:00 a.m. I received a phone call informing me that the meeting had been changed to 10:30. I went to my room to make sure I looked good, and even surrendered to using a bit of make-up. I changed into a fresh outfit and made my way down the stairway, right next to where the meeting would take place. I looked over and saw that it was already in progress. Two of my roommates and about eight other friends were sitting in a small group with our teacher. I walked over and sat down to join them.

But something was wrong. They were discussing business. They were discussing the trips they would be taking to various meditation centers, to give programs and make sure everyone was behaving themselves. These were not the people from my department. I realized with horror that this was not the meeting I was supposed to be in. I was in the wrong *darshan!*

I looked back into the carpeted lobby. At least 100 people sat patiently, waiting for their meetings. I turned back toward my teacher and the small group. As if I hadn't just crashed their meeting, they continued to discuss matters that were none of my business. What should I do now?

If I got up and walked away, surely my blunder would not go unnoticed. I would have to deal with the situation right then and there. I had hoped for an interaction with my teacher, but not like this! In addition, all the people waiting in the lobby would see what a silly thing I had done and would certainly laugh at me. Also, the truth is that I was right where I would have liked to be, at the feet of my teacher. I decided to postpone my fate.

After a few minutes, I started to loosen up and even began to chuckle with their jokes. I felt like a kamikaze pilot. I knew that inevitably there was going to be a confrontation about my being in the wrong place, so why not enjoy the ride down?

Finally, the jig was up. My teacher told one of the swamis, "Let's go around and have each person tell where they're going."

I wanted to laugh, but managed to control myself. She was always so creative. Each person gave their response, and finally it was my turn. My teacher broke the ice and asked the swami, "What is Kumuda doing here?" He very kindly tried to justify my presence by explaining that I had rushed to finish a batch of video edits for them.

But I knew it was a feeble attempt. I had to 'fess up. "Well, I was told to come down for a farewell *darshan*, but it appears I'm in the wrong *darshan*." With that, I bowed my head and stood up to walk away.

"Did I ask you to leave?" She asked sternly.

I turned and looked into her piercing, dark eyes. "No."

"Then why would you leave? What a big ego you must have to leave when I didn't even ask you to leave. How many years have you worked in the video department?"

I responded, "Six."

"And what have you learned in all that time?"

Inside, my mind was giving its unspoken commentary, "To keep my mouth shut at times like this."

I sat back down.

As the meeting continued, two other devotees made the same mistake I had, and wandered in. Both were asked to wait in the lobby. If I hadn't gotten the message yet, this was the punctuation. I would not have been there if it hadn't been God's will. You might ask, "Well yes, but what about the two people who were sent away?" Clearly, they too were brought there through God's will, specifically to be sent away.

I began to understand that having a big ego has nothing to do with praising oneself. Ego is the illusion that we are separate from the life process within which we exist. The part of me that got up to leave thought *I* had made a mistake. My teacher's chastisement made me realize that no mistakes are possible, including the one I thought I had made by getting up to leave. After this lesson, life became a little easier.

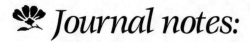 *Journal notes:*

A *poem about the monastic life*

What is it like to live in the ashram,
Being torn apart inside and out
only to be put back together the right way,
finally.

The comforting scent of burning frankincense
and myrrh,
the fragrance that must have carried Jesus
through his most trying times,
floats through the air,
lives in the strands of your hair,
and follows you even to the store.

The air is not just for breathing,
it is thick, vibrating.
It holds you and carries you, and loves you.
The power of the saints lives in the air they breathe,
and as I breathe their air,
my heart tastes the sweetness of their divine state.

Mornings come early here.
There is no debate:
should I roll over and sleep in?
No.

The Divine One is waiting for you
in his warm temple.
He wants to cradle you in his peace.
He wants to enfold you in his blanket of meditation,
in his blanket woven of dreams and purity.

The music of the chant begins before the sun explodes.
As the strains of love fly through the air,
my soul is lifted high, riding on the wave of sound.
As I chant the powerful Sanskrit syllables
long ago memorized,
now they are a part of me.
I exist in the vibration of sound,
as my heart, breath and mind unite to sing His praise.

Time is on hold.
Does it last for an hour and a half,
or does it connect with eternity?
The space of chanting may be repeated day after day,
but it is always the same time, the same space.
Troubles of the day — joy, guilt, fear, anxiety —
must wait outside.
Here there is just the sound that sparks the soul
and allows my entire being to sit in unity.

Then comes the time to work, selfless service.
Well, not always has my service been without desire,
yet it is given freely, without boundaries.
My service is the way I can give back
for all that has been given to me.

It is a way to perform actions
without being bound by my actions,
with devotion and heart-filled care.

Here, there is no need to focus on current news.
Why read and watch and hear over and over
about the waves of change
that come and go, endlessly?
Events will always arise and they will always subside.
They always have, and they always will.
Why not focus instead on the eternal spirit
inside the flux of the world, inside my heart,
inside the flow of the daily schedule?

In this place, there is Supreme Aloneness.
You are truly alone,
even in the midst of thousands of people.
Supreme Aloneness is not limiting, it is not lonely.
Supreme Aloneness is full and rich.
You feel your own sweet presence.
You have always been Supremely Alone
but you never knew it,
and now you do.

Action in itself is neither virtuous nor sinful.
The error lies in attributing it to our false individuality,
when really it emanates from God.

—*Papa Ramdas*

28.

She Still Thinks She Did It!

MY TEACHER HAD JUST ARRIVED back at the monastery for the summer, in time for a festive celebration of her birthday. A new devotee, Tony, was on the scene. He was an accomplished music-video director and would be overseeing the filming of the festivities. The monastery had three cameras and several novice cameramen. Tony brought a new professional flair, challenging all of us to move our skills to a higher level. He was also a very charismatic, strong-willed, and humorous man who I immediately liked and respected.

After the weekend, Tony was scheduled to fly to

Vancouver to work on a music video. Ralph asked Tony if he'd be willing to edit a video of the birthday celebrations while in Vancouver. Tony agreed, under the condition that I come along to assist him. I had no interest in leaving the monastery, certainly not now with my teacher back in town, but I accepted the assignment nonetheless.

I flew to Vancouver and met with Tony. It turned out things were busier than he had expected. He didn't know if he'd have time to make the video, after all. I asked what I could do to help get it done. He instructed me to log the tapes, noting every shot, and choosing the best ones for the video. I spent the next few days going through every tape, meticulously organizing and typing up log sheets describing each shot.

Then we went into the editing room for a two-day session. I immediately appreciated Tony's artistic sense. He looked for unnoticed moments, and would slow them down and juxtapose various images in unique and beautiful ways. Watching him, this style began to make sense to me. It was as though I had tapped into his mode of thinking, and could almost predict the effects as he chose them. Once again, I was witnessing the power of company, as my own artistic sense expanded.

Tony hadn't had a chance to watch any of the tapes, and depended on me to recommend the shots. At one point, he had to leave for a few hours, and entrusted me to work with the editor on one of the sections. As though I had been directing edit sessions all my life, I slipped into Tony's chair and somewhat into his mentality. The section I worked on came together with a style similar to his, indistinguishable as far as I could tell. It was a very intuitive process. The editor would look at me for the next shot, and I would quiet my mind and listen for inner guidance. I was even giving specific lengths of effects, down to the frame.

This was all fairly new to me. Our equipment back at the monastery was decent, but not quite professional. We didn't even have a way to record time-code numbers on the tapes, making it difficult to precisely control the parameters of each edit.

During this week, Tony worked hard to build up my self-esteem. Over and over, he told me what a great editor I was and how the monastery didn't really give me the respect I deserved. He said I should demand that we get time-code in the video department, and that I be treated as a professional. His responses were absolutely appropriate in a worldly context, but they clashed with my simple monastic surrender.

Nevertheless, I returned to New York with the video as well as a fairly inflated ego, though I didn't realize this at the time. I met a friend in the hallway and told her all about Tony's encouragement, explaining, "I think he's right. I need to demand more respect and insist on getting the equipment I need to do a good job." The power of company had affected me on more levels than I knew. I must have sounded like a typical Hollywood player.

I walked into the video room and prepared to show the birthday tape to my teacher through a cable connected to her house. She had gathered there with a few devotees so they could watch it together. As the video ended, the phone next to me rang. I picked it up and heard a woman's voice. I couldn't quite tell if it was my teacher or another Indian woman. "That was a great video."

I replied, "I'm glad you liked it."

The person on the other end was on a speaker phone, and I could hear some giggling in the background. This made me a little uncomfortable. Were they laughing at something I had said?

The unidentified voice continued, "We didn't know you had such a great skill. Tell me, from where did you learn this great skill?"

I was confused. The wording of this question alarmed me. It seemed to be a set-up. The truth is that I didn't know I had so much skill either, until this past week. Tony had mentioned that he was going to tell my teacher and Ralph what a great editor I was. Maybe she was referring to something he had said. I hesitantly replied, "I don't know. Through the years, I guess."

Again, I heard giggling, then a click, and the phone went dead. I was left feeling perplexed. I had a sense of having done something wrong, but couldn't imagine what it might be. All morning long, I tried to figure out what was going on.

While walking through the woods after lunch, I encountered one of the monks. He called me over and hinted, "It seems that you still haven't lost what you came here to lose."

It took me a moment to understand that he was talking about my ego. I asked, "What did I do wrong?"

He looked off into the trees. "You took credit for Tony's work."

I was surprised to hear this. It hadn't occurred to me that my words might have sounded that way. I tried to explain to him that I had been responding within the context of our teacher's questions, and also that I had contributed to the video substantially. He didn't seem interested in my explanations.

That afternoon I told one of my friends what had happened. I predicted, "I just know she's going to talk about it during the program tonight." I remembered her birthday talk several years earlier when she had praised me so profusely. Would the karmic scales be balanced tonight?

Late that afternoon, I sat down for the program, not sure if my prediction would come true. It didn't make sense that she would denounce me publicly for something so insignificant, yet something inside was preparing me for a new challenge.

My teacher began to speak.

"The poet saint Kabir said, 'When I was enrapt in myself, O beloved, your face was hidden from me. Now that I see you, I am no more I. I know now, this path of love is much too narrow. Two cannot walk here, only one.'"

I wasn't quite sure what this poem had to do with my situation, but I suspected it might be the opening to a talk about my ego.

My suspicions were correct.

She told the whole story about how this wonderful music-video director made an extraordinary production of the birthday celebration, and how an unnamed person in the video department had taken credit for his work. She even imitated my response to the question regarding where I had learned such a great skill. "Through the years, I guess," she recounted with a look of incredulous astonishment. The audience made *tsk-tsk* sounds, as they shook their heads in judgment.

The story sounded especially awful the way she told it. It appeared as though I had stayed in the monastery while this guy flew somewhere and edited the video all by himself. It wasn't that she didn't know I had gone to Vancouver. She was fudging the story, giving me the clue I needed, the blossom hidden beneath barbed thorns. I now understood that this lesson was not about anything I had done specifically. It was not a call for me to start analyzing my actions or feeling guilty. I had come back to the monastery with a budding arrogance, and she was going to chop it off before it took root in my karmic soil.

I sat in the audience listening to the story. If it hadn't been about me, I would have been laughing with everyone else about this poor schmuck who clearly didn't have a clue. But this time I *was* the schmuck.

She continued, "If I hadn't liked the video, the person would probably have said, 'Well, I didn't have anything to do with it, it was that guy in Vancouver.'" The audience roared with laughter. I don't remember the exact words, they weren't all recorded. Because something strange happened during her talk — the power went out.

These kinds of power outages happened occasionally during talks in India, but this was the first time it happened in upstate New York. Her mike lost its power. The video decks scrunched the tapes, and clicked loudly as they snapped off. The entire sound system took a power hit. There was my teacher trying to bust me, and nobody could hear her words. She stopped and waited for the power to come back on.

In a minute or so, the video and audio machines snapped back to life and began rolling once again. The sound system popped back on, and the lecture continued. "Can you imagine? What a big ego this person must have to take credit for somebody else's work!"

By this time, I was roasting. I didn't know if it was a wonderful or an awful experience, but it was unquestionably intense. This powerful moment blotted out everything else in my mind. All of my thoughts stopped. I was just *there*, an outlet of consciousness observing the play. It had nothing to do with me, and yet all of it had to do with me.

Many other hints about the deeper nature of this lesson were also woven through her talk, but I was too stunned to really digest them at the time. She explained, "No matter what Baba did — no matter how much work he did, no matter how much he sacrificed himself — he always repeated, 'I do nothing. My guru does everything. I sit under the wish-fulfilling tree of my supreme guru, and through his grace, everything takes place.'"

Suddenly, the power went out again.

I became alarmed as this coincidence repeated. My first thought was, "Who is doing that?" I felt as though some ethereal being was trying to protect me. But I didn't want to be protected from this blessing, regardless of its harsh form. I looked at the picture of my first teacher hanging above our current teacher's chair. "Baba, please," I prayed, "It's okay, I can handle it."

I heard the videotapes being scrunched again as the electricity came back on. It was all so dramatic and confusing. A part of me wanted to laugh, while another part was horrified. And beneath it all was a deep peace, just watching in a nonjudgmental way.

Eventually the talk ended, and we began to chant. Usually, I'd sway and sing loudly, but this night I sat stiffly, barely able to recite the words. I looked at my teacher and mentally asked for her grace. "Please help me to have right understanding about what is happening."

After a few moments, she looked at me. I expected a scowl, but she surprised me with a big, bright smile. I could almost hear her saying, "What can I do? It's my job to free you from your ego!" I couldn't believe that she would give such a generous smile after expressing so much displeasure with me. Nevertheless, just in case I was mistaken and the smile had been intended for someone seated next to me, I chose to not go up in the *darshan* line that night. I didn't quite have the guts to meet her face to face.

The next morning, I was working on a new edit. There was going to be a course entitled "From the Finite to the Infinite," and I had been asked to come up with a video for it. I started to mix Sanskrit chanting with classical music, over video footage of flames licking up in slow motion around shots of galaxies. While compositing all this, I received a phone call. My teacher wanted to see me outside the front door of the monastery. I took a moment to center myself, put on my mental and emotional armor, and headed toward my fate.

My teacher was seated with a few devotees. I bowed and sat before her. She was not smiling.

"How dare you take credit for Tony's work?"

It was clear that we were not going to ease into this.

I mustered up my courage and tried to explain the situation. "I knew that you knew that Tony made the video. I thought you were saying I did a good job assisting him."

My words seemed to shock her. Turning to the other devotees, she exclaimed, "She STILL thinks she did it!"

They seemed to be just as appalled by my explanation. What had I said wrong? I tried again, this time adding a little more detail. "You see, Tony was working on another video at the time, and I chose the shots and helped with the editing."

She looked as though I had just uttered the most ridiculous statement in the world. "She STILL thinks she did it!"

Now I was sweating. I decided maybe it would be good to abridge my description significantly. "I logged the tapes."

"She STILL thinks she did it!"

I was practically ready to say I had just made the coffee, when I glanced toward the monk seated next to me. He gave me a look of encouragement that somehow helped me to know what to say. With an inner shift, I started to realize that this was not about who did what. It had nothing to do with the video or with Tony. I glimpsed that we were dealing with an entirely different level of identification with action. It was the universal energy that did everything. Every moment was born anew from that ever-creative consciousness. The person who logged the tapes in Vancouver was not the same person sitting before my teacher today. In that moment, I opened up into a new vision of the universal play. I had heard the words "I am not the doer," being quoted in the past, but now I glimpsed the deeper meaning behind these words. I looked my teacher right in the eye and said with complete honesty, "I had nothing to do with that video."

She gave a slight nod, and paused for a moment. Even though she was acting stern with me, I was feeling peaceful and exhilarated. I loved being carried into new understandings, even though the external circumstances seemed to be harsh. My heart was happy just to be in her presence. Her bright energy soothed my soul as we began the next phase of this lesson.

She began insulting me. "Look at her face, her ghost face....See how stiff she sits? She's more stiff than that pillar....Have you seen how she walks? There is so much ego in her walk.... None of her videos are any good." She turned to a woman sitting there. "Aren't her videos lousy?"

The woman had always told me what a good editor I was and how much she liked my work. But this was a game and she had to play her role. She agreed with my teacher, "Yes, her videos are quite mediocre."

This drama went on for some time. Not one particle of me felt insulted in the least. There is no way that anyone watching could have known what was taking place beneath the surface. First of all, every time my teacher recited another criticism of me, I would immediately turn it right back and mentally ask her to heal and remove the problem. She was pulling out qualities that had been blocking me from the freedom I sought. She handed them to me one by one, and I offered each one back to her purifying force. We were working together. The process was intuitive and natural. I didn't understand all the deeper implications of what was happening, yet my subconscious intelligence saw this as an opportunity for inner cleansing and embraced it.

Her words also reflected back to me certain insecurities I had. I worried that I was stiff and boring, and had a lot of ego. Everything she mentioned had a ring of familiarity. These were my fears about myself. As she enumerated my faults for the next twenty minutes or so, I noticed how silly they sounded. I realized, "Hey, I'm not really so bad!" Her vocalization of my deepest fears helped to dissolve my identification with them.

All I could do was look at her with a totally open heart. I was so grateful for whatever guru-surgery she was doing. I could feel myself becoming lighter, more and more filled with a vibrant energy.

She continued, "Look at her. Nothing gets to her. She's like Mount Meru (a mountain in India)." Then she turned to me, "You've got the toughest shell of anyone here. I've been trying to break your shell for years, and I can't do it!" She threw her hands up in a gesture of exasperation.

I looked into her eyes and prayed silently with all my might, "Please don't give up on me. Break my shell. Make me free!"

Here I had been trying not to respond emotionally to her taunts, and now it seemed that was exactly what she had wanted me to do. She wanted me to get in touch with my deeply hidden emotions, but even after all her efforts, I had remained completely still and unmoved. I knew this shell she referred to was the hard covering of defense mechanisms that had sheltered me throughout my difficult childhood. I wasn't quite ready to let go of this dear old friend, my protective shell.

Eventually, I was dismissed and went back to the editing room. Still in a state of shock, I took refuge in my creative work. But as I looked at the images on the screen, I began to see blue flames over them. I closed my eyes. The blue flames continued to play across my inner field of vision. I opened my eyes and looked around. Still there. For four days, I saw blue flames.

The next day I ran into a friend who had witnessed the encounter. She'd had her own amazing vision, which synchronized surprisingly with mine. As our teacher started to question me about taking credit for Tony's work, my friend saw blue flames shooting from her toward me. But, she said, they stayed circling around my body. Each time I gave a response and received another reprimand, more blue flames would surround me. Finally, when I uttered, "I had nothing to do with that video," my friend saw the mass of blue flames enter into me.

Years later came another chapter of this lesson. After leaving the ashram and meeting with immediate success in Hollywood, I wrote to my teacher about the discomfort I was experiencing with all the praise that was being directed toward me. After all the labor she had done to help free me from egotistical identification with my actions, it almost seemed as though my co-workers and bosses were conspiring to puff me up.

She responded in a letter. "You should understand that I am very proud of you, particularly with the praises of your boss, because if he is praising you so profusely, that means that your stay in the ashram has borne complete fruit. All your training comes from living here, therefore you need not feel shy about the compliments that you receive. You should learn to offer them to the *Shakti*, to the Great Guiding Force."

When a sage is angry, he is no longer a sage.

—*The Talmud*

29.

Taming the Beast

EIGHT YEARS AFTER ARRIVING at the monastery, my journey took another major shift. After telling me specifically to send a certain video to the monastery in India, Ralph then told our teacher that I had sent the tape without permission. I was awakened in the middle of the night with a phone call. Ralph was on a speaker phone, and judging from the pauses in his speech, my teacher was listening as well. He scolded me for sending the tape without permission. It seems kind of strange that I didn't defend myself and say, "But you told me to send it!" At the time, it just wasn't my way. I knew that he knew he had told me to send it.

The next morning, I was informed that my service assignment had changed. I would be working in the garden now instead of the video department. I had a two-sided response to this. On one hand I thought it was pretty lousy that this man had been able to lie and get me booted out of video. But at the same time, I had a sense that the change was perfect. It had nothing to do with him, ultimately. As Jesus sang to Pilate in "Jesus Christ Superstar," "You have nothing in your hands. Any power you have comes to you from far beyond. Everything is fixed, and you can't change it." Ralph too was just a pawn in this karmic game.

Later that day, I sat in our beautiful garden under the sweet sun, plucking deadheads off rose bushes. A smile grew on my face. No more responsibilities, no more deadlines. Just sitting there, embraced by nature, touching her beautiful handiwork, repeating my mantra, watching my breath move in and out, thinking about life once again. Bliss began to pulse through my body, my heart. This is what I had come here for, after all, this peace. I began to hear the words of inner wisdom that had been guiding me through all the previous years. My life had been too full and busy to really sit quietly and hear the words, even though I had felt their guidance. Now I could listen to the teachings of my heart and soul for hours every day.

At one point, I was shoveling horse manure into the garden bed just outside a long glass hallway, on clear display to all the well-dressed executive-type residents. I couldn't help but chuckle to myself as they walked by and glanced out the window, trying not to stare. I could imagine the anxiety they must feel seeing me, a long-term, hardworking resident, shoveling mounds of horse manure all week long. Would they be next?

That week, I went shopping at a local store and found the perfect addition to the scene, a large T-shirt with the slogan,

"Are we having fun yet?" I would have worn the questionable shirt, had a friend not caught me at the cash register and insisted that it would be in poor taste.

I was pleased to see my surrendered response to this potentially painful turn of events, and felt it showed that I had risen above the level of petty anger and frustration. A few months later, I found out differently.

One of the managers asked me if I'd like to work in the cowshed. At the time, there was only one cow, but a new, pregnant cow would be arriving in a few days. A dairy farmer from Ireland had been taking care of the barn thus far, but it was going to be too much work for one person. With my love for animals, I knew I was going to like this new position. The next morning, I put on my blue-jean overalls and stepped into the cowshed, eager to begin this new service.

I was met with an icy-cold stare.

The dairy farmer did not want an assistant. This big macho man was not happy to have *anybody* invading his personal space, much less a city slicker *girl!* In a way, I couldn't really blame him. I certainly would have enjoyed the privacy as much as he.

One of the first things Patrick did was to position me *behind* the cow and tell me to milk her. I had never even touched a cow, much less milked one, so I just pulled on her udders. Nothing came out, but I kept trying.

"Are you sure there's milk in there?" I asked.

"Yep, she's full o' milk," he replied, glaring at me as I continued to pull the udders at different angles, to no avail.

Suddenly, the cow lifted her tail and splashed a big shower of urine on top of my head. Patrick laughed heartily at his practical joke.

He did act a little friendlier to me afterwards, but he was

inconsistent. One day, he'd be nice and welcoming, and the next he would be running around, throwing buckets across the barn, yelling at the top of his lungs. I had never witnessed such supermacho behavior before. It was interesting, but disconcerting at the same time. I would have preferred to have observed it through a one-way mirror.

After a few days, the new cow arrived. We received a message that our teacher wanted to see both animals together. Excited at the prospect of spending time with our teacher, we attached leashes to the cows, and headed toward the gardens. I was a little nervous about walking such a huge creature on just a small leash. I had to hold tightly, because the cow kept pulling away. She seemed none too happy to have this unknown person guiding her leash, while her beloved caretaker was walking *another cow!*

The woman in charge of landscaping had recently reprimanded us for allowing the cows to walk on the grass. Their hooves left only barely noticeable dents in the lawn, but this woman was very insistent that we walk them only on the pavement. However, the cement was hard on the cow's feet, so they kept pulling off toward the grass. Since our teacher had personally asked to see the cows, we decided to allow them to walk slowly on the edge of the grass.

As we reached our teacher, she told us to release the cows from their leashes. This did not sound like a good idea. What if they ran out into the nearby street? But our faith was stronger than our doubts, so Patrick and I unleashed our respective cows. They took off running, but didn't run away. The two cows dashed up and down the garden hills together, like two huge puppies playing with one another. They'd run up one slope and slide down another, tearing up the sod with playful bovine glee. I couldn't help but chuckle, thinking about the poor landscaping woman. So much for a few subtle hoofprints along the edge of lawn! And she couldn't say anything about this, because it had been at our teacher's request. We all laughed with delight, watching the cows play. I wondered how on earth we would ever catch them.

At that point, my teacher spoke without even looking at me. "Kumuda, go get Lakshmi." Lakshmi was the cow who had been there for about a year. Here were these two enormous animals bucking wildly across the garden, and my teacher was asking me to get one of them? It was testing time again. This was a direct command, and I was somehow going to accomplish it.

I moved into a place of faith and set out to get the cow. As I neared the area where the two 1500-pound cows were romping, Lakshmi looked over at me and stopped. She walked slowly to where I was standing, and stood still as I put her leash on. Then she walked right next to me as I brought her effortlessly to our teacher. One of the lessons of this challenge seemed to be that a centered state of mind could placate even a wild animal. Too bad I didn't learn this lesson well enough to use it with Patrick.

One day we'd be sipping fresh warm cups of milk together, telling stories; and the next day I'd walk in to an icy silence or a raging fury, with him throwing buckets across the barn, and shouting words I hadn't heard in many years.

I think this may have been a balancing lesson to the one I had learned with Ralph. That situation had taught me surrender and detachment; this one was teaching me to deal properly with situations in which detachment was not forthcoming. In this case, I couldn't really be centered and peaceful about the situation, and so my apparent detachment was not genuine. You can't fake spiritual attainments. I was getting more upset each day, but not expressing myself. The resentment started to build inside me like a mass of weeds.

Maybe if I had been open and honest at the time, we could have discussed things, and come to understand one another. However, I didn't really know how to communicate with this man. We were from such different lifestyles. Instead, I let the poison of anger build up silently, until it began to push its way out, expressing itself subconsciously through my actions, my voice, and my words. Some of it was obvious, but most of the anger festered beneath the surface. Where had this inner fury come from? I thought I was better than that! Where was my equanimity, my peaceful state of mind?

Part of the problem was that this challenge came at a time when I was weaning myself from many years of working in the video department. There, I had listened to the most sublime wisdom of the ages all day, every day. I would read transcripts, look for quotes in scriptures, and put together artistic expressions about the highest experiences and wisdom. No matter what anybody said or did to me, there was always a teaching speaking to me in the next moment, guiding me into a higher perspective.

For year after year, my awareness had been held high by the bridge of these videotapes. Whenever I lost my focus on my quest for eternal truth, I would be reminded by a line from one of my teacher's lectures. This had been an great blessing.

But now it was gone. No more videotapes; no more audiotapes; no more transcripts, research, or artistic expressions. Just this big brute giving me a hard time.

I thought it might help if I delved into meditation. Maybe that would bring back my peace. But there was one obstacle. Way back before my first winter in the monastery, I had asked my first teacher, "I'll be staying here for the winter, working alone in the video department. Should I meditate whenever I'm moved to, or be more disciplined about it?"

At the time, I would usually sit for meditation for one hour each morning. That was a common length of time for daily meditation on this path. But truthfully, I had entered a period where the state of meditation continued while I played instruments or did my work. Sometimes I could hardly finish the bookkeeping, because my eyes would keep rolling up, carrying me into deep states of meditation. Because of this, I hadn't been too upset when my first teacher replied, "You don't have to sit for meditation anymore. *Seva* (service) is the highest meditation."

He hadn't said I *should not* meditate anymore, but that I didn't have to. After this, I only meditated when the energy pulled me to turn within. I often pondered why he might have steered me away from sitting for meditation. Maybe he could see in my eyes the many hours I had spent exploring my unconscious. Maybe he could see that my assignment now was to integrate those spaces into *this* world, into my work. Or perhaps he was guiding me to experience the natural state of inner absorption where meditation becomes smoothly integrated throughout one's experience of life.

> *I don't have to close my eyes or plug my ears;*
> *I don't torture my body in the slightest.*
> *With my eyes wide open I laugh and laugh with joy,*
> *Seeing His beautiful form in everyone.*

> —KABIR

For the next eight years, I rarely sat for meditation, although I was living in a meditation monastery. After editing so many talks about the importance of disciplined meditation,

I did sometimes feel a little guilty that I wasn't doing it myself. Nevertheless, my teacher had told me, "You don't have to sit for meditation anymore. *Seva* is the highest meditation."

It had been easy to see my video service as meditation. There I would sit cross-legged, watching the highest truths pass before my eyes for up to sixteen hours a day. Often, I'd fall into deep meditative states while a video was playing.

But now I was doing all these physical, worldly things: milking cows, shoveling dung, wheeling barrows, and dealing with this macho creep every day. I was no longer living in a meditative state. I wondered if it would be helpful to start sitting for meditation again. Maybe the inner spaces could bring me to a higher awareness from which I could see the cowshed situation with greater perspective, and respond to it more appropriately. Maybe meditation would heal my frustration and bring me back into the flow.

After so many years of peacefulness, now I was walking around unstable and upset, angry and frustrated. I needed to meditate, so I wrote to my teacher. I repeated what our first teacher had said, and asked for her blessings to begin meditating regularly again.

It was like magic. The letter had barely left the front door when I was drawn into a deep state of inner peace. From that day on, I woke up extra early every morning to meditate. I even set my top bunk up as a meditation area. This was going to be great. Though my teacher was in India at the time, somehow her subtle consciousness seemed to have heard my request, answering through the blessing of all these beautiful meditations.

Two weeks later, her external reply arrived. I took the precious letter up to my new meditation bunk. Holding it close to my heart, I moved into meditation. I wanted to receive

her words from a completely open space. Slowly, I opened the
envelope and unfolded the beautiful stationery. My teacher's
response was placed in quotes: "*Ah, Kumuda. No meditation.*"

No meditation?

What a surprise!

I put the letter back into its envelope, and began to
dismantle my new meditation bunk. I took any directive
from my guru very seriously, and this one was quite simple
and clear.

From then on, I would actively keep myself from moving
into meditation. During the evening programs and
workshops, we would have meditation sessions. All the other
devotees would be seated in the darkness, trying to quiet their
minds by repeating the mantra and watching their breath.
And there I would be, trying to keep my mind thinking so I
wouldn't fall into meditation. Maybe it was the complete loss
of meditation in my life that made me so vulnerable to my
lower nature in the cowshed.

The thing that upset me most was that nobody seemed
to care. I hadn't taken my teacher's advice at the time when
she told me to stand up for myself. Now I was trying to do
it, but my efforts all seemed to be in vain. After so many
years of not using that "standing up for myself muscle," it
appeared to have atrophied. I was somehow unable to
communicate the problem sufficiently. Perhaps because I
had waited so long in frustrated silence, the agitation built
up inside me to such a degree that it distorted all my
intentions. I told the managers that this guy would kick the
cows in anger, and that I was afraid he might harm me in
one of his violent rages. I was shocked to hear them just
laugh it off, "Oh yes, Patrick can be bullheaded, can't he?
Ha ha." This just made me angrier. After all these years of

going through so much and never complaining, everyone was ignoring the problem and acting as though I was just a whiner. What injustice! What disrespect! My ego dukes were up and I was ready for battle.

Meanwhile, Patrick started to act meaner and meaner, more and more angry towards me. When I suggested that we use a nonpoisonous cleanser for the cow's feeding and drinking bins, he poured Lysol over them. Then he'd set up really dangerous tasks for me to do. Once he insisted that I wheel the barrow filled with cow dung over a series of wooden planks so precariously balanced that there could have easily been a disaster. If I questioned anything, he'd fly into a rage, yelling about how incompetent I was. And then, again, there would be those few good days sprinkled in, when we would drink fresh milk and feed cookies to the cows and ourselves, while sharing personal stories with each other.

This emotional roller coaster was taking its toll on me. I just wanted someone in charge to magically fix the problem. And so I complained about it to everybody — my friends, acquaintances, and the managers again and again. I became a complaint machine. I spent much of my free time telling all the horror stories about Patrick's violent actions and bad attitude. If I had been acting from a higher space, it would have been possible to use the instruction from the Chinese philosopher Sun Tzu. "Build your adversary a golden bridge over which to retreat." Make it easy for them to be helpful to you. Instead of attacking the person, find a way to help them feel good about themselves and about you.

Early one morning, I showed up to do my work, and found that Patrick had locked the barn doors. He tossed out a bag of my belongings and bellowed, "You'll not be working here anymore! Don't come back!"

He couldn't do that! This was the service that I had been assigned to do. I had grown to really love these cows. I lovingly bathed and stroked them every day. The vet once said our cows were cleaner than most people he knew. They were my pets, the first source of sweet affection I'd known in a long time. And now I was being ripped away from them because this jerk didn't feel like having me around anymore. You couldn't go around firing people here; it just wasn't allowed! But when I appealed to the managers, they said that maybe it was for the best, after all.

I had lost the battle, as well as my illusion of detachment.

I had been drawn right down into this macho bullfighting energy. Maybe it had to do with being around cows. But the funny thing is that the animals were so sweet and kind, and *we* were the ones acting like animals. The unresolved tension of this period remained with me for a long time. I felt violated, disrespected, and uncared for. It triggered an overwhelming echo of victimization from my past. When all of these contracted feelings took over my peaceful state of mind, I just didn't know what to do with them.

Instead of maintaining my normally silent nature, I continued to complain. I wanted to let go and move on with my life, but I couldn't. It was all too unfair.

But then summer came, bringing its own new challenges. We were working very hard to build an outdoor pavilion, and I was pick-axing, shoveling, planting, and even running huge excavators and front-loader tractors, for hours and hours each day. The cowshed became a vague memory as all of my energy was turned toward this new project.

Everything you do has a quality
which comes back to you in some way.
Every action takes a form in the invisible world,
which may be different from how you thought it would appear.
A crime is committed, and a gallows begins to be built.
One does not look like the other, but they correspond.
Accept the results of what you've done in anger,
or for greed, or to elevate your ego. Don't blame fate!

—*RUMI*

30.

UNDO WHAT
YOU HAVE DONE

NOW I HAD BEEN LIVING in the monastery for nearly ten years. As the summer began to wind down, my teacher told me it was time for me to leave. This decree did not come in a sweet or gentle form. In fact, the circumstances were so harsh that I wondered if they were intended specifically to make me more receptive to the idea of leaving.

The previous months had been very difficult physically and emotionally. The garden work had become heavy labor, and the hours were long and exhausting. Even after our new pavilion was inaugurated, there were still so many rocks to move, trees to plant, gardens to maintain, and acres of sod to lay. Those of us on the garden staff were rarely even able to make it to the evening programs. What had been a fairly pleasant romp through monastic life was quickly becoming boring and laborious. The woman in charge of the garden was a tough cookie and liked to show off how hard and long we could work, assuming perhaps that our surrender would reflect positively on her.

Along with all this physical challenge was the absence of a creative outlet. I'd always had some channel for expression, whether music, painting, writing or film making. Now there was just mindless hard work, day after day. My creative juices were building inside like a pressure cooker.

Many of the residents would simply have asked our teacher for an assignment change under these circumstances, but I was trying to maintain a state of acceptance. Nevertheless, my surrender was not true. I was trying to be surrendered, but each day was getting more difficult.

During this time, I received a phone call from my family. They were going to have a special party for my grandmother's 80th birthday and wanted me to come. I had visited them twice during the previous ten years. We had very little in common. My parents and grandmother were not thrilled that I was living in some strange religious place, but they didn't really care enough to find out anything about what it was about. And whenever they did say anything, I'd explain that I was happy there.

While visiting my family this time, I was disheartened to find that I could no longer say I was happy at the monastery. The words would not come out of me. It wasn't true anymore. At one point my grandmother and I were speaking alone. With tears in her eyes, she asked what I was doing with my life. "How can you be digging holes in the earth? You should be a doctor! You should have servants doing that kind of work for you! They don't really care about you."

I didn't really pay much attention to her, but when I arrived back at the monastery, things got worse. I couldn't bear it anymore, the long hours, the strenuous work, and the harshness of the supervisors.

My *shell* had finally been broken, and I found myself overwhelmed with emotion and vulnerability. If someone was kind to me, I would be overcome by waves of gratitude and sentimentality. If someone was unkind, I was hurt to the core. All the defense mechanisms that had protected me from my feelings were gone, and the flames of raw emotion leapt up at every turn.

I didn't know what to do. I wanted to talk to my teacher about it, but what would I say? I withdrew into a deep depression, walking through each day in a state of burning unrest. It got to the point where I even asked my friends not to talk to me. I could no longer speak. The pain would not allow words to come through. After two weeks of this, I realized that I had crossed into an inner hell. I had to tell my teacher. I needed her help. Hopefully she would understand that the garden wasn't really working for me, and find another department that would be better suited to my interests.

With trepidation, I walked up in the *darshan* line. There were so many people all around. I wondered if I should postpone the encounter and think about this further, but my depression was too deep. Even if she became angry, I had to tell her what I was going through.

I moved close to her, face to face, and whispered, "Some things happened when I visited my family, and I'm experiencing a lot of turmoil." This was not how I had planned to introduce the problem, but I was nervous, and the words didn't follow my plan.

She pointed to a spot next to her chair. "Go over there." Ralph was seated there, assisting with the flow of the *darshan* line.

He asked me to tell him what was going on. I had only meant to use my family trip to place the turmoil in a time line context, not to insinuate that the problem began there. But my words were not coming out the way I wanted them to. "I visited my family recently, and some things happened. I've been experiencing a lot of turmoil and confusion, and I can't break out of it."

He listened and then leaned over to tell my teacher what I had said.

She asked, "What happened there?"

I tried to put the problem into words, but was too overwhelmed by the intense energy around her. My brain cells were being zapped, and all my rehearsals went down the tubes. "Well, one thing is that my grandmother talked to me and it just raised these doubts. I didn't have the strength to resist it." What the hell was I talking about? I watched as words came out that had nothing to do with what I had intended to say.

She looked at me as if to say, "So, big deal!"

Then Ralph interjected to ask, "What did she say?"

I couldn't find a way out from this uncontrollable path of conversation, and so I continued. "She said, 'What are you doing there all this time? You should go back to med school. They don't care about you.'"

Why was I saying all this? Why couldn't I just tell her I was creatively stifled? Why couldn't I ask for a service-assignment change? Who was making my lips express all this information that wasn't even relevant to the problem? I hadn't thought my grandmother's words affected me. She had no concept of the world I lived in, and couldn't understand that my goals were not based upon materialistic desires. At the time, her words had slid right by me. So what was she doing here now, entering this conversation between me and my guru?

When I explained that my grandmother had said, "They don't care about you," my teacher's concerned look turned fierce.

"And you believe her?"

I was lost in this whirlpool of words, from which I couldn't free myself. Of course, I hadn't believed her. My teacher had fed me, clothed me, and given me a place to live, work, and experience the essence of spiritual life. She brought me all the way to India, paid off my leftover student loan, sent me to video school in California, and gave me a chance to explore my artistic abilities and share them with open hearts around the world. Why had I brought this statement to her? What subconscious agenda was trying to break through my intentions?

I replied, "No, I didn't believe her. But it created this turmoil inside of me."

She scrunched her face. "I'd better stop talking to you or I'll get depressed." Her sarcasm almost brought a smile through my fog of gloom. Then she paused while continuing to interact with the row of four to five people at a time that had been coming in front of her throughout our conversation. She looked at me. "You should just leave and go out to work, so you don't spread your stuff to other people."

Ralph was watching, and seemed genuinely concerned by my unusually somber demeanor. He whispered, "You should have talked to someone — a swami or someone, instead of just dumping this on her. She expects more from you after all this time."

How had things gotten so out of hand?

Ralph said, "You should go and contemplate this."

I thought, "No kidding!"

I asked him if she was serious about my having to go out to work. I told him, "I want to stay here. I just want to be happy again like I've been all these years."

He replied, "Don't ask again, or she may insist on it."

My teacher turned back in my direction and said, "Maybe you just want attention — that's probably it. This grandmother thing, everybody uses the grandmother as an excuse for attention."

I replied, "Maybe that's it."

Ralph turned to me and asked, "Is it true?"

I replied, "She knows. It must be. Thank you."

I bowed my head and walked away from what was surely one of the strangest conversations I'd ever experienced. What had just taken place?

I went to the temple, and sat against the wall. I wanted to contemplate it all, but every time I started to analyze the event, my mind would be drawn into a stillness that stopped my thoughts. If I started to think about what was going to happen in the future, my worries would also dissolve into this still space. It was as though I was impelled so effectively into the present moment that there was no room for thought about past or future. All I could do was wait.

While working in the garden the next morning, I received a message to go for a meeting with my teacher. I had already been feeling the potency of the upcoming encounter. It was as though the event created ripples on the lake of time that became even more tangible as I walked toward the meeting room.

My teacher was there, along with five or six other people. I bowed my head and sat before her. She looked at me sternly and said, "Tell them what you told me last night."

I was relieved to have an opportunity to try and say it the way I had intended. But as soon as I started choosing my words, she directed, "Tell them exactly what you said. You'll have your chance to speak."

I tried to become focused once again in the present moment. Part of me was concerned about the tone this meeting was taking, while another part was cheering the undeniable power of it all. Mostly, I was relieved that we were going to deal with the difficulties I had been going through. By this point, I was surrendered and willing to do whatever was asked of me. There was nothing to do but let go and be carried by the waves of destiny.

After I repeated our discussion of the previous evening, my teacher instructed, "Tell your life history." This surprised me because she had never asked about my life before. I moved into what felt almost like a trance state. It was powerful to be sitting right in front of my teacher, her attention focussed on me and my situation. The "dark night of the soul" I'd experienced for the past few weeks made it easier for me to let go of ego-consciousness. In this still space, words began to move through me. Slowly, each word arose from deep inside and moved up and out as speech. It was not so much that I was *thinking* of what to say. Rather, I was watching, witnessing, while certain long-forgotten highlights from my life were expressed through me.

As I recited the basic facts, my teacher watched me intently. I felt that her energy was entering into each event I invoked, infusing my life history with her grace. It was as though she was blessing my past from within the present moment. Here was this childhood and adolescence that I had blocked out of my mind, and she was walking through it with me.

My teacher asked some of the people there what they thought my problem was. A well-known author suggested that perhaps I was going through a dry spell. My teacher replied, "No, it's not a dry spell. With a dry spell, you feel numb. She's in *turmoil*." Another man who didn't even know me suggested that maybe I was angry because I had been moved from a high prestige service like video editing, into the garden.

My teacher looked at me. "Is it true? Are you angry?"

I replied, "No, I'm not angry at all."

She responded, "Yes, you are."

What could I say? The truth was that, even if I was angry, I probably wouldn't have known it. I was never allowed to be angry throughout my childhood. That would have elicited more punishment. I had learned to put my emotions off to the side, where even *I* was unaware of them. So maybe she was right. Maybe I was angry.

Then she brought up a familiar taunt. "I don't know why you would be angry about being moved out of video. Your videos were an embarrassment to the foundation." During previous years, I had received several letters from her, pressuring me to "make progress in the skill that you have got," because "So far, you have not produced anything that is close to being acceptable."

As she brought up the topic once again during this

intense meeting, I wanted to express something that had been a burden on my heart. I had tried so hard to make good videos for her, but clearly my efforts had failed. I explained, "That's one reason I feel so bad. I feel like I let you down."

My teacher turned her head to the side. I felt that she didn't want me to see that my words had touched her.

I whispered, "It's true."

She turned back and looked directly into my eyes. This is difficult to describe, but I actually felt her awareness entering through my eyes. I could feel it travel down into a deep core of my being. Then I could feel her looking into my soul. It was like a *souloscopy*. After a few moments, I sensed her consciousness moving back up through my body, and then exiting from my eyes once again. She had made her decision.

"You should go out and work in the world."

In a state of surrendered shock, I asked, "Where should I go, and what should I do?" The last time she told me to go out to work, it had ended up being a short-term, local job. I didn't think I'd get off so easy this time, but anything was possible.

She looked at me very sternly and said, "Go wherever you want and do whatever you want." My heart sunk as I felt that she didn't really care where I went or what I did. She was going to let me go just like that. She was pushing me away.

Then she added a surprise. "But you should pay back every penny that has been spent on you. That way when you die you won't have to die with a guilty conscience."

This must sound like an awful thing for her to say. I had never heard of her giving such an instruction to someone before. Here I had worked so hard for ten years, and she was telling me to pay back my room and board? But I knew it had nothing to do with money.

Her external words sounded one way, while internally I heard quite another message. This command made my heart smile. It was her way of giving me the strength to go out there and do well. She believed in me. She was imparting the faith and incentive I needed for this next phase of my life.

I had no desire for money, success or fame, but because she had given me this directive, I was able to go out there and do it for *her*. I wouldn't settle for less than she deserved. I wasn't so good at taking care of myself, but I had enough enthusiasm and devotion to do even the impossible for my beloved. I could become successful for her, while remaining free from the bondage of worldly ambition.

> *Constantly unattached,*
> *perform that action which is thy duty.*
> *Indeed, by performing action while unattached,*
> *Man attains the Supreme.*

—*THE BHAGAVAD GITA*

I walked away from the meeting in a state of shock. My body was pulsing with adrenaline, but the turmoil had lifted. I had a new challenge to meet, a new command to fulfill. I was back in warrior mode. She hadn't told me to leave right away, but I always tried to follow my teacher's directives promptly. This one was so intense that it felt as though I were holding a big ball of fire. I was going to have to face my fear of leaving, and I'd better do it quickly.

I made plans to leave for Los Angeles in one week. One of the summer guests kindly offered me the use of his little cottage there for a month. With only one week left, I was busy. I had to make a demo reel of my video work, put together a resume, say goodbye to old friends, pack my belongings, and get advice about what to do once I got to L.A. I was in red-hot, command-following mode. I was just *doing*. No thinking, no worrying. Just doing whatever was required to leave in a week.

In the midst of all this, someone mentioned that they had seen a note for me pinned to the community message board. I went to the lobby and saw a tiny piece of paper tacked up on the board with my name typed on it. Typed? That was strange. Who would type a message on such a small piece of paper?

I opened the paper and saw the sentence, *"Praise Patrick."*

What the hell was this? Who put this here? Was it Patrick? A friend of his? What was this all about? I was stunned. In the middle of all this flurry of activity, to get a cryptic message like this? It re-triggered all the emotions I had gone through the previous winter in the cowshed. I didn't know what to do with this anonymous message. Was it from my teacher? How could I know?

I walked away from the board and managed to calm down enough to look at the evidence before me. Maybe it was a joke, or maybe it was a command. What would a good disciple do? Well, on the possibility that this was a message from my teacher, I had to go for it. *Praise Patrick.* I wondered, did that mean praise him in my mind? Nah, that would have been too easy. Clearly, I was to find him and praise him personally. I didn't know why, and I certainly didn't want to do it. But in that fraction of a moment, there was a shift of awareness and I had a breakthrough. I didn't care anymore about the battle. In a few short days, I would be in a whole new world, far from these walls I had grown to love. Why not praise him? What would it hurt?

Coincidentally, I happened to pass Patrick a few hours later while walking along the forest path to the dining hall. I felt that running into him out of the thousands of people staying there was a sign that indeed this was something I was meant to do. I was supposed to praise him. Even if the note on the board had been some kind of prank, still the universe was telling me, "*Here he is. Do it!*"

I walked up to him and smiled as I called his name. I told him that I was going to be moving to Los Angeles in a few days. And I reached into my heart and found words of praise for him that were true. I told him I was sorry for being so sensitive and angry. I told him that I knew how incredibly devoted he was. I told him that he was really a very nice man, and that it was a shame we hadn't gotten along. I also apologized for any trouble I might have caused him. This was really difficult, because I knew it wouldn't be enough just to pay him lip-service. I had to find a place inside myself that knew this man was worthy of praise. What a struggle that was! Only my devotion to my teacher and my dedication to the spiritual journey could have motivated me to break through this one.

It also took a leap to apologize without expecting any kind of admission in return. It didn't matter what *he* had done. It became clear that my karmic job was to work on *my* responses, not to judge someone else's. Nevertheless, Patrick gave me a very sweet smile, and said some kind words to me, as well. He also apologized, and we gave each other a long, loving hug. It really did feel good to hug an adversary. I felt as though I were being rinsed clean of the cobwebs of anger and hatred that had formed around my heart.

Patrick gave me a big smile and said in that bellowing voice of his, "I give you my blessings!" I walked away, nearly moved to tears. It was a relief to have completed this challenging directive. Now I could get on with the pressing matters at hand.

Later that afternoon, I walked by the message board and noticed some typed messages for other people. I knew it was an invasion of privacy, but decided to open one to see if there was any indication of who may have sent it. It was in the same typed print as mine. I opened the message and saw that it was signed by one of my teacher's secretaries. So it *had* been from her.

Feeling confident about having passed this test, I jumped back into my preparations for leaving. But that evening, I passed by the message board once again and couldn't help but glance.

There was another typed message for me.

Oh my. My body got all hot and tensed. The adrenaline was flowing as I opened up this new command.

"Undo what you have done. Praise Patrick to others."

My heart sank into my stomach. Undo what I have done? At first, I felt a glimmer of outrage at this message, but it soon melted away into a deeper understanding of the cowshed period as a karmic lesson and test. And what had I done? I had bad-mouthed Patrick everywhere. I had complained about him, judged him, and tattled on him. I had intentionally harmed his reputation. This was not a karma I wanted hanging over my head, especially in Hollywood, a town known for its backbiting.

With great internal effort, I was able to rise above all my resistance and acquire a higher perspective. *Undo what you have done. Praise Patrick to others.* I did it. I threw away my ego and ran around trying to find anyone I might have talked with about the cowshed situation in the past. One by one, I explained that I was going to be leaving in a few days, and how I realized that those problems last year with Patrick had stemmed from my own hypersensitivity. Then I would give a whole list of all the good qualities I had seen in him. I'm sure some of these people wondered what I was babbling about. Most were probably so shocked by the news that I had been asked to leave, that the rest of my discourse went by unnoticed.

It helped that Patrick had been so kind to me that afternoon. For the next week, I praised him profusely, and more or less sincerely. I really tried to mean what I said. To fulfill this task properly, I had to move beyond my judgmental ideas of right and wrong. It's not that it was alright that this guy was mean to me or violent with the cows. That was not the point. I had focused on his faults so intently that I had brought myself down to a low level of gossip and revenge. It's like the story about a priest who lived across the street from a prostitute.

The priest would peek out of his window every day, watching as each sleazy man entered the woman's sinful abode. He would shake his head and pray for her evil soul. He could only imagine all of the disgusting actions that must go on there. Now, in the meantime, the prostitute would also look out her window. Sometimes she would see the priest returning home from church. She imagined that he would go inside and pray to God. She admired him so for his pious life.

One day, they both died. As they knocked on the pearly gates, the doors opened for the prostitute, but remained closed for the priest. Feeling the heat of flames licking at his heels, the priest cried out. "Why? Why did this sinful woman make it into Heaven and I, who have given my entire life to God, am being sent to Hell!?! How can this be?"

A voice spoke through the ether. "Oh, priest. You spent your time focusing on sin and evil. Your mind was filled with all kinds of degraded acts. This woman was in an unfortunate situation, yet day and night she contemplated your goodness. In imagining your love for God, she thought of God more than you. While you obsessed over her sins, she was imagining how pure *your* thoughts must be. Therefore, it is just and fair that each of you reaps the fruits of your own thoughts."

Too bad they always seem to tell us these things when we're already at the pearly gates! But unlike the poor priest, I had been given a chance to change my destiny before it was too late.

I had to undo what I had done. Not only did I have to work to mend this man's reputation, but I had to change my vision to see his goodness. I had to see his divinity, his good heart, his great qualities.

I gave my spiel to more than forty people during that week. No book could ever have taught me so much about the repercussions of my actions.

Just two days before I was scheduled to leave for Los Angeles, the financial officer of the monastery handed me an envelope. "This is for you."

It was from my teacher. I wondered if it contained another message, or perhaps a new challenge. Maybe it was an itemized bill from the last ten years? With anticipation, I walked back to my room. I sat on the bed and closed my eyes, moving into a state of inner openness. Then, I carefully opened the envelope flap.

Inside were thirty of the most beautiful, crisp hundred-dollar bills I had ever seen. This currency seemed to shimmer with light. It was money that had been donated by devotees to support the work of the monastery, offered out of gratitude to God. I knew these bills would be a great blessing on my new journey.

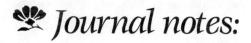 *Journal notes:*

A poem about leaving the monastery

Oh, how I hoped my entire life
would be lived in this safe place.
Away from the evils of the world,
away from my own unconfronted fears.

The monastic life is not easy,
but it is a cocoon of purity,
a bubble of "sattva", the pure quality
amidst this age of "kali", darkness.

I never wanted to leave,
but, damn, I knew one day I would.
The thought of my awaiting destiny
struck fear in my heart,
left me trembling and sweating at night.
Why must I be pushed out of heaven
like a fallen angel
who has lost his wings?
Will I lose my power?
Will I lose my understanding?
O God, please don't allow me to lose my devotion.

Will I be able to support myself?
Will I be alone?
Or. . .
is it possible. . .
that God really does exist within me?

O God, please follow me, stay with me.
Guide me through the jungle of the world.
Keep me safe from outer negativities.
Keep my inner state free and good.
I know I must go.
My lessons await me.
I must have faith.
That is all I have now.
No outer support,
no early morning strains of love,
no flowing schedule,
no thick shakti air to absorb,
to hold me up through anything.
Faith, faith, faith,
I must become the embodiment of faith.

You must make tracks into the unknown.

—*THOREAU*

31.

THE GREAT
GUIDING FORCE

WHAT WAS IT LIKE TO RE-ENTER "the world" after spending ten years living in a monastic environment? Or, let's rephrase that. What was it like to enter Hollywood, the epitome of illusion, after spending so many years seeking only eternal truth?

From the moment I left the doors of my beloved monastery, I experienced a constant, flowing mixture of emotions, thoughts and feelings. The world brought me confusion, surprise, peace, excitement, fear, motivation, and many new lessons. One of the challenging moments came when I realized it would be best to use my American name in work situations. Whenever I'd introduce myself to someone as *Kumuda*, there would be some inevitable question about the origin of this exotic name. I didn't want to lie, but I also didn't want people to know too much about my past right away. Not everyone would have a favorable view of guru's and monasteries. So after ten years of being Kumuda, I realized I would have to become Sharon once again. It was not an easy transition.

In a way, I resented having to answer to this name. Sharon had been locked away long ago with all the painful childhood memories associated with her. As far as I was concerned, Sharon had been a victim, while Kumuda was spiritual and powerful. I did not want to become Sharon again.

Soon after moving to Los Angeles, I received a letter from my teacher, which gave a subtle guidance for this situation. At first I was horrified to see that the secretary had typed my American name on the envelope. I was *not* Sharon Janis, certainly not to my teacher! I was still *KUMUDA!*

Feeling distraught, I tore open the envelope and unfolded the letter. It began, "Dear Kumuda. . . "

Immediately, a deeper message was revealed. I was to be Sharon Janis on the outside, and Kumuda inside. In a way this made sense. Why throw a pure soul like Kumuda out into this gnarly world? I wanted to keep that part of myself safe and clean. I didn't want her to be looking for jobs, struggling with mundane desires and goals, or even carrying the burden of success. No, Kumuda would represent the part of myself that remained free from the burning flames of worldliness, the lotus flower that lived in mud, yet remained free from stain.

I began to use the name *Sharon Janis* for my work. Sometimes it would take a while for me to remember when someone asked for my name. Either I would answer, "Ku. . . Sharon," or I'd just take an uncommonly long time to answer this seemingly simple request. One person even asked me, "Is that a hard question?"

After leaving this monastic environment that been my home for so long, I did not ease gently into the mundane world. Instead, I started my new life by editing a brand new tabloid show called "Hard Copy."

"Hard Copy" had just purchased two complex editing systems that were rare in Los Angeles. The operations manager was having a hard time finding any editors who were able to use the set-up. When I called to apply for the job, he scheduled me to take a day of training, along with seven fellows who were also up for the position.

These guys had been professional editors for quite some time. I was the least experienced person in the group, by far. I immediately became concerned about my obvious disadvantage in this arena. It didn't look like I had any chance of landing the job. I didn't even know most of the basic terms used in editing television shows, since my experience had all come from the monastery.

At that point, I would likely have given up, told everyone there it was nice to meet them, and left. Why spend all day working so hard and feeling so inadequate when I had no chance of getting the job anyway? Under normal conditions, I would have probably gone out and found myself a nice little job editing for a small company. I would have started at the bottom, which was clearly where I belonged in terms of experience.

I had little personal ambition in terms of career. All I needed was enough money for a place to live, hopefully on my own after so many years with roommates. I needed a car and enough cash for necessities. Nevertheless, one thing stopped me from settling for a simple, sparse life: my guru's command.

If I settled for a job paying $10 or even $20 an hour, how could I ever repay this elusive "debt" my guru had placed upon me? Even though I knew her direction really did not have to do with money, it was important that I act as though it did. I couldn't settle. I had to shoot for the highest.

Wherever I'd apply, the interviewer would ask how much money I had made in my last job. How could I say $100 or even $500 per month? I would have been laughed out of Hollywood. Yet, part of my discipline was also to be truthful whenever possible. And so, when asked this question, I'd simply answer "Oh, thirty to thirty-five." They would, of course, think I meant "Thirty to thirty-five thousand per year," while I'd chuckle inwardly at the unspoken "cents per hour."

Now things had changed. I was infused with ambition. I wanted to make a lot of money, even though I was not personally attached to making a lot of money. I wanted to achieve great worldly success, even though I couldn't care less about success. This paradox brought to mind one of the main teachings of the *Bhagavad Gita*.

This powerful text teaches the importance of performing actions without desiring the fruits of our actions. It explains that non-action is not really a viable alternative to greed-based action, because it is impossible to not act. The entire universe is constantly performing actions.

This ancient scripture discusses many pitfalls that can get in the way of the higher experiences available to us. Detachment can quickly become inertia. Inspiration can become fanaticism. Even purity can become dogmatic judgment. How can we free ourselves from all these potential downfalls? The *Bhagavad Gita* explains that the key is to remain balanced above and beyond these unavoidable qualities. This was the lesson before me now. I had to play the game of worldliness without becoming trapped by it.

No longer was it enough for me to live as a simple monk. I had to meet the new challenges unfolding before me. I had to surrender in a new way. The movies and television shows I had shunned for so many years were now going to become a major part of my life. Not only would I watch them, but I'd watch them over and over, using my creative energy to focus on every word, every image. My purity was no longer to be based on living a clean, pure life, chanting and contemplating spiritual wisdom all day long. Now my purity would consist of surrendering, even to living in this impure world, because it was God's will that I do so. The final statement of the *Bhagavad Gita* was ringing in my heart, "I will do thy bidding."

Just as I would never have refused a command of my guru, now I had to learn that this entire universe is the guru, the teacher. I had to accept what was being presented to me, without being defensive or resistant. This was the jewel I had received from the monastery, this surrender to God's will, to the infinite beneficence of Universal Perfection. I had to keep that alive. I had to allow my body, mind and heart to go through this new branch of destiny, without getting in the way. I had to play this instrument of Hollywood lifestyle, as I might have stepped back and allowed that inner energy to play the drum or harmonium through my being. This was the new challenge for me.

Courage attracts miracles.

—GURUMAYI CHIDVILASANANDA

I decided to stay in the training session for the "Hard Copy" job, in spite of the apparent futility of doing so. Surprisingly, after about five hours, the playing field had become more level. Even though I didn't know as much as these other editors did to begin with, I processed the new information quickly.

In the end, I was the only editor who even went back to "Hard Copy" to apply for the job. The others didn't think they would be able to keep up with all the complex operations. It would take too long to learn these three ridiculously complex systems that made up the "Hard Copy" editing room. I'm sure they'd all worked in many other places using more user-friendly equipment. Why put themselves under that kind of stress and pressure for some freelance work when they could just find a job with more familiar editing systems?

But, for me, this was a unique opportunity. Yes, it would take effort, and yes, I knew it would be stressful to attempt something so difficult. But I wanted a job; I needed a job. This was an amazing possibility for someone who had so little experience with professional editing. I arranged to spend my next two weekends at "Hard Copy," practicing and studying all the manuals.

The operations manager was impressed by my perseverance, and hired me. My first assignment was to edit a three-part "sex survey," working with a man-and-woman producer team who had no idea that I was completely new to the show, the equipment, and virtually the entire world. I was certainly new to a three-part series on sexual fantasy!

The producers wanted all kinds of snazzy effects. This was "Hard Copy's" first season, and their style was really wild and glitzy. Snazzy effects required even more complex equipment operations. I spent that week thinking harder than I had ever thought before. I was constantly on the hot seat. Still, I must have put together a decent act, because the two producers had no idea I had just come from a monastery, or that I had never done this kind of editing before. Their suspicions only arose when the man asked me to cut a shot of Michelle Pfeiffer into the celebrity fantasy montage. I asked who she was, and they both looked at me as though I were joking. The woman producer teased, "What planet did *you* come from?"

I thought, "If you only knew. . . ."

The three-part series was very educational for me. I hadn't discussed or even thought about sex for ten years. I really didn't know much about it, except what can be assumed logically, i.e., what goes where. But these people were talking about things like G-spots and fantasizing. They interviewed one group of people, asking, "How much money would it take for you to give up sex for a month, and how much for a year?" I was shocked by their answers. These people were asking for thousands, even millions of dollars! One huge, husky woman even declared, "Nothing could make me stop that!" We enjoyed imitating her during the long days of editing.

It took whatever little energy remained in my brain after all the technical concerns to try to act normal in responding to all this new information. Here we were joking about sex, and I was pretending to know what we were joking about. The experience was as challenging as anything I had ever experienced.

The "Hard Copy" job was on a freelance basis, so I continued to seek other work. I edited several music videos, did a stint at CBS News, and put together a "Candid Camera" special with Allen Funt himself. I knew my karmas had seriously shifted when I was hired to write and edit a trailer for the film, "Life of Sin."

Four months after arriving in Los Angeles, I went to Disney Studios to apply for a job with their budding "Prime-Nine News," the largest local news operation in the world. While filling out the forms, I looked up to see Mark, the operations manager from "Hard Copy."

I asked him, "What are you doing here?"

He replied, "I'm running this whole show, just tripled my salary. What are you doing here?"

I held up the application, "Applying for an editing job."

Mark said, "Great, you're hired." He had been impressed by my dedication in coming in for two full weekends to learn the equipment, and had also received good reports from the producers I'd worked with. He walked me upstairs to introduce me to the vice-president and station manager.

Mark praised me to the skies to them. I had no idea this boss thought so highly of me. I had never been praised so much in my life. This was my first experience of being schmoozed.

All the other editors for this show had been carefully chosen from news organizations around the country—the best of the best. And here I was, having had practically no experience with editing news, hired right off the bat. Not only was I totally unfamiliar with the terms and traditions of news production, but I barely even knew what had been going on in the world for the past decade. Nevertheless, I took the job.

There couldn't have been a better way to catch up on worldly events than to edit the news. I was actually surprised to see how little had really happened in all those years, considering the thousands of magazines, newspapers and television shows that had been constantly produced throughout the decade.

In news editing, deadlines can be extremely tight. An event occurs, and the footage is rushed to the station either via satellite or tapes. I'd often have just a few minutes to edit a piece, using all the best shots. These were known as "crash and burn" stories, because they had to be put together under intense pressure. I soon became known as the "crash queen," because I'd edit the pieces in whatever time was allowed, while remaining totally calm and even joking around with the nervous reporters and writers who were sure there was no way to finish their story in time. I loved these challenges, because they gave me an opportunity to tap into the same kind of surrender I had learned in the monastery.

These situations gave me a chance to step back and watch in awe and gratitude as everything always seemed to come through quickly and beautifully. I would just say "yes" to any project, knowing the *Great Guiding Force* would somehow fulfill my commitments.

Content to do any kind of work, I didn't mind putting in extra time and effort to do a good job. After all, I had just spent ten years offering every action to God. That is not a habit easily broken, nor should it be. As a matter of fact, one of my co-editors at Disney had to lecture me that I was supposed to put in for a missed lunch even if I hadn't been hungry when asked to work through the hour. I wasn't used to getting paid for my work, and so it took me a few years to get as greedy and pathetic as my co-workers. At the time I was enthusiastic and willing even to work on my own time to put extra care into a project. With all this dedication, I was honored with many awards during my first few years in Hollywood.

I won an Emmy award (along with seven nominations), two Golden Mikes, an International New York Festival, National Associated Press, two L.A. Press Club Awards, and more. I received first-place awards as "best editor" for Los Angeles, and "best news feature editing" for the state of California. Within three years, I had been honored with more than fifteen local, national and international awards.

This gave me quite a bit of prestige around the studio. Reporters would wheel and deal to get me as their editor. Barely a single day went by when I didn't hear some form of extreme praise for my work at least once. When my specials would air, the news anchors would introduce them as, "Brought to you with the magical touch of our own Sharon Janis." And so, as fate would have it, in the very building in which "Star Trek" and "I Love Lucy" were filmed, I had the chance to experience a taste of Hollywood stardom.

By the summer of '92, I had been living in Los Angeles for nearly three years. Our monastery had hundreds of meditation centers all over the world, formed for the purpose of giving devotees a local place to come together, chant, meditate, and study the teachings and scriptures of our path. One of the reasons I had chosen to move to Los Angeles was because there was a large community and center there. I had met many of the California-based devotees over the years, and they seemed like quite a friendly, open group.

However, when I arrived, there were some unexpected snags in the form of several people who seemed threatened by my presence. Unfortunately, they were the main coordinators of the center. They weren't much nicer to the other devotees. It seemed as though they were using their position to work out their own power lessons, taking advantage of the good hearts and devotion of the other devotees who for the most part tried to acquiesce and accept their harshness. I had been in similar situations in the main monastery with some of the more difficult people. There, I had tried to move with the flow, to understand the greater lessons being given through challenging circumstances. But this time I had a choice as to whether I would involve myself with disturbing people and situations.

The adversity that used to be such fodder for growth in New York was now unacceptable to me. It was no longer okay for people to be disrespectful to me or to one another, especially in the name of spirituality. I attended fewer and fewer programs at the center, and began to take refuge in my Hollywood work. Perhaps there was an underlying reason the universe brought these difficult people to me at this time. Maybe this friction was necessary to wean me from my dependence on the external form of this path, so I could learn some of the other lessons waiting on my karmic plate.

The funny thing is that when I left the monastery I had been concerned that people in the *world* might be unfriendly. In an unexpected turn of events, the people I met at jobs and even on the street were wonderful. Folks I didn't even know often took time to help me or give friendly advice.

One day, I was driving along Third Avenue, thinking about this paradox. "Why are some of the people at the meditation center so mean-spirited, while the so-called *worldly* people are acting so kind? Why are these supposedly nonspiritual people following the teachings of our path better than our own devotees?"

I flipped my signal to get into the right-turn lane. The car behind me in that lane would neither speed past nor let me in. I gave a friendly tap of the horn to get their attention, but they just would not let me in. I thought the universe was giving me a clear message that rude people are everywhere, not just at the meditation center. I caught the lesson and slowed down, nearly to a stop. The car finally went past me, and I slipped into the lane behind it. There, on the back window of this car was a decal from the local meditation center, "See God in Each Other"! In the driver's seat was one of the center people I'd had a hard time with. I learned from this that it is very easy to put a decal on your car, or to repeat a phrase that you have read, but much more difficult to really imbibe a teaching into your heart.

As the years went by, I became more and more dedicated to my Hollywood work. This was where I found my joy now. Our TV station even allowed me to produce my own uplifting pieces for special occasions, so I felt I was doing service to humanity as well.

Maybe I would have checked out other spiritual activities in the area, but this kind of "promiscuity" was frowned upon by some of the people at the meditation center. I learned this a few years later when I started attending services at a nearby church. A rumor spread through the community that I had left the path to become a "born-again Christian." This was the kind of silliness that was beginning to grate on my nerves. What place did this kind of gossip have in the search for eternal truth? If I was being blessed by teachings through another avenue, how could that be a bad thing? Several people were speaking of me as though I had become some sort of traitor.

Remembering once again that this universe is conscious

and purposeful, I tried to discern what the lesson might be. After all, even if these people were acting off the wall, it was God's wall, ultimately. Along with this, my teacher also began to change her external relationship with me. With each passing year, she seemed less and less disposed to give me external guidance. What was the message? Was my next step to move away from this path? My heart sank at the thought.

Moving on from people and situations was never difficult for me. When the karmic pull left a friendship or job, I would simply end it. The universe would always give hints. And if I didn't heed the hints, they'd become more bothersome and disruptive until I had no choice but to make the required changes. Now it seemed as though I was being pushed away from the spiritual path I loved so dearly. This time I resisted more than ever.

It is only by doubting
that we eventually come to the truth.

—CICERO

32.

THE
WISH-FULFILLING TREE

FTER TWO AND A HALF YEARS, I left Disney and was getting ready to begin editing and co-producing my first low-budget feature film (trust me, you've never heard of it). The movie was being produced by bodybuilder Franco Columbu, and his best friend Arnold was going to be in it. In a few months, I would be spending Thanksgiving evening chatting about "mooovies" with the *Terminator* himself. But first I took the opportunity to visit the upstate New York monastery for five days.

This pilgrimage brought up some feelings of apprehension and anxiety. While living there, I had been used to meeting challenges from the peaceful space that comes with spiritual practice. However, after living in Los Angeles for nearly three years, I was no longer keeping the kind of discipline that had been so easy to maintain in the monastery. I was afraid my new Hollywood-style persona would clash with the quiet recluse I used to be. For the next five days, I would not be Emmy award-winner Sharon Janis, but Kumuda, the (supposedly) humble disciple. Could my ego shrink quickly enough to handle the lessons awaiting me there? Was my faith still strong enough to carry me through the challenges? My sense of anxiety continued to build during the cross-country flight.

 *Journal notes:*

A poem written during this confusing time

What to do in this state?
Discomfort surrounds me
and clouds the mind.
Illusion shoots arrows
Through my understanding.
My heart cries out in grief,
And darkness shrouds my eyes.
Still, through the clouds
Your Grace shines
Like the light of dawn,
beckoning to me:

Come,
Go through this time.
Remember,
All things will pass.
Your sorrow
Will become joy once again,
Joy made deeper
and clearer
By the burning flames
of pain.

But, my beloved Master,
I can't see you clearly
Though I know you are here
And can hear your call.
Please appear before me
In a more tangible form
Speak to me,
Write to me,
Remind me of your love for me.
I shouldn't forget
But at times
I do.

Know that I love you
Know that I'm thinking of you
With great care
And compassion,
Loving the greatness you cannot see
within yourself.
I know you are suffering.
I can feel your pain
In my heart.
Didn't you know?

My Glorious Master,
My saint of Grace,
I can hear your words
Resounding in my heart
And I'm so ashamed to question
Is it really you,
Or could I be playing tricks on myself?
I know you're so busy
But please.
Speak to me,
Write to me,
Remind me of your love for me.
I shouldn't forget
But at times
I do.

My child,
I wish you would understand
And know how deep my love can be.
How sad that you
Can even slightly doubt
That I speak through your heart.
How sad that a rich man could doubt
the authenticity of his jewels,
And live in poverty.
I am here for you
As I always have been
And always will be.
Have faith, my child,
Trust that which is worthy of your trust.

A shuttle service from the monastery came to pick another woman and me up from the airport. She introduced herself as Robin. As we set off on our 2- to 3-hour drive, I made small talk with her. She didn't really seem too interested in chatting with me, though she wasn't blatantly impolite.

Under normal circumstances, I would have just sat quietly. But I was already feeling anxious. Robin's lack of interest in me brought my feelings of insecurity to the surface. Because of this, there was a subtle flavor of bragging behind my words. I wanted her to know that I was somebody important. I wanted to see a look of admiration and interest in her eyes. I wanted her to believe that I was special, so that I could remember it myself.

However, Robin wasn't impressed. I was starting to feel more and more insecure about myself. It was not a good omen for this visit that the one person I was riding with didn't seem to like me. Back in Hollywood, it seemed as though *everyone* was impressed with me.

Somewhere between mentioning that I was going to be starting my first feature film soon and tossing out a few Sanskrit terms, I moved the conversation into more daring territory. It is not that I was sitting there consciously trying to come up with ways to impress her. But, my deeper insecurities were expressing themselves through me, guiding the conversation with their hidden motives. I told Robin that every time I came to visit the monastery, I *always* saw our teacher within the first ten minutes. I spoke these words as if challenging fate itself, as though I were so connected with the underlying forces of this universe that I could dare to declare something so unpredictable.

Robin looked as though she thought I was odd, but finally there was a flicker of admiration behind her eyes. What if it were true? She certainly would like to see our teacher as much as anyone. I had managed to elicit a glimmer of interest, though it wasn't anywhere near what would have given me the boost of confidence I was seeking. Nevertheless, it was *something* to hold onto as I tried to pull myself out from the mire of self-doubt.

When we arrived at the monastery doors, there was no guru in sight, so Robin and I went to our respective rooms to drop off our luggage. Then, I headed downstairs to visit the temple. Robin and I both arrived in the shoeroom at the same time. As we took off our shoes, Robin smirked at me and asked, "So where is she? I thought you always see her within ten minutes?" It wasn't that Robin was a sarcastic person, but she had been listening to my obnoxious routine for the past three hours. I'm sure she wanted to teach me a lesson. It had already been ten minutes since we had arrived, and the guru was nowhere to be seen. I mumbled a discouraged response.

We went to kneel in reverence before the bronze statue of our grandfather guru, which sat inside the temple. The temple itself was locked, so we paid our respects from outside the glass doors. I arrived feeling like a real dolt. But as I knelt and touched my head to the ground, the magic of surrender began to enter me. I moved into a state of *witness consciousness*, where I could see that I had acted like an idiot, but I wasn't identifying with the part of myself that had acted like an idiot. Once again, there was the awareness that everything was fine, everything was perfect. No place for guilt or shame; no need for embarrassment or fear. Whatever had happened was perfect, and whatever was going to happen would be perfect.

Through this posture of surrender, kneeling before an image which represented the Divine Force, I had taken refuge in the awareness that it is only *that* Force which moves through all. I was able to let go of my insecurities and step back. Layers of defense mechanisms and wrong understandings opened up to reveal the light of truth they had been obscuring from my sight. Feeling rejuvenated in spirit, I stood up and turned to go to the chanting hall. Robin stayed with her head bowed.

As I turned the corner, there. . .
walking down the hallway. . .
was none other than. . .

Yes. It was her!

My heart leapt as I saw her heading in my direction. She stopped at the doorway of the hall to look in on the chant for a moment. I stood off to the side, watching. She was walking with her secretary and one of the women swamis. As she turned, my teacher looked at me with deep, piercing eyes. She gave a mischievous smile, and said, "Ah, it's the famous one!"

I was shocked to hear her call me that for several reasons. First of all, I had just been feeling pretty insecure about myself for the last few hours. And here was the one person whose opinion I most treasured, calling me famous. It was said with more of a friendly tone than sarcastic, though still with that mischievous smile.

It didn't even occur to me that she might be referring to

the success I had already achieved. I wondered, "Does she think I want to be famous? Does she think I've got the ego of a famous person?" Or was she giving a concealed message to the higher consciousness that expresses through my life?

One of the Indian scriptures explains that even the mundane words of a great sage are *mantras*, potent declarations. I had previously understood this to mean that their teachings were powerful. But one week before my trip to the monastery, I'd had a new revelation into the depth of meaning in this statement.

Kathaa japaha:
His mundane conversation
constitutes the invocation of prayer.

—THE SHIVA SUTRAS

I had recently been hired to co-produce and edit the feature film with Arnold Schwarzenegger's best friend. Here I was preparing to work on a feature film, having had no experience at all in editing dramatic shows of any kind (although I didn't quite tell the producer that!). There was no logical reason for me to have gotten the job. It is considered almost impossible for a news editor to move into film editing. I had never edited a single drama scene. I had never even read a script or heard of script notes. Nor had I ever used the kind of equipment I would be using to edit the film. Technically, there was no reason I should have this job.

A week before my trip, I had been lying in bed, mulling all this over in my head. Many events from the past few years became strung together, and I realized that so many of my wishes had been fulfilled!

I had come to Los Angeles hoping to get a job with Disney; I got a job with Disney. I wished I could live in Santa Monica; there I was. I wished I could win an Emmy award; and I had. I wished I could edit a feature film. My eyes widened as I remembered a story my teacher used to tell about a man who sat under a "wish-fulfilling tree."

Walking through the wilderness alone one day, a poor man happened upon a large tree. Settling down into its cool shade, he closed his eyes and began to daydream. How nice it would be to have a beautiful woman sitting there beside him. Suddenly, he felt a presence, and opened his eyes to find an exquisite woman sitting there, looking at him with big, beautiful eyes.

"Such a glorious woman," he thought. "I wish we had fancy servants here to bring us delicious food and wine." Suddenly, they appeared.

The man sat with his beautiful new friend, eating, drinking and having a wonderful time, when he stopped to think. "I wished for a woman, and a woman appeared. I wished for servants, and servants appeared. I wished for delicious food, and there it was. There must be a demon around here!" And the demon appeared.

"Oh, no! He's going to eat me alive!" End of story.

So I thought of how I now found myself in a similar position, that I seemed to have been sitting under a wish-fulfilling tree. Yes, I had to put effort into all of the accomplishments that had come my way, but clearly these boons had also come from a deeper place. My wishes were somehow being amplified into the world as it manifested around me.

Filled with gratitude, I began to hear inside myself the words my teacher had spoken when she told me to leave the monastery. "Go wherever you want and do whatever you want."

I had heard those words originally as being said with impatience and indifference. I felt bad at the time, because I interpreted them to mean that my teacher didn't really care what happened to me anymore. But while lying in bed early that morning, I heard the same words being spoken in her sweet, loving voice, "Go wherever you want...and do whatever you want...." It was like a song — so beautiful, such a positive affirmation, a great blessing.

She had disguised the gift with a stern exterior, perhaps so my ego wouldn't grab onto it and ruin everything. "My guru said I can do whatever I want!"

Only now could I finally appreciate what had been given years earlier.

You cannot teach a man anything;
you can only help him find it within himself.

~ GALILEO GALILEI

And so, as I arrived one week later, here was my teacher saying to me, "Ah, it's the famous one." After my recent revelation, I was keenly aware of her words. She joked with her secretary and the swami, asking if they knew how famous I had become. They certainly did! I stood there with a sheepish grin, not quite understanding what the point was, but knowing there was more going on than I could comprehend.

At that point, the woman I had bragged to on the shuttle bus turned the corner and stopped with a jolt as she saw us there. There we were, my teacher and me, just as I had boasted to her earlier. "I always see her within ten minutes of arriving." So maybe it was fifteen minutes instead of ten. It was still impressive. After wallowing in, regretting, and then transcending my pettiness and insecurity, I had been vindicated and even exalted by the hand of fate.

A man saw Mullah Nasrudin searching
for something on the ground.
"What have you lost, Mullah?" he asked.
"My key," said the Mullah.
So the man went down on his knees too,
and they both looked for the lost key.
After a time, the other man asked,
"Where exactly did you drop it?"
"In my house," replied the Mullah.
"Then why are you looking here?"
"There is more light here than inside my house."

—*A TRADITIONAL MIDDLE EASTERN STORY*

33.

WHERE IS THE KEY?

URING THIS FIRST DAY of my five-day visit to the monastery, some of the garden workers saw me and thought I might be able to help them out. Several gardening projects were taking place behind the main building. The largest was the construction of a huge hill. For weeks, a line of trucks had been driving in and out of the gates, dumping load after load of soil onto the pile. Ralph was now in charge of the monastery gardens, and he had quite the extravagant flair.

The garden folks happened to have a meeting with our teacher at lunchtime, and asked her if it would be okay for them to assign me to the gardening department during my stay. She nodded, but as they stood up to leave, she added, "Kumuda should be in charge."

This statement made no logical sense. There were already several very skilled department heads supervising all the projects. And now I, with hardly any gardening background — I, who was only going to be there for five days, was to be *in charge*? When they told me this, I had to laugh.

I was brought outside to speak with the man who had been overseeing all the garden work before I came along to be in charge. For him, my appearance was a source of stress. In the monastery, you might go along doing your work as if it were an actual business. But there was a unique infrastructure that would sometimes jump out and surprise you when rules were changed, positions rearranged, and projects canceled or redone over and over again. The work in this place was not about efficiency. We were on a quest for eternal Truth. We were treading a spiritual path to which we had committed ourselves. This is why we were there instead of working for a company in the city. We wanted to be *worked on*. We wanted our false expectations to be crushed. We wanted our egos to be broken. We just didn't always like it when it actually happened!

So this guy didn't know what to expect from me. He probably thought I was going to come in with a big power trip, and that my teacher had given me this position of authority because I had major control issues. He looked at me with a concerned face and said, "I'm not really sure what it means that you're supposed to be in charge."

We were standing in front of the huge mountain of soil that had been amassed over the past few weeks. I pointed at it and said, "Well, for starters, you should get rid of that pile of dirt over there."

He looked stunned for a moment, and then realized that I was joking. He's a very serious fellow, and I think this was the only time I saw him come even close to laughing. Between the long hours, the hard work, and then my being put "in charge," his emotional resistance must have worn quite thin. So he did manage to crack up at my joke.

Now there was a new command from my teacher, more potent words amid this *power of her word* lesson. "Kumuda should be in charge." It was a personal command, an important instruction to the consciousness that lived through me. I realized that, in a way, I was on my own now. I had to move into the next limb of this journey, and learn to receive guidance from within. My teachers had often declared that "the disciple must become the guru." It was time for me to discover the meaning behind this statement.

Kumuda should be in charge. It was time for this bird to find her wings and fly. Thus began an inner shift that was incredibly painful and difficult, as I grieved the loss of my teacher's external guidance in my life. This time there was no statue, no next guru to pacify me. I had to go deeper. I had to become a channel of grace unto myself. It didn't come easy.

❧ *Journal notes:*

A poem about the inevitable transition

The desert sands, dry and coarse,
remembering a different time.
Seems so long ago.

A time of showers,
frequent and sweet,
nourishing the roots,
Sprinkling the faces with shimmering light,
feeding the stream of the heart
as it overfills its banks
and carries my soul with it
into spaces neither here nor there.

The heart remembers.

The world takes its toll.
It teaches great lessons
but destroys even as it gives.

The rain of the world is hard,
so different from the soft sprinkle of grace.
It's like the rain on a Hollywood set.
You can control it to some degree,
but you can't make it be real.

My heart has never loved as it loved You.
What passes for love out here
can't touch the complete devotion
and absorption
I knew in your house.

I know there is no turning back time,
nor should there be.
The lessons of the world have been good,
sometimes easy, sometimes hard,
but expanding in their own way,

giving even as they destroy.
Giving knowledge as they
take away knowledge.
Shifting from one incomplete view to another.

Sometimes I go inside myself
and this wisdom is there,
this inner knowledge
so far beyond day-to-day thoughts.
It guides me in understanding
more about what is really going on here:
The energy flows of the universe,
the undifferentiated force that refracts
through the mirrors of the senses
to create the illusion of experience.

That energy moves through me,
moves my body to heal
and opens up channels of blocked energy.
Uses my breathing to
nourish body and soul,
shows me worlds far greater than
this transitory world of accomplishment.

It's the next phase of my evolution.
I can't judge from within it

if it is higher or lower,
better or worse.
It's just next.

EPILOGUE

DURING THE NEXT FEW YEARS, I lost much of my enthusiasm for work and spirituality. I went through the motions of life, but not with the inspiration I had known when everything I did was in service to my beloved. Anyone watching from outside would have thought I was very ambitious and motivated. After all, I was editing and associate producing the top two children's shows in the world, "Power Rangers," and "X-MEN." I was raking in big bucks and working hard, often seven days a week. People must have thought I was thrilled with such great success.

In truth, it was just service. It was the final teaching of the *Bhagavad Gita,* "I will do thy bidding." It was also a distraction to keep myself from having to feel the deep loss I was suffering. I was working myself into the ground, because I just didn't know what else to do.

Then came the earthquake, shaking me from my worldly dream. But even with this awakening, I still didn't know how to proceed with the next step on my life journey. I was too entrenched in the illusion around me to know what to do. Instead, I continued to work at an exhausting pace. Inevitably, I fell ill.

It may seem strange to thank God for an illness, but even if it had been fatal, I would have gone with gratitude in my heart. Due to this trauma, I was forced for the first time in my life to stop, and to remember.

Then, while sitting quietly one day, through the deep inner stillness echoed a clear and welcome holy command, fulfilling the promise of my spiritual teachers as this benediction came now from within myself, in my own powerful voice. "First, you have to share what you have learned."

With the same dedication and inspiration I had known when asked to perform a service to my beloved, I sat down, and began to write....

Correspondence to the author can be sent to:

Sharon Janis
449 Santa Fe Drive, #624
Encinitas, CA 92024

The name Blue Dove signifies peace and spirituality. Blue Dove Press publishes books by and about saints and sages of all religions of the world as well as other spiritually and inspirationally oriented topics. To receive our free catalog or to get on our mailing list contact:

BLUE DOVE PRESS
P. O. Box 261611
San Diego, CA 92196

Phone: (619) 271-0490
Orders: (800) 691-1008
FAX:(619) 271-5695
E-mail: bdp@bluedove.com
http://www.bluedove.com